TAKE
COMFORT

Encouraging Words From Second Corinthians

BOB RUSSELL

**STANDARD
PUBLISHING**
Cincinnati, Ohio

Unless otherwise noted, all Scripture quotations are from the HOLY BIBLE: NEW INTERNATIONAL VERSION, Copyright © 1973, 1978, 1984 by the International Bible Society. Used by permission of Zondervan Bible Publishers.

Scriptures cited NASB are from the New American Standard Bible, © 1978 by the Lockman Foundation. Scriptures cited KJV are from the King James version.

Library of Congress Cataloging-in-Publication Data:

Russell, Bob, 1943-
Take comfort: encouraging words from Second Corinthians / Bob Russell.
  p. cm.
ISBN 0-87403-844-8
  1. Bible. N.T. Corinthians, 2nd — Sermons. 2. Sermons, American. 3. Christian Churches and Churches of Christ — Sermons. 4. Encouragement — Religious aspects — Christianity — Sermons. I. Title.
  BS2675.4.R87 1991
  252'.0663 — dc20   91-11266
                                                             CIP

Copyright © 1991. The Living Word, Inc.
Published by The STANDARD PUBLISHING Company, Cincinnati, Ohio.
A division of STANDEX INTERNATIONAL Corporation. Printed in U.S.A.

Contents

Comfort-Able Living

2 Corinthians 1:1-11

A COWBOY ON THE WESTERN FRONTIER came across an Indian lying flat with his ear to the ground. The Indian said, "Wagon, four horses, two passengers, woman wearing calico gown, heavy man driving, thirty minutes away."

"That's amazing!" the cowboy said. "And you can tell all that just by putting your ear to the ground?"

"No!" the aggravated Indian said. "Him run over me half hour ago."

Have you ever felt like that Indian? Maybe people have deliberately run over you. A friend, mate, co-worker, or employee has knocked you down and left you deeply wounded. Or maybe circumstances have flattened you. Your health is broken; your house has burned down; a financial risk you took hasn't worked out; a loved one has died. And just when you need encouragement, people seem oblivious to your hurt, or they misinterpret your actions and ask, "Why are you so down in the dumps?"

The Corinthian church was a troubled church full of hurting people. In his first letter to them, Paul had to confront all kinds of problems—everything from division to immorality among their members. Unfortunately, after they received his first letter, matters grew worse, and Paul had to make what he called "a painful visit" to confront the troublemakers. Still the problems were not resolved, so Paul sent his co-worker, Titus, to Corinth to help them get things straightened out. Finally, after several months, Paul received word from Titus that the church was improving. Paul then wrote what we call 2 Corinthians to express his appreciation for their improvement and to encourage the church to remain faithful. He emphasized the special resources available to Christians who are hurting.

5

At one time or another everyone needs *encouragement*. That's a key word in 2 Corinthians. Sometimes translated *comfort*, the word is used twenty-nine times in this letter, eighteen times as a verb and eleven as a noun. In spite of all the hardships that he faced, Paul was able to write a letter of encouragement because Jesus Christ had transformed their behavior and his attitude.

A poet wrote,

> Two men looked out from prison bars,
> The one saw mud, the other stars.

Whether you see dirt or beauty in life doesn't depend on your vantage point, but on your perspective. Four truths from these opening verses should comfort all of us when life runs us down.

Hardships Are Part of Every Life

The two greatest human needs met by God are forgiveness and comfort. Everyone is a sinner and needs God's grace; everyone is a sufferer and needs God's peace. Suffering is a normal part of every Christian life, just as sin is. "The sufferings of Christ flow over into our lives" (2 Corinthians 1:5). Jesus said that in the world we are going to have trouble just as He had trouble. Savonarola said, "The Christian is called to do good and to suffer evil."

Our culture today is trying to convince us that we should never have to hurt. Overindulgent parents try to exempt their children from every unpleasant experience. "I don't want my children to have it as rough as I had it as a child," they say. "I don't want them to hurt." So children don't know the pain of discipline, the unpleasantness of hard work, or the disappointment of denial. They grow up thinking that all of life is supposed to be peaches and cream. When life gets difficult, they want to bail out. One of the reasons we have such a drug and alcohol problem in our society is that people are trying to escape suffering. They say, "I have so much pressure in my marriage and so much pressure on my job that I've got to find a way out. When I take these chemicals, I feel at peace; I feel better."

Now we have an accommodating theology to support the philosophy that life can and should be free from pain. We call it the "Health and Wealth Gospel." Media ministers will tell you that if you really confess all of your sins and dedicate your life to God, you will always be happy, healthy, and prosperous.

The Bible teaches us from the very beginning that suffering is a natural part of every life lived in this contaminated world. Just after Adam and Eve disobeyed God and had eaten of the forbidden fruit, God said to Eve, "I will greatly increase your pains in childbearing; with pain you will give birth to children" (Genesis 3:16).

I remember how proud I was when our second child was born. He weighed ten pounds, and I thought that I had really done something special. I marched into my wife's room all smiles.

She spoke two words: "Never again."

Every one of us is here today because a woman suffered to bring us into the world. We've tried to reduce that suffering by anesthesia and by the natural childbirth procedure, but it's still there.

The man was supposed to suffer, too. God told Adam that, because he had eaten of the tree, "Cursed is the ground because of you; through painful toil you will eat of it all the days of your life. It will produce thorns and thistles for you, and you will eat the plants of the field. By the sweat of your brow you will eat your food" (Genesis 3:17-19). Every time we sit down to a meal, we're eating because somebody has suffered to provide that food. All the automation in the world has not eliminated the pain of farming. It's one of the most difficult jobs in the world to clear the field and to plow and plant and cultivate and finally to harvest the crop.

A friend who works in a local meat packing firm said that working in a slaughterhouse is one of the worst jobs in the world. There's the squealing of the animals, the flashing of knives, frequent injuries, terrible stench, and low pay. The meat and vegetables we eat are on the table because somebody has suffered to provide them.

Paul used two examples to illustrate that no one is exempt from suffering. The first example was Jesus. "The sufferings of Christ flow over into our lives" (2 Corinthians 1:5). From the beginning of His life, Jesus was lonely and rejected, a victim of criticism, and acquainted with grief. If Jesus was perfect and He suffered, how can we expect to be exempt? God had one Son without sin, but He had no sons without suffering.

The second example was Paul himself.

> We do not want you to be uninformed, brothers, about the hardships we suffered in the province of Asia. We were under great pressure, far beyond our ability to endure, so that we despaired even of life (2 Corinthians 1:8).

We think that pressure is a twentieth-century experience only, because we are under a lot of stress. But we probably don't experience the kind of pressure that Paul faced. He had to work part-time in order to pay for his missionary trips (1 Corinthians 9:6, 12; 1 Thessalonians 2:9; 2 Thessalonians 3:8). He had physical problems that kept dragging him down (2 Corinthians 12:7). He was lonely. He endured the tension of constant travel and the disappointment of people who rejected the gospel. His enemies even had a contract out on his life. That's pressure. That's suffering.

If Jesus suffered (He was perfect), and if Paul suffered (he was the most zealous Christian there ever was), then so will we. "Do not be surprised at the painful trial you are suffering, as though something strange were happening to you" (1 Peter 4:12). It happens to everybody. You're no different.

One preacher said that in his small community, each of two Christian families had a family member commit suicide the same week. Both families tried to conceal the real cause of death. "We don't understand how God could let this happen," the first family said. "Nobody in the world understands how we feel right now. We hurt more than anybody." Hours later, the second family said, "We don't understand how God could let this happen to us. Nobody understands how we feel. We hurt so badly, there's nobody who understands." He couldn't tell either family that at that very moment in that little town of 15,000, another family was going through the same experience. "Man is born to trouble as surely as sparks fly upward" (Job 5:7).

Hardships Provide an Opportunity to Receive God's Comfort

We are so egotistical we think we can be self-reliant. We think if we can just make enough money, buy enough insurance, and have enough savings, every future contingency will be covered and we won't have to depend on God. If we can just get enough education, we'll establish our own guidelines for right and wrong and we won't need the Bible. If we can just belong to enough organizations and meet enough people and be popular enough, we'll have plenty of relationships and we won't need the church. If we can just invent the right kind of medical procedures and the right kind of pills, we'll be able to prevent diseases and prevent pregnancies, and we won't have to abide by God's restrictions. The whole philosophy of humanism, so prevalent today, is simply that people can rely on themselves. But Paul said, "This happened that we might not rely on ourselves but on God" (2 Corinthians 1:9). God occasionally permits hardships in life to knock us to our knees to remind us that, in Jesus' words, "apart from me you can do nothing" (John 15:5).

Years ago, I awakened one morning to hear a radio announcer saying, "Robert Kennedy has been shot." I was half asleep and thought it must have been a replay of the assassination of President Kennedy. But as I awakened, I realized that Robert Kennedy, campaigning for the presidency in Los Angeles, had been shot and killed.

I thought about all the tragedies that had befallen the Kennedy family: a child born retarded; a son killed in a plane crash; Joseph Kennedy, the father, had a stroke; John F. Kennedy assassinated as President; and now Robert Kennedy shot and killed.

Later in the day, on the car radio, I heard the announcer say, "Rose Kennedy has gone to church to pray." She had money, power, and family, but she went to church to pray because there was no place else to go. Regardless of your status or wealth or influence, there will be times when suffering comes into your life, and you'll have no place else to go. People need the Lord.

Not all troubles are God's discipline of His people. Many troubles that come in life are just the natural consequences of living in a sinful world. Some people get AIDS because they disobey God's commandments, but other people get AIDS from having a blood transfusion. They haven't been disobedient; they just live in a contaminated world. We shouldn't interpret every hardship that comes along as God's disciplining us, but God can use any hardship as a means of developing maturity.

> Endure hardship as discipline; God is treating you as sons. For what son is not disciplined by his father? If you are not disciplined (and everyone undergoes discipline), then you are illegitimate children and not true sons. Moreover, we have all had human fathers who disciplined us and we respected them for it. How much more should we submit to the Father of our spirits and live! Our fathers disciplined us for a little while as they thought best; but God disciplines us for our good, that we may share in his holiness. No discipline seems pleasant at the time, but painful. Later on, however, it produces a harvest of righteousness and peace for those who have been trained by it (Hebrews 12:7-11).

When the sufferings come, it's important that we turn to God and not run from Him; we rely on God and not resent Him.

J. Vernon McGee tells what happened when he and some other boys got caught skipping school one day to go fishing. The principal called them into the office and said, "Boys, I know you've skipped school and I'm going to whip every one of you."

McGee was petrified. He had been a good boy; he'd never been whipped before. But an older, more experienced boy told him, "When he whips you, don't run—he'll wear you out. When he whips you, as hard as it is, move a little closer to him, so he won't have as much leverage and it won't hurt as much." McGee said that was some of the best advice he had ever received in his life. He was the first to be whipped. It stung like mad, but for the second blow he moved closer, then closer, and it didn't hurt as much.

That same principle applies to the Christian life. When there's pain, there's a real temptation for us to withdraw from God, blame God, and get angry at God, but this only intensifies the pain. As tough as it is, if we move closer to God, it hurts less. "Cease striving and know that I am God" (Psalm 46:10, NASB). One of the most tender moments in the life of a parent comes just after a child has been disciplined, and the child curls up on the parent's lap to have his tears wiped away and his parent's love reaffirmed. That's the way it ought to be in our relationship with God.

Hardships Equip Us to Comfort Others

God "comforts us in all our troubles, so that we can comfort those in any trouble with the comfort we ourselves have received" (2 Corinthians 1:4). Until you have experienced hurt in a similar way, you really don't sympathize with hurting people the way you can afterwards. If you have a child who is mentally retarded or physically limited, then you better understand people who have a similar child. If you are prone to depression, you can identify with people who are melancholy in spirit. If you've ever had a kidney stone attack, you can be sympathetic with other people who have had kidney stone attacks.

My son, Rusty, had an internship at a small country church where he preached every other Sunday night. He called on people in hospitals and taught lessons; he did the work of the ministry and he really enjoyed it. The previous two summers in college, Rusty had worked in an office job and a construction job. When I asked him how he liked his internship, he said, "Dad, it sure beats working!" But since he has gone to Bible college and since he's beginning to think about preaching, he's able to understand me better, and it has deepened our relationship.

Rusty's best contribution that summer came when a little five-year-old boy had to have an operation to straighten his crossed eyes. This young man was petrified, but Rusty had had the same operation when he was a boy. He went to talk with the boy about it and was a great comfort to him.

When you go through hurt, God enables you to identify with somebody else who had a similar experience. William Carey said that his mother lost a child, and that's where she got her soft eyes. That's why other mothers ran to her when they lost a child.

That's the whole theory behind support groups. No one understands the struggles of alcohol addiction like an alcoholic. No one understands the agony of divorce like somebody who has been through it. Nobody understands the embarrassment of having a family member in prison like somebody who has dealt with this problem. If we can get these people together, they can encourage one another and comfort one another. God allows all of us to suffer so that we are able to comfort others who go through a similar experience.

Paul gave praise to "the Father of compassion and the God of all comfort" (2 Corinthians 1:3). I think there is a difference between compassion and comfort. Compassion has to do with understanding; comfort has to do with sharing. You can be sympathetic but not be of any help. Comfort puts compassion into action.

A little girl took first aid training. Several weeks later, she burst into the house all excited and said, "Mother, I saw a terrible accident and I used my first aid training."

"What did you do?" the mother said.

"I saw all that blood and I sat down on the curb and put my head between my legs so I wouldn't pass out!" she answered.

The training that God has given us is not for ourselves, but to identify with the problems of others and to assist. The word *comfort* means "to call alongside." The comforter listens, encourages, shares.

> Suppose a brother or sister is without clothes and daily food. If one of you says to him, "Go, I wish you well; keep warm and well fed," but does nothing about his physical needs, what good is it? In the same way, faith by itself, if it is not accompanied by action, is dead (James 2:15-17).

Compassion, if it's not accompanied by comfort, is dead, too. The comforter comes alongside. The comforter takes the initiative to make a phone call or write a note or make a visit or give the sufferer a tap on the shoulder saying, "I've been there. I can help. I care about you."

Pat Rogers was a member of our church who had to have her arm and shoulder amputated because of a malignancy. What a traumatic experience! One of the first visitors to her bedside in the hospital was Don Stansbury, another member of our church, who years before had lost an arm in a construction accident. Don's visit meant a lot to Pat, even though she didn't know him well. She said, "Don told me before I could expect others to accept me I had to accept myself." Any of the rest of us could have said that, but it would have seemed shallow and meaningless. But when it came from somebody who had been there, it had depth and meaning. Don did more than sympathize and identify with Pat—he contacted her and was a comfort.

> If we are distressed, it is for your comfort and salvation; if we are comforted, it is for your comfort, which produces in you patient endurance of the same sufferings we suffer. And our hope for you is firm, because we know that just as you share in our sufferings, so also you share in our comfort (2 Corinthians 1:6, 7).

If you are experiencing a deep hurt and you don't understand it, there's going to be a day in the future when God will use that hurt to comfort somebody else if you will be alert to it.

Hardships Enable Us to Testify of Our Faith

Any kind of hardship you go through puts the spotlight on your faith. The world is watching to see whether you are consistent, and they especially notice how you react when you're in trouble. Stephen Brown suggests that, for every pagan who undergoes cancer, there's a Christian who goes through cancer so the world can tell the difference. For every pagan who goes through bankruptcy, there's a Christian who goes through bankruptcy so the world can tell the difference. That's the reason Paul said, "If we are distressed, it is for your comfort and salvation." Since Paul was faithful, a lot of people were able to be saved. "Then many will give thanks on our behalf for the gracious favor granted us" (2 Corinthians 1:11).

> I urge you, as aliens and strangers in the world, to abstain from sinful desires, which war against your soul. Live such good lives among the pagans that, though they accuse you of doing wrong, they may see your good deeds and glorify God on the day he visits us (1 Peter 2:11, 12).

A construction worker climbed up on the superstructure of a tall building under construction and started doing some welding at night. It was damp and he slipped. He caught himself by his fingertips on a ledge. He tried with everything he had to pull himself up, but he didn't have the strength to do it. He just hung there screaming for somebody to help, but the noise of traffic was too great and nobody heard. His arms ached and his fingers became numb. Finally, he could hold on no longer, and he just let go, expecting to plunge to his death—not knowing that just a foot below him, unseen in the darkness, was the platform of a scaffolding. Instead of falling, he landed safely on the platform.

Maybe you've been hanging on for dear life. Maybe you're going through a hurt and you've been desperately trying to pull yourself up and resolve the situation on your own. Or you've cried out to other people, and they can't help you either. Maybe it's time to release yourself to the Lord and trust Him that He will provide.

That comfort is available to you. It's the promise of Jesus, who promised not to leave His disciples alone, but to send the *Comforter*, the Holy Spirit, to be with them (John 16:7, KJV). When you surrender to Jesus Christ, the Comforter comes to pick you up when you fall, to soothe you when you're hurt, to strengthen you through your suffering. As noted above, the word *comfort* means "to call alongside." God wants to call *you* alongside himself, but you have to humble yourself and not rely on your own strength. You have to rely on God and turn it over to Him, believing that "in all things God works for the good of those who love him" (Romans 8:28).

> I've had many tears and sorrows,
> I've had questions for tomorrow,
> there have been times I didn't know right from wrong.
> But in every situation,
> God gave blessed consolation,
> that my trials come to only make me strong.
> Through it all, through it all,
> I've learned to depend on Jesus,
> I've learned to trust in God.
> Through it all I've learned to depend upon the Lord.
> So I thank Him for the mountains
> and I thank Him for the valleys
> and I thank Him for the storms He's brought me through.
> For if I'd never had a problem,
> I'd never know that He could solve them
> and I wouldn't know what faith in God could do.[1]

---

[1] Andrae Crouch, "Through It All," © Copyright 1971 by Manna Music, Inc., 25510 Avenue Stanford, Valencia, CA 91355. International copyright secured. All rights reserved. Used by permission.

A Standard for Leadership

2 Corinthians 1:12 — 2:4

A RE WE EXPECTING TOO MUCH of our leaders?

For a while, it appeared there would not be anybody left to run for President in 1988. Gary Hart dropped out of the campaign after the press disclosed that he had been unfaithful to his wife. Senator Joe Biden withdrew his hat from the ring when the press revealed he had plagiarized a speech and exaggerated his credentials. Pat Robertson and Jesse Jackson, according to the press, were not morally pure in their premarital relationships, and, even though that had been many years earlier, their candidacies were shaken. A film clip of then Vice President George Bush reminded viewers that he had made a flippant and inappropriate remark about his opponent, Geraldine Ferraro, during the 1984 election. The press bends over backwards to prove that it is fair—dredging up dirt about everybody. It makes us wonder whether anyone can withstand the investigating eye of the media.

Are we expecting too much of our leaders? Are we setting unrealistic standards? Will we reach the point where nobody is qualified to lead?

There's no question that the press is looking more carefully at the private lives of public officials. That can be taken to extreme, of course, but, for the most part, I think it is good. There ought to be a consistency between what people say and what they are. If the scrutiny of the press holds public figures accountable for that kind of integrity, then we are better off for it. No one who frequently betrays his stated convictions should be considered qualified to lead.

In 2 Corinthians, Paul defended his qualifications as a leader. He set down some realistic standards that we can still use today to measure the people we elect to office—or to measure the spiritual leaders we follow. Better still, we ourselves ought to measure up to those standards in our own leadership roles in the home, church, school, or business.

Integrity

Paul was a man of honest character. "This is our boast," he wrote. "Our conscience testifies that we have conducted ourselves in the world, and especially in our relations with you, in the holiness and sincerity that are from God" (2 Corinthians 1:12). Three words in that verse outline what integrity is. The first is *conscience*. Paul served with a clear conscience.

Conscience is the inner faculty that approves when we do right and accuses when we do wrong. In order to be reliable, the conscience must be properly programmed and obeyed. Warren Wiersbe says, "The conscience is the window that lets in the light, and if the window gets dirty because we disobey, the light gets dimmer and dimmer." If we obey the conscience, and it's been programmed properly, we can serve with a clear conscience. Paul said that his conscience testified that he had conducted himself properly. Paul could have withstood the scrutiny of the press in his private life because he walked his talk.

Gary Hart was bitter about the fact that the press disclosed his private moral life. He insisted that what he did in private had nothing to do with his public service. I suggest that one's private life has everything to do with his public service. If a man cannot be trusted to be reliable in the most sacred vows of his life, how can he be trusted with secondary promises?

The second word is *holiness*. That's part of integrity. *Holiness* simply means being different from the world, being separate from the sins of the world. We don't have a right to expect spiritual leaders to be perfect, but we do have a right to expect the general direction of their lives to be different, to be separate from the sins of the flesh.

It is disappointing to discover those in leadership emulating the world in its greed, lust, and indulgence. After Jim and Tammy Bakker had months to repent, they were still advertising a telephone number people could call for inside information about them. "For $1.50, we'll disclose to you how Jerry Falwell really stole our ministry from us. Then, if you'll call back again tomorrow [and put some more money into our coffers], we'll tell you more." That's not holy. That's emulating the greed of this world.

Paul's motives were also *sincere*. That's the third word. Paul said he conducted himself "in . . . holiness and sincerity" (2 Corinthians 1:12). The word *sincere* comes from a Latin word meaning "without wax." The Greek word means "sun tested." The ancients made fine porcelain vases that were very expensive. Sometimes, when a vase was heated in the kiln, it would crack. Dishonest merchants would pour pearly white wax over the cracks, which would hide the flaws unless the vase were held up to the sunlight. Honest merchants would advertise their porcelain "*sinacera*" — without wax—no cracks, no covering of the flaws. When sincerity flows from our lives, there's no deception. There's no embellishing the truth for personal advantage. When the Son of God shines through and tests our lives, the absence of cracks will guarantee the presence of truth.

Bobby Jones was playing golf in an important tournament. His ball was in the rough. As he addressed the ball, his clubhead hit a twig that moved the ball. He turned and said to his caddy, "I moved the ball; count that a penalty stroke."

The caddy said, "Mr. Jones, I didn't see it; nobody else did, either."

"I saw it," Jones said. "That's enough."

That's integrity, a clear conscience that results in right living. There are still people of integrity in the world. They may not have the most charisma and they may not be the most self-promoting, but we must search them out and put them in positions of leadership.

When God wanted to appoint a king over Israel, He didn't choose the most obvious. He went to the home of a poor shepherd by the name of Jesse. Jesse's youngest son, David, was not very impressive in appearance perhaps, but "he chose David . . . to be the shepherd of his people. . . . and David shepherded them with integrity of heart" (Psalm 78:70-72).

Clarity

"We do not write you anything you cannot read or understand" (2 Corinthians 1:13). When you're dealing with critical matters, it is important that you speak the truth clearly.

Russ Summay of our church was my flight instructor when I learned to fly. He's one of those guys who can tell the truth clearly so you don't forget it. "Do not fly in bad weather or at night," he told me. "Ninety percent of accidents in small aircraft happen under those conditions.

"If you're flying in the daytime at 5,000 feet and the engine quits, you can just look down and spot a field and coast the plane down and land safely," he explained. "If it's at night and the engine quits, you coast down in the darkness until you get near the ground. Then you turn on the landing lights. If you don't like what you see, turn the lights off."

I've never forgotten that lesson. It was pretty clear.

When we're dealing with life and death matters, and especially with eternal matters, we need to speak clearly. There were no hidden motives in Paul's behavior and no hidden meanings in his communications. He said what he meant. That didn't always make him popular, but he knew he was dealing with matters too important to be vague.

Modern leaders are being urged to be deliberately deceptive. In *The Wall Street Journal* some time ago, David Brooks reviewed a book by Robert McElvain entitled, *The End of the Conservative Era: Liberalism After Reagan*. The thrust of the book was that politicians must be very careful about the words they use. The words they use have to meet the needs of people regardless of the reality, he says. McElvain suggests that politicians in this era should not use words like *liberal,* which turn people off. They should use words like *progressive,* because surveys show that only twelve to twenty-three percent of the populace reacts negatively to it.

> In the rush to appeal to the evolving taste, words are used to seduce and not to explain. Leading politicians in the . . . 90's should do their best to identify themselves with newness while espousing family and community themes with all their traditional connotations.

He urges the politicians to be vague when stating their position on abortion, for example, because precise positions (Geraldine Ferraro had one) may offend a large number of people. Then he adds, "There's a great opening here for liberal leadership that would speak of values and offer hope and not talk about problems and limits all the time."

In other words, be vague; be deceptive; don't let your exact views be known. Some of those views will alienate voters who really vote by charisma and not by content anyway. Leaders should use familiar words like "family" when in reality they don't mean a traditional family, but just a group of people who live together.

The same kind of duplicity takes place in theological circles, where some church leaders use terms they don't mean. They talk about the Word of God, when in reality they don't believe all the Bible to be the Word of God. They talk about the resurrection of Jesus from the dead, but they don't believe in the bodily resurrection—they just mean that Jesus' memory or His teaching lives on. The Mormons speak of Jesus as the "son of God," but they don't mean that He is God in the flesh; they mean He's *a* son of God the way we can all be sons of God.

Leaders worth following state their positions clearly, and we who follow have a responsibility to ask direct questions: "What is your stance on abortion?" "How do you feel about the freedom of the church?" "What about homosexual rights?" In the church, we need to ask: "What do you believe about the integrity of the Bible?"

Scripture says we need to speak the truth in love (Ephesians 4:15), but we need to speak the *truth*, and truth is seldom vague. When Jesus stood on trial before the Sanhedrin, the high priest was flustered because the witnesses were contradicting each other. Finally he looked Jesus squarely in the eye and asked, "Are you the Messiah or not?"

Jesus said, "I am, and one day you're going to see the Son of God coming in power and glory."

The high priest tore his garment and said, "We don't need any more witnesses. This is blasphemy! He claims to be the Messiah."

Because He stood for the truth, Jesus died. He could have been vague. He could have been evasive. But He spoke clearly. That's the reason He is worth following!

Transparency

There should be an unashamed openness about a leader. Paul was being criticized by some of his enemies for changing his plans. He had told them in a previous communication (cf. 1 Corinthians 4:19; 16:5) that he would stop by Corinth and visit with them on his way to Macedonia, and then stop by on the way back home and see them a second time. But then Paul changed his plans. Circumstances resulted in a change of itinerary, and it appeared on the surface that Paul was unreliable.

When you consider Paul's travel schedule, you have to be impressed that this kind of thing didn't happen more frequently than it did. When you travel, plans can be interrupted.

A man at the airport said to the airline clerk, "I want you to send this bag to Chicago, this one to Atlanta, and this one to New York."

The clerk said, "Sir, we can't do that."

"Oh, yes, you can!" the man said. "You did it last week and I didn't even ask you to."

Paul did a lot of traveling. Sometimes his plans were interrupted. He was open about why this change of itinerary occurred. "When I planned to visit you, I didn't do it lightly," he said. "I don't make my plans in a worldly manner so that in the same breath I say yes and no. As surely as God is faithful, that's not the case. The reason I changed my plans was that I knew if I came it would be a painful visit; you had not repented, and if I came there was going to be another confrontation. The timing wasn't right." (See 2 Corinthians 1:15—2:1.) He was open and transparent about why he had changed.

I had a high school teacher who would make spelling errors on the chalkboard. We'd say, "Miss McCabe, you misspelled such and such."

She'd say, "I know. I just wanted to make sure you were watching."

A good leader is open about mistakes. There's always a temptation to try to cover over and appear to be infallible. In reality, however, people are much more supportive of transparency than they are of perfection.

Some preachers at a conference in Georgia told how Wayne Smith helped them a few years ago. Wayne is the minister of the highly-regarded Southland Christian Church in Lexington, Kentucky—a church of some 4000 members. "We were all country preachers," one of them said, "and we held him in such high esteem, we felt intimidated around him. When he was introduced, he got up to speak with tears in his eyes. He said, 'Men, I'm in trouble. Some men in my church took me out to eat the other day, and they told me my preaching was shallow and I needed to study more, and now I'm hurting.'"

Then they ministered to Wayne, and he ministered to them. His transparency encouraged them to realize they weren't alone in receiving criticism. If you pretend to be perfect, people admire you at a distance for a while. But if you're transparent, they'll love you up close for a long time.

We can't expect leaders to be infallible or never to change their minds. Everybody makes mistakes. If we're wanting somebody who is flawless, we'll never find anybody who is qualified to lead. Good leaders try to minimize their mistakes, but they admit it when errors occur. And good followers know how to forgive and to be flexible.

In my ministry at Southeast Christian Church, I've occasionally had to admit serious mistakes. Years ago, we had a million-dollar offering to finance a building project. I told the congregation this would be a "once-in-a-lifetime sacrifice." Three years later, we needed $400,000 to complete the building. Our leaders concluded the one solution was to have another special offering. I announced, "We told you three years ago that the building-fund offering would be a 'once-in-a-lifetime sacrifice.' We were wrong. We will call this the 'second annual once-in-a-lifetime offering'!" People laughed and seemed to appreciate the humor.

We just have to admit we don't always see the future. We try to tell the truth, but sometimes circumstances change and we turn out to be wrong. People can accept mistakes if they feel their leaders are being honest. What they can't accept is deliberately being lied to. They resent the kind of pride that refuses to admit mistakes.

Humility

For a spiritual leader, humility means dependence on Christ and not on himself. Paul admitted that he changed his mind, but he pointed to Christ as the only one whose promises are completely reliable. "For the Son of God, Jesus Christ, who was preached among you by me . . . was not 'Yes' and 'No,' but in him it has always been 'Yes.' For no matter how many promises God has made, they are 'Yes' in Christ" (2 Corinthians 1:19, 20). Paul admitted he sometimes said one thing and did another because he couldn't see the future. But that's never the case with Jesus. Jesus sees the future. When He makes a promise, you can write it down. It is going to be fulfilled. He never fails. "It is God who makes both us and you stand firm in Christ. He anointed us, set his seal of ownership on us, and put his Spirit in our hearts as a deposit, guaranteeing what is to come" (2 Corinthians 1:21, 22).

If I buy a suit and put a twenty-dollar deposit on it, that means I'm going to come and pick it up after it's altered. When you became a Christian, God put a deposit on you, His Holy Spirit, which means when Christ returns, He's going to take you with Him. You can count on that. It is reliable because Christ's promises are firm.

A spiritual leader should exalt Christ and not himself. Secular leaders are expected to promote themselves, but even they ought to have enough humility to acknowledge they don't have all the answers. Abraham Lincoln once said, "I've been driven to my knees many times by the overwhelming conviction that I had no place else to go." Beware of the leader who has all the answers. Nobody does.

Spiritual leaders are here to promote Jesus. Beware of the spiritual leader whose name is always up front, who's always promoting his own stuff. It's the leader's task to point you to Jesus Christ. When John the Baptist saw some of his followers going after Jesus, John said, "He must increase, but I must decrease" (John 3:30, NASB). That should be the slogan of all spiritual leaders.

Many times in our church, when people get up to sing or perform on the platform, we don't even tell their names. Some of them have pretty impressive credentials, but it's not important. What's important is that they are exalting Christ. We try not to have the staff's name emblazoned over everything. Jesus is Lord of the church, and spiritual leaders have a right to be followed only if they follow the example of Jesus—or of Paul, who said, "Follow me because I follow Christ." In one pulpit there is taped a little verse of Scripture that has been there a long time. It simply says, "Sir, we would see Jesus."

Sensitivity

Years ago I received a telephone call from my mother informing me that my dad had been in a car wreck. Her very first words were, "Now your dad's not hurt, but there's been an accident." I didn't experience any anxiety because my mother anticipated what my feelings would be. She was much more sensitive than another lady, who called on another occasion to tell me why my son was late getting home.

"Mr. Russell, there's been an accident," she said. "We're sorry that Rusty is late. Now he's not involved, but it's right outside our house and he can't get out of the driveway."

Between the time she said, "There's been an accident" and "he's not involved," I nearly had a coronary!

One of the most important ingredients in leadership is relating to people. In 1 Corinthians, Paul listed a number of spiritual gifts, but then he said, "I'm going to show you a more excellent way. It doesn't make any difference how many languages I speak or how much power I have; it doesn't make any difference how dedicated I am; if I don't have love, it profits me nothing." (See 1 Corinthians 12:31—13:3.)

A Sensitive Leader Is Perceptive

Perceptiveness is the ability to see life from another perspective. It's the ability to see the big picture. Paul was perceptive about the feelings of the Corinthians. "It was in order to spare you that I did not return to Corinth," he told them (cf. 2 Corinthians 1:23).

The Corinthians were out of line. Paul had already chastised them in a letter and in what he called "a painful visit." When he received word from Titus that the situation still had not been corrected, he decided not to visit them again because it would not accomplish anything but to hurt them more deeply. He looked at the big picture. We sometimes think of the apostle Paul as being a very severe person—and he could be stern on occasion—but Paul was also sensitive to the feelings of people. He anticipated how they would react. He was tough and yet tender.

How sensitive are you to the feelings of people around you? All around us, every day, are people who need understanding. All around us are people who hurt. Sometimes they put on masks, but people are going through divorce, they're going through an alcohol or drug addiction, or they're going through severe financial problems. Even if they're not, other irritating problems nag at people every day. If we're not perceptive, if we don't look beneath the surface, we're not going to anticipate their feelings or be responsive to their needs.

I rode in a hospital elevator with a young mother taking her tiny baby home. With her was her husband, the grandparents, and a little girl about three years of age. The elevator stopped on the way down and a woman stepped on. "You're taking the baby home today?" she asked them, and everybody in the family beamed.

Instantly this lady stooped down to the three-year-old girl. "You must be a very special little girl to have a new baby come into your house," she said. "You know that now you have a new member in your family and you're going to have to be mother's helper, aren't you?"

I was moved by that woman's sensitivity. She knew that everyone tends to focus on the infant to the point that the three-year-old could feel jealous.

We could all use an added dose of that kind of sensitivity. It's easy for doctors, nurses, and dentists to see their patients as Case #238 instead of as people with hurts and anxieties, who need understanding and tenderness. It's easy for coaches of young children to see some of their ball players as liabilities to winning rather than as little persons with low self-esteem who need encouragement. Husbands need to remember that wives are not just robots grinding out a performance—they're people who need support and attention and encouragement.

A cartoon showed a wife standing in the middle of a house that was in complete disarray. She was saying to her husband, "You ask me what I do all day long? Well, today I didn't do it and here it is!"

Jesus was always perceptive about the feelings of people. He knew what was in their hearts. When a woman brought an alabaster box of perfume and poured all the expensive contents on His head, the disciples criticized her for such waste. But Jesus knew what she was thinking and feeling. "Leave her alone," He said. "She did what she could. She poured perfume on my body beforehand to prepare for my burial. I tell you the truth, wherever the gospel is preached throughout the world, what she has done will also be told, in memory of her" (Mark 14:6-9).

A Sensitive Leader Treats Subordinates With Respect

A real test of your sensitivity is how you treat people who are under your authority. A salesman in Miami telephoned his boss in Chicago. "I'm trapped in a hurricane," he said. "The highways are flooded; I can't drive out. There are no buses or trains, and the airport is shut down. I can't get out of here. What should I do?"

The boss answered, "Begin your two-week vacation today."

Just about all of us are in positions of leadership at one time or another, from baby-sitting to parenting; from being captain of the cheerleaders to being executive of a corporation; from serving as youth representative to becoming an elder in the church. When you're in a position of leadership, do you treat those under you with respect?

Paul had authority over the Corinthians spiritually. At the beginning of his letter he reminded them that he was an apostle of Jesus by the will of God. Paul could have pulled rank on them. He could have shown his authority and said, "If you don't obey, I'm going to excommunicate you," but he didn't. He wrote, "Not that we lord it over your faith, but we work with you for your joy" (2 Corinthians 1:24). To another church he wrote, "As apostles of Christ we could have been a burden to you, but we were gentle among you, like a mother caring for her little children" (1 Thessalonians 2:6, 7). Because Paul tempered his authority with sensitivity, little people sometimes took advantage of him and didn't respect him. But mature people, who knew Paul the best, loved him and served him for joy.

All of us know people in authority who lack sensitivity. They disregard the feelings of their subordinates. They treat them as inferior, they love to lead by intimidation, they love to enforce the rules rigidly, and they get ego gratification from being able to tell people what to do.

Usually the people who have the most trouble with authority are people who are the least accustomed to having it. General Pershing lit a cigarette during a blackout in World War I. A corporal barked, "Put out that light!" Then he saw it was General Pershing and apologized.

Pershing just patted him on the back and said, "That's all right, son. Just be glad I wasn't a lieutenant!"

Immature preachers can become very authoritarian. They scold and bark orders at their congregations. Some elders, when they first get the position, act like they're not supposed to enjoy things anymore. They want to lord their position over people rather than to serve them. "Be shepherds of God's flock that is under your care, . . . not lording it over those entrusted to you, but being examples to the flock," wrote Peter (1 Peter 5:2, 3). Relax in that leadership role. Sometimes you have to give guidance, but do it as one working with people, not lording it over them. The most effective leaders are those who understand people and treat them with respect.

Civil War historian Shelby Foote commented on the popularity of General U. S. Grant. He said Grant's men loved him because he identified with and understood their circumstances. On many occasions, when the Union army was making a tedious march, the men would look up and unexpectedly see General Grant on his horse beside them. They called him "a dusty man on a dusty road." He wasn't on an ego trip. He wasn't lording it over them or intimidating them. He was working with them for their mutual benefit.

A Sensitive Leader Openly Expresses Affection

Paul expressed his love for the people at Corinth in three ways. First, he admitted his vulnerability. "I made up my mind that I would not make another painful visit to you. For if I grieve you, who is left to make me glad but you whom I have grieved?" (2 Corinthians 2:1, 2). A lesser man would say, "If you don't like what I'm telling you, then good riddance. I can do without you." But Paul said he didn't want to alienate them because he needed them. "I wrote as I did so that when I came I should not be distressed by those who ought to make me rejoice" (2 Corinthians 2:3). He openly admitted, "You have the ability to make me rejoice, or to make me distressed. I'm vulnerable."

Some people are terrified of being vulnerable. If they admit they care, that means they can be hurt, so they don't admit they care. If they shed tears, people might laugh, so they don't cry. If they confess their faults, they can be betrayed, so they don't confess their faults. They go through life with a shell around them, never letting anybody know what is going on inside, never identifying with other people's feelings or letting other people identify with them. As a result, they lose the capacity to express love. To love and be sensitive to people, we have to make ourselves vulnerable.

Jesus was not ashamed to admit how he felt. He stood outside Jerusalem and wept. He said, "I wanted you to come to me, but you wouldn't." He wept at the tomb of Lazarus because He cared so much for him. He was so vulnerable that He was crucified by the very people He loved.

The second way Paul expressed affection was by practicing affirmation. "I had confidence in all of you, that you would all share my joy" (2 Corinthians 2:3). That's a short phrase, but it's important. Paul had gone through all kinds of trouble with these people, but still he said he had confidence in them that they would do better. It must have meant a lot to the Corinthians to have Paul say that. If we are going to be sensitive to people's needs, we have to understand the importance of affirmation.

I read somewhere that it takes forty compliments to offset one discouraging remark. I don't know how those things are calculated, but I think that sounds about right. The way to express our love is not through correction, but through encouragement. In educational circles, it's called "positive reinforcement." It's the sensitivity that sees the need in other people for a boost or a complimentary word. We seem to operate on the assumption that behaving correctly is what people are supposed to do; so, when they behave correctly, we don't say anything. We only speak up when there's wrong behavior, and we have to try to correct it. But it produces better results and communicates affection when we reinforce through positive affirmation.

Some friends asked me to sign one of my books they were going to send to Dr. LeRoy Lawson in Mesa, Arizona. I trembled a little. There are few people whom I respect more than Dr. Lawson. He preaches at a church that has a 3500-seat sanctuary, he has served as president of many institutions, and he's written many books himself. I never considered myself a writer, and I wondered what Dr. Lawson would think of my book.

A few weeks later, I got a letter from Dr. Lawson. It read,

> I can't tell you, Bob, how pleased I am to have you join the ranks of our book publishing works. We've been waiting a long time to hear from you. I hope this is only the first of many to come. Thank you for what you mean to me and what you are contributing to our brotherhood for the cause of Christ. I'm proud to call you my friend.
>
> Your brother,
> LeRoy Lawson.

For half an hour after I received that letter, I was like Barney Fife just after he'd made a big arrest. I strutted into the office and began telling the secretary how we'd do the next book. It was sensitive of Dr. Lawson to take the time to write a letter to affirm me. It motivated me to do more because I appreciated his confidence in me.

I get a lot of positive strokes, and I need them. But what about the people who work in the nursery or with the children? What about the elders and the chairman of the board? What about the widow who comes to church by herself, or the divorcée who comes with three children? Hardly anybody notices how desperately they need somebody to affirm them, to be sensitive enough to say, "I believe in you. I admire you. You're special."

Jesus was like that. He could affirm people who were less than perfect and motivate them to good behavior. He said to a woman caught in the act of adultery, "I believe you can do better; go and sin no more." He could say to weak, vacillating Simon Peter, "You're going to be a rock." He could say to uneducated, uncultured disciples, "You fellows have the responsibility to take the gospel to the whole world. I think you can do it." And they did. He expressed love by affirming them.

A third way Paul expressed affection was by verbalizing his feelings. "I wrote you out of great distress and anguish of heart and with many tears, not to grieve you but to let you know the depth of my love for you" (2 Corinthians 2:4). Love can be expressed in many ways—giving time, sacrificing money, paying attention, giving a gentle touch or look or some other gesture of affirmation—but we need to verbalize it, too. How long has it been since you actually said to your mate, "I love you"? How long has it been since you wrote your parents or your grandparents, not asking for money, but just to tell them, "I care about you"? When was the last time you told your child—or somebody close to you—"I love you"? Someday it will be too late.

When my younger son, Phil, was nine years old, I'd give him a hug and a kiss before he went to bed. One night, he got in bed and said, "Mom, I can't remember if Dad kissed me good night tonight." So I tiptoed up the steps and bolted through the door like I was a monster. I dived in his bed and we wrestled and tickled and hugged, and then we lay there for ten minutes and talked in the darkness.

The next night he got in bed and said, "Mom, I can't remember if Dad kissed me good night tonight." So I tiptoed up the steps and bolted through the door and we wrestled and talked the same way. Soon it became a tradition, every night.

Then one night his mother was away, and, after spending that time with Phil, I walked by his older brother's room and called, "Good night, Russ."

He said, "Good night, Dad."

I suddenly realized that I had not been very sensitive to my older son's needs. He heard us every night in the next room wrestling and carrying on, and then I'd just walk by his room and call, "Good night, Russ." That's not very sensitive.

"But he's fourteen," I thought to myself. "He's old enough to know that I love him, and you don't kiss a boy who's fourteen—but maybe I should try. . . ."

Without warning, I bolted through his door and dived on his bed and wrestled with him (and nearly got whipped, if I remember) and I lay there with him for some time, and I finally said some things that are hard for me to say: "Russ, I just want you to know I really think you're special and I appreciate you and I love you very much."

"OK, Dad; no problem," he said.

I felt better, though, because I had expressed it.

The next morning was Saturday morning, and Russ was getting ready to go somewhere. "Dad," he said, "could you come in here a minute?" He was a little self-conscious, and he stumbled a little bit, but he said, "I just want to thank you for coming in last night."

You never get too old for love. When was the last time you expressed to those closest to you, "I want you to know you're very special to me and I love you"? Do you think that's corny? It's one of the tougher things you'll ever do, but someday, when they're gone, you'll be glad you did.

That's one of the things that was so wonderful about Jesus. He wasn't too proud to say it. "As my Father loves me, so I love you. As I love you, I want you to love one another." Then He demonstrated His love beyond words by going to the cross and dying. "Greater love has no one than this, that he lay down his life for his friends" (John 15:13).

As you look back over those characteristics, do you see why Jesus is the only one worth following? He's the only one who has integrity; they could find no fault in Him, even though they scrutinized. He spoke so clearly the common people heard Him gladly. He was transparent; there was no pretense in Him. He was so humble that, even though He was God in the flesh, He washed feet. He was sensitive to our needs — so sensitive that He gave His life on the cross.

He alone is worthy of our total allegiance.

Restoring the Backslider

2 Corinthians 2:5-11

WHAT DO YOU DO when a Christian friend begins to drift away from the Lord?

Let's say you have a friend who hasn't been to church for two months, and you sense that he is really becoming infatuated with the materialism of this world. What do you say? Or suppose you have a Christian relative who is becoming increasingly dependent on alcohol. What do you do? If you go out to eat and see another church member walk in, arm in arm with someone other than his or her mate—and there's obviously something wrong going on between them—do you do anything? When a church member is spreading slander and being divisive, how do you respond? If you work with a Christian employer who you know is cheating people out of money. He is flagrantly, continuously dishonest. What do you say?

How do you confront and restore the backslider? It's the easiest thing in the world to look the other way and just passively hope that everything will take care of itself. After all, Matthew 7:1 says, "Do not judge, or you too will be judged." Who am I to tell another Christian how he is supposed to live? But Galatians 6:1 says, "If someone is caught in a sin, you who are spiritual should restore him gently." How do you reconcile those two verses of Scripture? Just what are we supposed to do when another Christian begins to drift away from God?

A Man's Flagrant Sin

There was a serious problem at Corinth. A man in the church was entangled in a flagrant and continuous sin. Paul said this person had caused

29

much grief. He had grieved the church, he had grieved Paul, and he had probably brought a lot of grief to his family and to himself.

Sometimes reading a letter is like listening to half a phone conversation. If you don't know what's being said on the other end, you have to put the pieces together. Paul was discussing forgiveness for a Christian who had repented, but he didn't tell us who he was or what he had done. You have to go back to Paul's first letter to the Corinthians to get an idea of the situation he was probably talking about. "It is actually reported that there is sexual immorality among you, and of a kind that does not occur even among pagans: A man has his father's wife" (1 Corinthians 5:1). A man in the church was living openly in incest. Paul was aghast—it was even worse than what normally went on in the world.

Apparently, it was common knowledge in that church. "And you are proud!" Paul added (1 Corinthians 5:2). The church was proud of its tolerant spirit. They were a magnanimous church—they didn't condemn anybody. This man was probably an influential member of the community, and they were just proud to have him as a member of their church. But Paul said, "Shouldn't you rather have been filled with grief and have put out of your fellowship the man who did this?" (1 Corinthians 5:2). Instead of boasting about what a tolerant church they were, they should have put this man out of the fellowship. He was ruining their testimony.

The very word church—*ekklesia*—means "called out." We're called out from the world to be pure, to be different. When we're not, the world laughs at us. Rather than be tolerant of sin, we ought to be so distraught that we would put a flagrant sinner out of our fellowship. The Corinthian church was to say to the man and to the community, "This person is no longer a member of the church. He is no longer to be regarded as a Christian."

The purpose of such action is to restore the sinner. The church is to confront *flagrant* sin. The Bible does not instruct church leaders to be undercover agents, privately investigating the lives of Christians and confronting every misdeed. In fact, for the most part we are to overlook people's faults. "Love covers over a multitude of sins," said Peter (1 Peter 4:8).

In Matthew 13 Jesus told a parable about an enemy who came and sowed weeds in a farmer's wheat field. When the servants discovered it, they asked the farmer, "Do you want us to go and pull them up?"

"No," he answered, "because while you are pulling the weeds, you may root up the wheat with them. Let both grow together until the harvest." At harvest time, they would be gathered up and separated (Matthew 13:24-30). In the same passage, Jesus said,

> The kingdom of heaven is like a net that was let down into the lake and caught all kinds of fish. When it was full, the fishermen pulled it up on the shore. Then they sat down and collected the good fish in baskets, but threw the bad away. This is how it will be at the end of the age. The angels will come and separate the wicked from the righteous (Matthew 13:47-49).

Don't get disturbed because the church isn't 100% pure. Jesus taught us to expect imperfection. He will separate the real from the false at the end of the age. He's the only one capable of doing that. We're not able to discern the difference sometimes. Frankly, I'm glad He doesn't eliminate everybody who's imperfect, or we would all be cast aside. But when the offenses are flagrant, when they are continuous, and when they threaten the testimony of the church, then they must be confronted.

John Wilson of Springfield, Ohio, suggested that the church has to determine whether it has measles or cancer. If it's just measles, let it go and it will get better. But if it's cancer, then it has to be confronted. The leaders of the church have to be discerning enough to tell the difference between malignancy and measles.

The Church's Responsibility

The Corinthian church took disciplinary action. At first, they were tolerant, but Paul told them, "When you are assembled in the name of our Lord Jesus and I am with you in spirit, and the power of our Lord Jesus is present, hand this man over to Satan, so that the sinful nature may be destroyed and his spirit saved on the day of the Lord" (1 Corinthians 5:4). Eventually, they confronted the situation and corrected it according to Paul's instructions.

The purpose of this kind of disciplinary action is to restore the backslider. "Hand this man over to Satan, so that the sinful nature may be destroyed and his spirit saved" (1 Corinthians 5:5). That means, put him back out into the world. Let him know that he is no longer welcome in the fellowship of the church. He's no longer included. It is hoped that, once he's cut off from the fellowship of the church, he will feel lonely. He'll see that sin grinds him down. Like the prodigal son in the pigsty, he will say, "I have sinned. . . . I am no longer worthy," and he will repent. But that will not happen if Christians continue to befriend him and grant him all the privileges of the church.

The second purpose is to restore the purity of the church. We say, "One rotten apple spoils the barrel." Paul said, "Your boasting is not good.

Don't you know that a little yeast works through the whole batch of dough?" (1 Corinthians 5:6). If you don't excise this malignancy, he told them, the whole church is going to be affected. Young people will see this behavior and think it's permissible. The world will ridicule you, Christ will be blasphemed, people will lose respect, and the Spirit will be quenched. So Paul told them to withdraw fellowship from the man: "I have written you in my letter not to associate with sexually immoral people—not at all meaning the people of this world who are immoral, or the greedy and swindlers, or idolaters. In that case you would have to leave this world" (1 Corinthians 5:9, 10). If you didn't associate with worldly people, you'd never go out your front door—you'd never go to work, you'd never go to a ball game. "But now," Paul wrote, "I am writing you that you must not associate with anyone who *calls himself a brother* but is sexually immoral or greedy, an idolater or a slanderer, a drunkard or a swindler. With such a man do not even eat" (1 Corinthians 5:11). You can't prevent someone from coming to church if he continues to do so even after you say he is no longer a member, but you can withdraw your fellowship. You can let him know that you don't consider him a brother any more. Otherwise, he has little motivation to change.

All of this sounds cruel and unloving if you don't understand that it's the last resort. Paul is not saying whenever someone in the church makes a bad mistake, the church should immediately kick him out. A three-step series of approaches is to be made to restore the backslider quickly, lovingly, and quietly. If those steps are followed, the discipline will seldom reach this extreme.

The first step is *self-examination*. "Do not judge, or you too will be judged," Jesus said. "For in the same way you judge others, you will be judged, and with the measure you use, it will be measured to you" (Matthew 7:1, 2). Before you judge other people, you ought to be willing to impose the same standards on yourself.

> Why do you look at the speck of sawdust in your brother's eye and pay no attention to the plank in your own eye? How can you say to your brother, "Let me take the speck out of your eye," when all the time there is a plank in your own eye? You hypocrite, first take the plank out of your own eye, and then you will see clearly to remove the speck from your brother's eye (Matthew 7:3-5).

You notice that your brother has a speck in his eye and it hurts. He needs somebody to help him remove it, but first you need to examine yourself.

Do you have the same sin? Then repent of it. Is your motive pure, or are you just going to give him a piece of your mind?

The second step is *gentle confrontation.* "Brothers, if someone is caught in a sin, you who are spiritual should restore him gently. But watch yourself, or you also may be tempted" (Galatians 6:1). *You who are spiritual* doesn't mean you who are *perfect;* nobody is perfect. It means those of you who are trying to be obedient; those of you who are walking by the Spirit. If you are not spiritual, if you're not mature enough to do it, then don't go. Just keep silent about the matter.

The word *restore* means to "reset a broken limb" or to "reset a dislocated bone." If you have a broken bone, you want the physician to be gentle. Likewise, we are to restore the sinner gently. When I was a boy, a part-time chiropractor, part-time farmer lived next door. When I dislocated my shoulder, my parents took me to see him, and he treated me like one of his cows. He grabbed that arm and whipped it around, and he finally said, "Yeah, I think he has a dislocated shoulder!" If you're hurting, you want the physician to be gentle. If somebody is hurting in sin, be gentle. Don't use inflammatory language. Don't be angry or harsh.

Richard Strauss, in his book, *Getting Along With Each Other,* says,

> Suppose a Christian wife is fuming as she rides home from a party with her husband. The atmosphere in the car is so thick you can cut it with a knife. He has flitted from one person to another all evening, mostly females, and left the wife to fend for herself. He never so much as spoke to her all night long. On the way home she's thinking about what she is going to say. She's thinking, "Boy, you made a fool out of yourself tonight. Everyone saw what a big flirt you are, Mr. Casanova. You wowed all the ladies tonight, didn't you? You don't care two cents about me, do you?"[2]

She needs to confront her husband, but that kind of confrontation is not going to be effective. It's going to start an all-night war because there's no gentleness, no self-examination. Strauss suggests that, instead of using "you" messages, we ought to use "I" messages, which are more gentle. Rather than say, "You never think about me . . . you made a fool of yourself . . . you don't love me," it would be better to say, "I felt rejected . . . I felt lonely . . . I felt all by myself." Spoken gently, such words will help the husband to be less defensive, to respond in understanding, and to repent.

[2]Richard Strauss, *Getting Along With Each Other* (San Bernadino: Here's Life Publishers, 1985).

Caring Christians should not wait for the leaders of the church to confront such a person; they should take the initiative and gently confront him. "If your brother sins against you, go and show him his fault, just between the two of you" (Matthew 18:15).

At Christian service camp years ago, I stayed in the dorm with the other faculty. You're not allowed to smoke at Christian camp, but occasionally I'd hear somebody walk down the hallway and go into the rest room, and then I would smell cigarette smoke. Since the dorm was just for faculty, I concluded that it was a preacher going into the rest room to smoke. It took some courage, but I stepped out in the hallway and met him. I said, "I just want you to know that when you smoke in there, people can smell it. I'm afraid it's going to get you in trouble, and it may hurt your ministry. If you're going to smoke, do it in the open; or, better still, I don't think you ought to do it at all."

He said, "Thank you for telling me. I had the habit as a boy in high school, and I don't know why I've picked it up again."

Ten years later, that minister approached me again. "Remember when you spoke to me at camp?" he said. "I quit smoking, and I'm glad I did because it could have harmed my testimony."

I could have gone to the dean or to the other faculty members and said, "Have you noticed somebody smoking in there?" But, on that occasion, I think I did it right—I went to him personally and gently. Don't go to your family or to board members or to your friends—that's childish, egotistical, and cowardly. When you do that, you don't want to restore the person. You want sympathy; you want attention; you might even want revenge.

The third step is *group intervention*. What if you gently approach somebody, and he doesn't repent? "If he will not listen," Jesus said, "take one or two others along, so that 'every matter may be established by the testimony of two or three witnesses.' If he refuses to listen to them, tell it to the church" (Matthew 18:16, 17).

This hasn't been practiced much in Christian circles because it takes tremendous courage. However, secular counselors are now discovering the wisdom of this tactic. They call it "crisis intervention." If you have a loved one who is on the downward spiral of alcoholism, rather than waiting for him to hit rock bottom and hoping that he will turn to AA, they now suggest you get a group of four or five people close to the individual to confront him, tell him how the drinking is affecting them and affecting him, and beg him to go for treatment. They boast an eighty-percent success rate! Crisis intervention is regarded as something new—but it was prescribed 2,000 years ago by Jesus Christ. Saying to someone, "We love you too much to let you continue this behavior," is much better than discussing it with others in his absence.

Only after these steps have been taken do you take the step of *deliberate isolation*. "If he refuses to listen even to the church, treat him as you would a pagan or a tax collector" (Matthew 18:17). How do you treat a pagan? You still speak to him; you're still congenial; but you don't treat him as a brother. You don't invite him to Bible studies. You don't necessarily have him in your home. This is severe action, but remember: it's the last resort, and—even now—the purpose is *redemption*. As Paul put it, "so that the sinful nature may be destroyed and his spirit saved" (1 Corinthians 5:5).

If the person responds at any point in this process, the next step is *loving restoration*. Paul was addressing just such a situation in 2 Corinthians 2. "The punishment inflicted on him by the majority is sufficient for him. Now instead, you ought to forgive and comfort him so that he will not be overwhelmed by excessive sorrow" (2 Corinthians 2:6, 7).

A physician in Texas had several boys. The oldest was a gifted musician, and he went off to college to study the violin. His family was affluent, and provided for all of his needs. He went to college on the west coast, and he bought the whole dose of defiance and rebellion that was common at Berkeley in the 60s. When he came back home that first summer, he was intent upon setting the family straight. His attitude was condescending; his conversation was critical; his behavior was rebellious.

But his father was a man of integrity and courage. After a few conversations, the father could see what was happening, so he sat the boy down for a talk. The boy began making all kinds of demands and denying having done any wrong.

But the father stopped him. "Son," he said, "Everything you have, I bought. That violin—I want you to leave it here. The car you drive—leave it in the garage. The money in your pockets, the clothes in your closet—I want you to leave them here. I'm going to give you the shoes on your feet and the clothes on your back. I want you to leave the rest behind. Then you'll be free."

It's amazing the education that boy suddenly got as he stood there in the living room facing his father. He realized that he'd have nothing left if he departed. He realized he was a loser.

The father said, "Don't come back here until you can come back knowing what you did a year ago about how this home is run. It is run fairly, it is run Biblically—but I am the authority."

The son said, "Dad, let's talk this over." They negotiated for a while. The boy changed his attitude and today he's an outstanding Christian.

The Sinner Expressed Sorrow

Apparently, a similar transformation had taken place in the life of this man from Corinth. He became sorrowful for the evil he had done. He repented, and he asked the church to forgive him. He forsook the relationship and sought to make his life right with God.

Genuine repentance involves three phases. The first is *conviction* — open admission that I have sinned, that I have been wrong; I won't try to cover it over. The second is *contrition* — I am genuinely sorry for what I have done. "The sacrifices of God are a broken spirit; a broken and contrite heart" (Psalm 51:17). It's been said that "God loves the bent knee, the broken heart, and the wet eye." You don't repent with a sneer on your face. You don't repent with a chip on your shoulder. You don't drop out of church. There is the open admission of sin, and usually tears. Peter went out and wept bitterly after he realized that he had denied Jesus.

Third, there is *change*. Repentance means a change of mind, a change of direction. If a person says, "I was wrong, I'm sorry," but keeps behaving the same way, he hasn't really repented.

A little girl called down to her mother after she had been put to bed. She said, "Mom, I want a drink of water."

The mother said, "No, you've already had a drink of water. Go to sleep."

Ten minutes later the girl called, "Mom, I want a drink of water."

The mother sternly said, "I said go to sleep. You're not getting any more water."

Ten minutes later the girl called, "Mom, I want a drink of water."

The mother said, "Heather, if you ask for a drink of water one more time, I'm going to come up there and spank you."

There was a pause, and Heather said, "Mom, on your way up to spank me, would you bring me a drink of water?"

That's not repentance. There can be the admission of wrong and the acceptance of the punishment, but if there's no change of attitude and no change of behavior, we haven't repented. "Godly sorrow brings repentance that leads to salvation and leaves no regret, but worldly sorrow brings death" (2 Corinthians 7:10). Judas admitted he was wrong, and he felt badly about it. But instead of weeping bitterly, the way Peter did, Judas went out and killed himself because he was too proud to repent.

The Church Was to Forgive Him

Once this man in Corinth had repented, the church had a responsibility to restore him, forgive him, and reaffirm its love for him.

The great thing about God's forgiveness is that He not only forgives us, He forgets. He forgets all about the sin. The Bible says God buries our sin in the deepest sea, and He remembers it no more. Charles Swindoll says, "God buries our sins in the sea, and then He puts up a no fishing sign."

But some Christian people are miserly with their forgiveness. They pretend to bury it, but they mark it with a buoy so they can go out and dredge it up whenever it's convenient. Even though a person is genuinely repentant, twenty years later someone will say, "You know, she was pregnant before she got married," or, "They lived together for a year before they got married," or, "What's he doing teaching? He was divorced years ago." Paul said, if the church doesn't learn to forgive, then the genuinely repentant feel excessive sorrow. They feel an awesome burden of guilt to begin with, but if Christians can't forgive them, then that guilt is compounded, even though God has forgiven them. The church should be a place where repentant people are forgiven and welcomed with open arms.

Forgiveness has been defined as "relinquishing my right to retaliate." Christian forgiveness goes a step further. You not only release your right to retaliate, you do your best to restore the relationship.

That's not easy. That takes effort, and it takes time. That's what we want God to do for us; we don't want God to punish us for our sin. We want Him to continue to include us in His family. Paul said, "You ought to forgive and comfort him" (2 Corinthians 2:7). Recognize the person is hurting. Put an arm about his shoulder. Reaffirm your love for him. Whatever you did with him before, do it again. By doing so you're being obedient to God. Forgiveness is not an option, it's a commandment. "Forgive . . . one another . . . as the Lord forgave you" (Colossians 3:13).

We do so "in order that Satan might not outwit us. For we are not unaware of his schemes" (2 Corinthians 2:11). Satan is clever; he's a schemer. He is determined to destroy the church. He makes noises at the front door and sneaks in the back. He gets our guard up about liberalism, but then we're vulnerable to a legalistic spirit. We stand guard for the purity of the church, but then we risk becoming so unforgiving that nobody feels comfortable. The church has to be constantly alert lest Satan draw us in.

Paul is urging the church to be like Jesus, full of grace and truth. People ought to be able to look at the church and say, "That church stands for the truth. They teach and preach the Bible." But people also ought to be able to look at the church and say, "That church is full of grace, too. They've got people there who have had horrendous drug and alcohol problems, marital problems, moral problems, and legal problems—but they've been forgiven, they've been restored, and they've been accepted."

Dr. David Seamands is a counselor at Asbury College. In his best-selling book, *Healing for Damaged Emotions*,[3] Seamands points out that our forgiveness of ourselves and of other people is closely related to our concept of God. "Your view of God," he says, "will dictate how well you can forgive." He tells about a seminary student who was struggling with guilt about the past. He was an A student, but he was an emotional wreck.

Seamands asked him, "What is your view of God?"

The young man said, "I'll bring God's picture to you tomorrow."

Dr. Seamands said he could hardly wait; any theologian would be interested in seeing a "picture of God." He didn't know whether the student was going to use infra-red lights or laser beams or what.

The next day the young man came in with a picture of Ebenezer Scrooge. "That's my view of God," he said, and then he pointed to Tiny Tim. "Here I am."

No wonder the young man had a hard time forgiving himself and forgiving others. His view of God was one of a miserly, mean-spirited, angry Scrooge.

What's your concept of God? Do you see God as a Scrooge, a rigid legalist who stands ready to punish? If so, it's probably hard for you to forgive yourself and to forgive others. Or do you go to the other extreme and see God as a doting old grandfather who can't even see your sins, much less hold you accountable? If so, it's hard for you to stand for the truth.

Jesus came to reveal God to us. He was full of grace and full of truth, and He told us what God is like. God is like a loving father who had two sons. One son rebelled. He took his share of his father's money and went to a far country. His father let him go, because he was full of truth. In the far country, the son wasted his money, his mind, and his body. He spent it all. He finally ended up in a pigsty, feeding pigs. "This is wrong," he said. "I'm going to go back and ask my father to forgive me."

As he came home, the father was waiting. He ran to greet his son and forgive him, because he was full of grace. He could have made him work as a hired hand, but he restored him to sonship. He said, "This son of mine was dead and is alive again," and he welcomed him back with a celebration (Luke 15:11-24).

That's what God is like. He's waiting now to forgive you, regardless of whether your sin has been flagrant or hidden. The Bible says, "He that comes to me I will in no wise cast out." And if God doesn't cast them out, neither should we.

[3]Wheaton: Victor, 1981.

Finding
Peace of Mind

2 Corinthians 2:12-17

CHARLES KEATING, owner of the failed Lincoln Savings and Loan Association, was a little shook up as he left court on August 2, 1991. Keating, facing twenty counts of securities fraud, was leaving the courtroom after a pretrial hearing when a ninety-year-old former customer, Sarah Mandell, grabbed him by the lapels and began shaking him. "Give me back my money!" she cried.

We can all sympathize with Mrs. Mandell. In fact, in these days of an uncertain economy, we're all a little edgy. Is *my* bank safe? Will *my* life's savings be there when I need them?

It's not just the uncertainty of the economy that has us biting our nails, either. Each of us could list a dozen subjects that make it difficult for us to keep calm: a malignant tumor, a bitter divorce, aging parents, the Mid-East, the governor's race, a guilty conscience, an IRS audit, rebellious teenagers, transmission trouble, the Supreme Court. If there ever was a time when we need the peace of God that passes understanding, it is now.

Paul began this passage by saying, "I had no peace of mind." That's surprising because we usually think of inner peace as a natural result of being a Christian. But Paul admitted that during this period of his missionary journey, he did not have peace. "When I went to Troas to preach the gospel of Christ and found that the Lord had opened a door for me, I still had no peace of mind, because I did not find my brother Titus there. So I said good-by to them and went on to Macedonia" (2 Corinthians 2:12, 13). Paul had expected his co-worker to bring news about the troubled Corinthian church. Paul had sent a stern letter to that church, and now he wondered what their reaction would be.

39

When I'm away from my church on vacation, I think about it all the time. I call back in the afternoon on Sunday and ask, "How did the service go? Were there any responses to the invitation? What was the attendance? Did my replacement make me look bad?" I do that even when things are going well at the church. The Corinthian church was having serious problems, and Paul was trying to correct them from a distance. When Titus didn't arrive with the long-awaited report, Paul was so restless he couldn't stand it. He moved on to Macedonia for more information.

But Paul's anxiety was temporary. He quickly recovered his peace of mind because of his faith in God. Christians experience pressure and anxiety like everybody else, but our faith in Christ should enable us to handle that stress and live lives that are predominantly serene.

A Grateful Heart

After he identified the pressures on him, Paul changed the pace of his thoughts, and his key word is *thanks:* "Thanks be to God, who always leads us in triumphal procession in Christ" (2 Corinthians 2:14). He was reflecting the same attitude he encouraged the Philippian Christians to have:

> Do not be anxious about anything, but in everything, by prayer and petition, with thanksgiving, present your requests to God. And the peace of God, which transcends all understanding, will guard your hearts and your minds in Christ Jesus (Philippians 4:6, 7).

Circle that word, *thanksgiving.* When you complain about your problems, you increase your anxiety. When you praise God for His goodness, you increase your peace.

> When upon life's billows you are tempest tossed,
> When you are discouraged, thinking all is lost,
> Count your many blessings—name them one by one,
> And it will surprise you what the Lord hath done.[4]

Most of us aren't very good at that. Most of us are constant complainers. Nobody has ever had it better, yet we gripe continuously. We think it's a mark of sophistication to be critical or complaining, but it really is an indication of spiritual immaturity. We complain to get attention or sympathy.

[4]Johnson Oatman, Jr., "Count Your Blessings," 1897.

We think that it's harmless, but in reality it destroys our peace and arouses the wrath of God. "Now the people complained about their hardships in the hearing of the Lord, and when he heard them his anger was aroused" (Numbers 11:1).

Some children decided to play a trick on Grandpa. When he was asleep, they sprayed his moustache with bug spray. When he woke up, he sniffed and said, "Something stinks in this room." He went into the kitchen and said, "The kitchen stinks." He went outside and said, "The whole world stinks!" It wasn't the world—Grandpa needed to clean up under his nose. There's something wrong with us that we complain that the whole world stinks. We don't like the schools, we don't like our house, we don't like our jobs, we don't like our families. It doesn't matter how good we have it—we still find something to gripe about. We eat some good food at a restaurant, but we go home complaining about the service or how drafty it was. I hear people at church who find some little thing to complain about all the time, and yet they would freely tell you they love the church.

We are almost professional complainers. If we got paid for it, we'd be millionaires.

Two elderly women went to an orchestra concert. On the way home, one asked the other, "How did you like it?"

The other woman said, "The way that first violinist blew his nose after the first selection just ruined the entire evening for me."

Some people miss the entire concert of life and focus in on the blowing of a nose. That complaining mind etches dissatisfaction and unrest in our lives. We have done it so often it has become second nature to us. Many of us have little peace because we praise so little and complain so much. "I complained, and my spirit was overwhelmed" (Psalm 77:3, KJV).

Sometimes I think we would be more grateful if God gave us less. Take, for example, the changing of the leaves—they are spectacular in the fall. I wonder what would happen if the leaves didn't change. Some little county in eastern Kentucky would decide to spray paint all their leaves and make them as pretty as the ones we see every fall. People would travel for miles to see that. They would pay ten dollars a carload.

Fall colors are spectacular, but so abundant we take them for granted. We can drive through our own neighborhoods to see the changing of the leaves, but we don't appreciate them. I mentioned to someone about how pretty the leaves were. The man said, "Boy, don't talk to me about leaves! If you had the kind of trees in your yard that I have. All that raking. . . ."

Now that may seem like a little thing, but when we do that, our greatest assets wind up sounding like liabilities. Our peace of mind is disturbed because we see only our problems. I really believe the most important step in developing inner peace is to quit complaining and start praising.

"Do everything without complaining" (Philippians 2:14). If you don't learn anything else in this chapter, learn that verse. "Do everything without complaining." Read it aloud: "Do everything without complaining." Now listen to yourself! As soon as you catch yourself griping, stop it. If you don't notice it, ask somebody close to you to help you. He will be delighted to point it out! And don't be angry with him when he reminds you you're complaining. Don't excuse yourself and say, "That's just my nature. I don't mean anything by it. It's just harmless." It is not harmless. It is spoiling your peace of mind. It is making people around you miserable.

Start praising! Find scores of things to thank God for. Make yourself a little rule: "Every time I catch myself complaining, I'm going to say, out loud, five things for which I'm grateful." You'll discover the peace of God that transcends all understanding beginning to take place in your life.

In his excellent book, *Money, Sex and Power*[5], Richard Foster emphasizes that the essential attitude for contentment in dissatisfied America is gratitude, whether you have little or much. He says, for example, when you wake up in the morning do you thank God for your night's sleep? Or do you complain that you have to get up in the morning?

You might answer, "I can't thank God for my night's sleep, because I'm a poor sleeper." If that thought has crossed your mind, you're the person God wants to deal with. You're negative. You're a complainer. The Bible calls you a grumbler. If you can't sleep, get up and walk around and thank God you can walk. Or go by the room of one of your children and thank God he's asleep.

Cultivating a spirit of thanksgiving is not easy in this ungrateful, critical society. Foster suggests that, once in a lifetime, we ought to go to the bank with our paycheck, cash it, and ask the bank to give us the money in one-dollar bills. Then we should come home and spread all those bills on the table so that we can visualize how good God has been to us and see how rich we really are.

If you're thinking, "Yes, but the dollar bill doesn't go as far as it used to," listen to yourself! You're the person God wants to deal with. You're a grumbler, a complainer—and it's ruining your attitude. Foster suggests that we should divide those dollars into stacks and say, "This is what I give for my house, this is how much goes for food, this is how much goes

---

[5]Richard J. Foster, *Money, Sex and Power: The Challenge of the Disciplined Life* (New York: Harper & Row, 1985).

to my car," and so on. But the first stack ought to be, "This is what we're going to give to God" — the first fruit of thanksgiving. Maybe when we visualize how good God has been, we'll begin to be thankful.

I remember one morning during a building program, my wife said, "You must be worried about something." She was right. I had tossed and turned all night worrying about trying to sell our old building and how to meet the additional costs we were running into on the new one. I lay there awhile thinking about the pressure. But I remembered to give thanks, so I began my quiet time that morning by saying, "Lord, thank You for my Christian parents, thank You for the school I went to, thank You for my wife and my healthy children, and thank You for this church."

As I was giving thanks, I remembered something. I remembered how much more fun it had been to play basketball when the pressure was on. I used to love to play in those critical games when every basket mattered, every pass was crucial, and every play was important. I said, "Thank you, Lord, to be a part of a church where every person is important, every Sunday is crucial, and where there is such growth that the pressure is on. Thank you for the pressure. I wouldn't want to be in a place where everything was routine." I got up from my place of prayer with a new sense of joy and peace for my role that day.

It really works. I challenge you — I beg you — stop griping and start praising. You don't have to be a Pollyanna and say, "There's nothing wrong in this world; it's all beautiful." Sometimes you have to identify and deal with a problem. But you can be thankful, you can be positive, and you can begin to experience the peace that passes understanding.

A Sense of Significance

"God . . . leads us in a triumphal procession in Christ and through us spreads everywhere the fragrance of the knowledge of Him" (2 Corinthians 2:14). We need to have the feeling that our lives count for something. Victor Frankl wrote, "There's nothing in the world which helps a person surmount difficulties, survive disappointments, keep healthy and happy, as the knowledge of a life task worthy of his dedication." Newly retired people sometimes discover that their retirement doesn't bring peace, but turmoil, because they no longer have a sense of importance.

Paul knew his life mattered to God. He compared the Christian life to a Roman triumph, the victory parade given to a conquering general. It was like the ticker-tape parade given to honor sports, political, and military heroes today. Warren Wiersbe describes it this way:

If a commander-in-chief won a complete victory over the enemy on foreign soil and if he killed at least 5,000 enemy soldiers and gained new territory for the emperor, then that commander-in-chief was entitled to a Roman triumph. The processional would include the commander riding in a golden chariot surrounded by his officers. The parade would also include a display of the spoils of battle as well as the captive enemy soldiers. The Roman priest would also be in the parade carrying burning incense to pay tribute to the victorious army. The procession would follow a special route through the city and would end at the Circus Maximus, where the helpless captives would entertain the people by fighting wild beasts. It was a special day in Rome when the citizens were treated to a full scale Roman triumph.[6]

We're part of that victory parade. Our commander-in-chief, Jesus Christ, came to foreign soil and completely defeated the enemy, Satan. He claimed the spoils of battle, lost souls who had been in bondage to the devil. The victorious general's sons would walk behind their father's chariot, basking in his victory. That's where believers are today, following in Christ's triumph. Our Heavenly Father has won, and we're glorying in His victory.

"We are to God the aroma of Christ among those who are being saved and those who are perishing. To the one we are the smell of death; to the other, the fragrance of life" (2 Corinthians 2:15, 16). The crucial task of every Christian is to be a testimony for Christ. To some, it's the aroma of life; to others, the aroma of death.

Have you ever noticed how different people will react differently to the same smell? I love the smell of a locker room — it reminds me of football. My wife can't stand that. A certain flower may remind you of a wedding; it might remind someone else of a funeral. In the Roman triumph, the burning incense was the smell of celebration and life to the victorious army. But to the chained captives marching to the arena in that parade, it was the stench of death. In the same way, Paul said Christians living in the world are a sweet smell to those who are being saved, but a stench to those who are lost. Genuine Christians love having other Christians around because it reminds them of salvation; but the nonbeliever hates being around dedicated Christians because he's reminded of his sin and his responsibility. To some, we have a smell of death; to the others, the fragrance of life.

My sister Rosanne is a joy to me. She's a counselor and a friend. When she planned our parents' fiftieth anniversary celebration, at her place of

[6]Warren Wiersbe, *Be Encouraged* (Wheaton: Victor, 1984).

business she was getting out some letters. Somebody in the office said, "Why don't you just make those copies on the office copy machine?"

"No, I don't think I will," she said.

"Why not?"

"Well, I just don't really think it's right for me to use the company's copy machine for my own personal business because that costs the company."

"I'm certainly glad I don't have to live with your conscience," the woman responded in a huff. "You are disgusting."

Sometimes our standards annoy people. It's easier to sin if they are convinced everybody else is doing it. But if there's one Christian who takes a stand for what is right, he may be considered an irritant. I don't like the smell of smoke, but that smell might save my life if it motivates me to run from a fire. The world may not like the fragrance of the Christian, but it just could be that smell will be a warning to spare them from eternal fire.

You may never know how far your influence is spreading. It's an awesome thing that your influence could determine somebody's eternal destiny. But that's what gives life meaning and peace. When you have a sense of meaning, you realize your life really counts for God. That gives you a sense of meaning and a sense of peace.

Pure Motives

"Unlike so many, we do not peddle the word of God for profit" (2 Corinthians 2:17). That word *peddle* carries a dishonest connotation. It was used of a wine merchant who diluted his product then sold it as pure. Paul was saying, "We don't mix the pure truth of the Word of God with any human philosophy. We don't water it down so it can be to our personal advantage and we can pad our own pockets." There were all kinds of hucksters of the gospel in Paul's day, and their ilk are still with us today.

A preacher on the west coast told about a loud Pentecostal woman in his church. Every time she saw him, she shouted, "Oh Brother Bob, it's so good to be in the Spirit today. Hallelujah, praise Jesus, isn't God good? Praise the Lord!"

One day there came to his church a family from the right side of the tracks. They drove up in a Mercedes; they were dressed immaculately; everything about them gave evidence of wealth. So he tried to have a dignified conversation with them in the hallway after the service. Out of the corner of his eye he saw this Pentecostal woman coming. He prayed, "Oh, Lord, you delivered Daniel from the lions' den and you delivered Jonah from the whale. . . ."

But she came anyway. "Oh, Brother Bob, it's so good to be in the Spirit today!" she began. "Hallelujah! Praise Jesus! I've got wonderful news to share with you—praise God!"

"Martha, can it wait until later?" he said.

"No, praise God, my rich uncle died and left me $200,000—and I'm going to give half of it to the building fund!"

He said, "Hallelujah! Praise Jesus! Isn't God good? Praise the Lord!"

What about your motives? Why do you say the things you say? Why do you sing the songs you sing? Do you come to church just because you have a chance to meet people and increase sales, or get up in front to lead because it's an ego boost? Paul said, "We don't peddle the Word of God for profit. Our motives are pure." There's no peace if there's constant deception within you. If you're always pretending, your conscience is going to bother you and there will be no peace. I urge you to be honest, refuse to fake it, be up front, be transparent, be real. Then you can sleep at night.

> When you get what you want in your struggle for self
>   and the world makes you king for a day,
> Then go to the mirror and look at yourself
>   and see what that guy has to say.
>
> For it isn't your father, mother or wife
>   whose judgment upon you must pass.
> The fellow whose verdict counts most in your life,
>   is the guy standing back from the glass.
>
> He's the fellow to please, never mind all the rest,
>   for he's with you clear up to the end.
> And you've passed your most dangerous, difficult test
>   if the guy in the glass is your friend.
>
> You may be like Jack Horner and chisel a plum
>   and think you're a wonderful guy.
> But the man in the glass says you're only a bum
>   if you can't look him straight in the eye.
>
> You can fool the whole world down the pathway of years
>   and get pats on the back as you pass.
> But your final reward will be heartaches and tears
>   if you've cheated the guy in the glass.[7]

[7]"The Guy in the Glass," source unknown.

The word *peace* is used about 200 times in the Bible, and it's almost always linked with *righteousness*. Righteousness almost always comes first. Righteousness and peace have kissed each other, the psalmist said. If there's no righteousness in your motive, there's no peace in your mind.

A Sure Destiny

Have you ever watched a tape-delayed broadcast of a ball game that you already knew your team had won? You're so happy about the victory, you decide to stay up until 1:00 A.M. to watch the game. Your whole attitude is different. Your team might get ten points behind, but you don't mind. You don't gripe about little things that happen. You don't get disturbed. You know in the end you're going to win—it's just a matter of how.

The great thing about being a Christian is that Christ has already won the victory. He won it at the cross. The book of Revelation tells us that, in the end, He's going to come in triumph. We can know as Christians we have eternal life. We know the outcome; we don't always know why there are detours or why there are problems, but we shouldn't be biting our nails and getting all uptight because we know in the end we're going to have the victory. "Christ leads in triumph, we are being saved, and we are the fragrance of life," Paul said.

> There is a place of quiet rest,
>> Near to the heart of God.
> A place where sin cannot molest,
>> Near to the heart of God.
>
> There is a place of full release,
>> Near to the heart of God.
> A place where all is joy and peace,
>> Near to the heart of God.
>
> Oh Jesus, blest Redeemer,
>> Sent from the heart of God,
> Hold us, who wait before Thee,
>> Near to the heart of God.[8]

Lowell W. (Bud) Paxton made millions of dollars with his creative idea for the Home Shopping Network on television. But Bud Paxton's life was

[8]Cleland B. McAfee, "Near to the Heart of God," 1901.

not at peace. There was a troubled marriage and a multitude of frustrations in his life. Then Bud became a Christian, and his whole value system was realigned. People now mattered more than things, eternity more than time.

On October 19, 1987, Paxton was scheduled to address the International Convention of Stockbrokers in Washington D.C., a gathering of 1800 stockbrokers or representatives of brokerage firms. But when he entered the room at 1:30, only about twenty people were there. Earlier in the day the stock market had started to plunge—a plunge that would go 508 points. The people in the room had panicked. Everybody left. Paxton said that, as he walked down the hallway of his Washington hotel, he soon quit counting the number of businessmen in expensive three-piece suits who were crying their eyes out because their lives were crumbling and their security was threatened.

Paxton himself lost over 100 million dollars on the stock market that day. His preacher asked him, "Aren't you really ruffled? How do you feel?"

He said, "I'm just thankful that my trust isn't in the things of this world."

> Command those who are rich in this present world not to be arrogant nor to put their hope in wealth, which is so uncertain, but to put their hope in God, who richly provides us with everything for our enjoyment. Command them to do good, to be rich in good deeds, and to be generous and willing to share. In this way they will lay up treasure for themselves as a firm foundation for the coming age, so that they may take hold of the life that is truly life (1 Timothy 6:17-19).

The Sunday after the stock market took that dramatic plunge, our church, on a normal day, had a near-record offering. I was proud of our people for remembering that there is no security in investing in this world, but there is security near to the heart of God.

Only when we place our trust in Jesus Christ can we develop a thankful heart, a significant task, an authentic motive, and an eternal destiny that will give us the peace that passes understanding.

The Confident Christian

2 Corinthians 3:1-6

THE CHRISTIAN SHOULD BE A HUMBLE PERSON.

The Christian should be a confident person.

How do you reconcile those two virtues? Christians are not supposed to have an inflated view of their importance. But neither are we to be insecure, plagued with constant feelings of self-doubt. We are to evaluate our gifts properly. The book of Romans gives us a clue: "Do not think of yourself more highly than you ought, but rather think of yourself with sober judgment, in accordance with the measure of faith God has given you" (Romans 12:3).

We are to be confident without being cocky, self-assured without being arrogant. A good athlete who does not believe in his ability will sit on the bench. A public speaker who is so nervous that he can't remember his speech will not be effective. An overly cautious driver who lacks confidence is a hazard on the highway.

Self-confidence is absolutely essential for the Christian as well. Confidence enhances the use of our spiritual gifts. Paul told Timothy, "Fan into flame the gift of God, which is in you through the laying on of my hands. For God did not give us a spirit of timidity, but a spirit of power, of love and of self-discipline" (2 Timothy 1:6, 7). If you lack confidence, you're not going to be able to teach, sing, encourage, or use effectively the gifts that God has given you.

Confidence also enhances our personal testimony. Can you imagine Lee Iacocca coming on television and timidly saying, "We hope our cars are OK; maybe you ought to try one"? No, he comes on with confidence and says, "If you can find a better car, buy it." And he becomes believable.

We Christian people should not be hesitant about our salvation. If we are apologetic about our beliefs, we're not going to convince anybody. But when we can say with confidence, "Christ has forgiven me. Christ has given me a new purpose in life," then our testimony is believable.

Confidence also enhances our personal joy. *Reader's Digest* reported recently that we are born with two innate fears—only two—the fear of falling and the fear of loud noises. All other fears are acquired. I believe that nearly all the others are from the adversary, and they need to be unlearned.

It is a terrible thing to go through life being afraid of people—insecure, inhibited, always lacking confidence. Life becomes a continuous, exhausting effort to avoid embarrassing yourself. There is a special joy that comes to people who aren't afraid any more. It is a wonderful thing to be able to say confidently with Paul, "I can do everything through [Christ] who gives me strength" (Philippians 4:13).

When Paul speaks of his confidence in the Christian life. He uses the word *competent* three times. That word means, "sufficient" or "qualified." It is the same word used in 2 Corinthians 2:16 where he asked, "Who is equal to such a task?" This passage gives the answer. The Christian can be equal to the task through Christ. Here are four ways that we can gain confidence as believers.

Resist the Temptation to Impress Others

Paul said, "Are we beginning to commend ourselves again? Or do we need, like some people, letters of recommendation to you or from you?" (2 Corinthians 3:1). Paul was not out to impress people, though he could have. He had impressive credentials. He was a world traveler and a brilliant man, but he refused to boast about himself to impress other people.

It's common today for athletes, politicians, and people in public office to try to commend themselves. When you have to write a resumé about yourself, you know what it is to have to commend yourself. It's a constant temptation to find some way to boast about your accomplishments so other people will esteem you.

I heard of a preacher who was proud that he had written a book. He got in the pulpit the Sunday after the book was published and prayed, "Oh God, Thou who hast also written a book. . . ." Sometimes we find pretty clever ways to commend ourselves. But Paul insisted, "I'm not here to try to impress you by boasting of myself, and I don't need letters of recommendations from other people, either."

In that day when the people traveled to a new community, they didn't have credit cards that could tell a person's credit rating instantly by computer, so they would establish their credibility by bringing letters of recommendation from influential people in other towns. These would be similar to letters of recommendation people now write for someone else to help them get hired for a job or admitted to a college. In the ancient world, as now, sometimes these written testimonials didn't mean very much because people would exaggerate or falsify.

One lazy employee was always changing jobs. He asked his boss for a letter of recommendation. The boss wanted to get rid of the slacker, but he didn't want to be dishonest by praising him falsely, so he wrote: "To Whom It May Concern: If you can get Bob Johnson to work for you, you will be extremely fortunate!" A preacher was asked to write a letter of recommendation for a church member who was completely obnoxious. The preacher didn't want to be dishonest, so he wrote: "When you come to know Tim Hawkins the way I know him, I'm confident you will feel about him exactly the way I do." Sometimes letters of recommendation don't mean very much. But Paul said he wasn't concerned about what other people felt about him. That was not the source of his confidence.

If your confidence is directly related to other people's opinions, you are going to be plagued with insecurity for three reasons. First of all, people are fickle. People can approve of you one day and then criticize you the next. One day the crowd said, "Hail, Jesus," and a few days later it was, "Nail Jesus." I've heard football fans at U of L football games praise Coach Howard Schnellenberger as a genius at the beginning of a game and berate him as a complete incompetent by the end of the game. If you don't understand that people are fickle and you put a lot of stock in their approval, you can be devastated.

The second reason you shouldn't put stock in people's opinion is that people are often wrong. One newspaper editor ripped Abraham Lincoln apart for his Gettysburg Address, saying his remarks were inappropriate and not worth mentioning. Thomas Edison's grade school teacher said he was stupid and would never learn. Walt Disney was fired from a newspaper whose editor said he had no creative ideas. Louisa May Alcott was told that she had no ideas worth the contemporary thought of her day. Fred Smith, the head of Federal Express, got the idea of a door-to-door delivery service while he was in college. He wrote his thesis on the idea and his professor gave him a C-minus, disapproving of the concept. Noah preached for 120 years and he had no converts except the seven other members of his family. If Noah's confidence had been directly related to people's response, he would have been devastated because people—even the majority of people—can be wrong.

The third reason you shouldn't put stock in people is because people's tastes are varied. What one person likes, another person may find repulsive. If you try to please everybody, then you'll be constantly frustrated and you'll lack confidence because people are so different.

Sometimes I think the toughest job in the church is music director. He tries to provide a variety of musical talent and songs so that everyone will hear his favorite style at one time or another. But what you really like, another person doesn't like. We sometimes get exactly opposite comments on the same worship service. One person will write a note that says, "Boy, that was really a live service today," and somebody else will say, "That wasn't very worshipful today."

I personally have a wide musical taste. I like everything from Willie Nelson to Johnny Cash and everything in between. I took a survey in a staff meeting recently because we had been hearing a lot of contemporary music in our services. I thought most of our congregation were like me, and they wanted to hear more southern gospel.

Our music director said, "No, I think most of the people like the contemporary styles better."

"Let's just take a survey of the staff," I said. "How many of you would prefer hearing the musical styles that the trio sings, contemporary music, as opposed to the style of the men's quartet, the gospel music?"

It was 9 to 2 against me. I was devastated that our staff had such low spiritual musical taste. I took the same survey among the elders and it was 10 to 1 agreeing with me. I was relieved to learn the real spiritual leaders have the same taste as I do!

If your sense of security too closely depends on other people's opinions, your life is going to be miserable. You've got to determine how God has gifted you and where God wants you to walk. Then walk in that way confidently, and don't be upset about how people feel. Remember, if you worry too much about what people think of you, you probably will be disappointed to discover how seldom they think of you at all!

Rejoice in the Endorsement of Other Believers

Paul didn't need to boast about himself. He didn't need to receive letters of endorsement, he said, because "You yourselves are our letter, written on our hearts, known and read by everybody" (2 Corinthians 3:2). Paul's endorsements were the changed lives of people he had led to Jesus

Christ. His record spoke for itself. Everyone could see the legitimacy of his ministry by the lives that he had won to the Lord every place he had been.

We evaluate a school by its students. We evaluate a company by its products. We evaluate a church and a ministry by the people who come to know the Lord through its influence.

God's people are open letters to their community. Many people will not read the Bible and will not listen to a religious broadcast, but they will read our lives and carefully observe whether the church and Jesus Christ are having a positive or negative effect on us.

One morning, driving to the church office, I wasn't alert at a yield sign and I pulled out right in front of a guy coming down another street. He had to slam on his brakes to avoid hitting me, and he was angry. He blared his horn at me and yelled and shook his fist. When I came to a stop sign, I waved back and called, "I'm sorry, I just didn't see it." But he wouldn't let up. He kept blaring at me and shaking his fist and screaming. Even a preacher can just take so much! So I shook my fist back at him, and then I turned left onto Hikes Lane, where my church is. He turned too. He was still right behind me, and there was little other traffic at that time in the morning. I thought, "If I pull in here at church, he might come by here every morning and see my car in the parking lot. And then he's going to draw some conclusions about who I am." So I just drove right on by and around the block!

It's not just preachers that people watch. You are a letter, too. People observe your life. They are watching to see whether Christ and your church are making a difference in your life. You are a testimony to Christ and to your local church.

If we are going to be confident Christians, we need to take satisfaction in the maturing process of those we influence. The world seeks confidence boosters through externals. You might think, "I'll be more confident if I can own a new car." So you buy a nice red sports car, and for three weeks you just think you're really something driving around in that. But eventually the newness wears off and your self-esteem goes down. "I'll be confident if I have a new wardrobe," you might think. "If I dress right, I'll feel right." So you buy some new clothes, but eventually that feeling wears off, too. "I'll be confident if I can get my doctorate," you say, or "if I can become president," or "if I can be sales manager," but those titles lose their impact as well.

Paul said he received his satisfaction not from something written in ink, but something written by the Spirit; not written on tablets of stone, but on the human heart. Christian parents, you ought to receive a real confidence

boost when you see your child come and accept Jesus Christ and be baptized into Him. Maybe they're not scholars, maybe they're not great athletes, but the thing that really matters, their relationship with Christ, is not
written with ink, or engraved on a trophy. It's written on their hearts.
Sunday-school teachers, when you see young people grow up and enter
the ministry, or when you see adults grow in the Lord, you should have a
real sense of satisfaction. If you invite your neighbors to come to church
and they keep coming, and eventually they give their lives to the Lord,
you get a sense of satisfaction from them.

I get an ego boost out of the numerical growth of my church, but that
confidence boost today can become a source of insecurity tomorrow, because that's external. If the attendance should drop, people would say,
"What's happening? What's wrong?" While I appreciate the numerical
growth, I get a greater sense of satisfaction out of seeing spiritual growth.
When I see people who were alcoholics come to know the Lord and clean
up their act and grow; when I see married couples that were having
trouble and, because of their love for Christ, they work it through and so-
lidify their relationship, that's a source of satisfaction and a confidence
booster for me. When I see young people work through rebelliousness and
remain true to the Lord; when I see people who were materialistic and
greedy begin to open up and become sacrificial and generous, that's a
tremendous boost to me. None of this is written in ink—it is written with
the Spirit on the human heart.

I went to visit the family of a thirty-nine-year-old woman who had died
of a stroke two days before. I saw the faith of her mother and father, her
husband, and her three daughters through that ordeal. I saw her Sunday-
school class bringing food and ministering to them even after midnight. I
heard her husband say, "I just don't know how people can go through this
kind of sorrow without Jesus Christ." I hurt for that family, but I was
proud of them, too. I have a sense of satisfaction when I see the maturing
faith of people who have come to put their confidence in Christ and not in
external things. Paul said we don't look at the things that are seen, but at
the things that are unseen, because the things that are seen are temporary.
The things that are unseen are eternal. (See 2 Corinthians 4:18.)

Rely on the Assurance of God's Provision

"Such confidence as this is ours through Christ before God. Not that we
are competent in ourselves to claim anything for ourselves, but our com-
petence comes from God" (2 Corinthians 3:4, 5). You can read all kinds of

books on how to build up your self-confidence or how to overcome an inferiority complex. Almost every one of those courses will tell you you've got to believe in yourself. But that's not true. If you put your confidence in yourself alone, that confidence will invariably be shaken, because no matter how talented you are, you are going to make mistakes. If you can't distinguish between your worth and your performance, that will be devastating to you. No matter how confident you become, there will be things you cannot control. You might have a heart attack, or you may discover your mate is unfaithful, or you might fail to get admitted to the medical school where you applied. No matter how confident you are, as you get older your talents begin to wane—you can't see as well, you don't remember as quickly, and your reflexes aren't as fast. But we can be confident as Christians because our confidence is not in ourselves but in God.

Do you know what the middle verse of the Bible is? If you took a plumb line, put it right down through the heart of the Bible, and found the middle verse, it would be Psalm 118:9, "It is better to take refuge in the Lord than to trust in princes." Don't place your confidence in people; trust in the Lord. God's promises never fail. His resources never run out. His memory never fades. His Word is always reliable. That's the reason Jesus said, "God cares for the grass of the fields and the birds of the air, and He will take care of you. Therefore do not worry about tomorrow." Paul told the Colossian Christians he thanked God "who has qualified you to share in the inheritance of the saints in the kingdom of light" (Colossians 1:12). That word *qualified* is the verb form of the same word he used in 2 Corinthians 3: 5, *competent*. "God has made you competent," he says. He has "strengthened [you] with all power according to his glorious might so that you may have great endurance and patience" (Colossians 1:11).

That's the secret! "I can do everything through him who gives me strength" (Philippians 4:13). I love that plaque that reads, "Lord, help me remember that there's nothing going to happen to me today that You and I can't handle together."

When I first learned to fly an airplane, I persuaded my mother-in-law to go up in the plane with me. It was the first time she had ever flown, which was a real testimony to her confidence in me. I tried to point out my house and the church building below, but she could barely look down. Her favorite part of the flight was when she got off after we had landed! She was so nervous, she was like the woman who said, "I never did put my whole weight down on the seat."

Most of us go through life all tensed up; we never do put our whole weight down on God. We think we've got everything under control, or if we don't, we're going to work at getting it under control. But God is the one who is really controlling everything, so we can relax. "Cast your cares on the Lord and He will sustain you; he will never let the righteous fall" (Psalm 55:22). It's a wonderful day when you realize, "I'm not in control. I'm not competent. But the Lord is, and He's the one who has everything under control. So I'll put my whole weight down on Him, and I'll quit being afraid."

Relax in the Freedom of the New Covenant

"He has made us competent as ministers of a new covenant—not of the letter but of the Spirit; for the letter kills, but the Spirit gives life" (2 Corinthians 3:6). We are not going to be confident Christians if we don't understand the important distinction between the Old Testament and the New Testament. In the Old Testament, people could earn God's favor by living a good life. If someone kept the Ten Commandments, God would bless and save him. But the problem was, nobody could keep the rules. Nobody ever completely obeyed, so nobody was ever confident of his salvation.

But in the New Testament, there's a whole new way of righteousness. Jesus Christ came and died on the cross. He knew you were incompetent. He knew you had sinned, but He took the burden of your sin on himself on the cross, and now, through Him, you can be saved. "It is by grace you have been saved, through faith—and this not from yourselves, it is the gift of God—not by works, so that no one can boast" (Ephesians 2:8, 9).

Paul Little[9] illustrated salvation in terms of swimming across the Pacific Ocean to Hawaii. Some people can swim ten feet and some can swim ten miles, but we're all in deep trouble, because we're all going to drown. But let's say that a cruise ship comes by and the captain says, "Get on board. I'm going to give you all a free trip to Hawaii." Everybody who got on board could relax and enjoy the trip for free. The people who would be the most reluctant to get on board that ship would be the people who were the best swimmers. They might want to flaunt their superiority.

Jesus Christ comes and says, "You can't make it. You can't do it on your own. You are all sinful. But I'll pay the price. I'll give you a free trip to Heaven if you'll just humble yourself and get on board." The most reluctant to get to respond are the good moral people. It's tough for them to admit they have sinned. It's tough for them to be humble enough to get

[9]*How to Give Away Your Faith* (Downer's Grove: IVP, 1988).

into the baptistery. They want to do it on their own. If your concept is you're going to be good so that God will love you and save you, you're never going to be confident because, no matter how good you are, it's never quite good enough. No matter how hard you try, even your good deeds have bad motives.

It is a wonderful day when you begin to understand that Christ has asked you aboard His ship of salvation. He's paying the price and you can relax.

Now if the captain of that cruise liner asked you to run a little errand during that trip to Hawaii, you would do it in a snap—not to earn the trip, but to show him you are appreciative. Our good deeds as Christians are just deeds of thankfulness that Jesus Christ has saved us. "If we claim to be without sin, we deceive ourselves and the truth is not in us. If we confess our sins, he is faithful and just and will forgive us our sins and purify us from all unrighteousness" (1 John 1:8, 9).

The Golden Gate Bridge in San Francisco was built between 1933 and 1937. During the first half of the construction, over a dozen men fell off the superstructure, falling as far as 700 feet to their death in the water below. Construction was halted, and a safety net, costing several hundred thousand dollars, was put under the bridge so that, if anybody fell, he would be caught. During the last half of construction, about six people fell, but their lives were spared. But during the last half of construction, the work proceeded at twenty-five percent greater efficiency. Knowing the net was there didn't make the workers careless, it made them more confident and more efficient.

As a Christian, you have a net below you called God's grace. When you stumble and fall, that net catches you and forgives you and reestablishes you in your role. When you understand about that net of grace, it doesn't make you careless. It makes you more confident and more self assured. It makes you more relaxed, happier, and more joyful in the Christian life.

> Amazing grace! how sweet the sound
>> That saved a wretch like me!
> I once was lost, but now am found,
>> Was blind, but now I see.[10]

Therefore, brothers, since we have confidence to enter the Most Holy Place by the blood of Jesus, . . . let us draw near to God with a sincere heart in full

[10]John Newton, "Amazing Grace," 1779.

assurance of faith, having our hearts sprinkled to cleanse us from a guilty conscience and having our bodies washed with pure water. Let us hold unswervingly to the hope we profess, for he who promised is faithful (Hebrews 10:19, 22, 23).

It's a wonderful day when we can be confident and say with Paul, "My sins are forgiven. My eternity is assured. My present is empowered. I can do everything through Him who gives me strength."

The Increasing Wonder of Christianity

2 Corinthians 3:7-18

HAVE YOU NOTICED how the thrills of this world decrease with time? A young person may get a big thrill out of listening to a tape of a rock singer over and over again, but eventually that thrill wears out and the tape is put on the shelf, never to be heard again. An adult may be excited to begin a new job, but it's not very long before he hates to hear the alarm ring in the morning.

A ninety-year-old couple sat on the front porch. The old man was overcome with the romance of the evening, and he said to his wife, "I'm proud of you."

"Huh?" she said.

"I'm proud of you."

"I'm tired of you, too," she said.

The world's pleasures decrease with repetition, and that's particularly true of sin. The Bible speaks of the pleasures of sin for a season. Sin brings an initial thrill, but it's followed by a decreasing fulfillment. The law of increased appetite and diminishing return takes over.

Christianity is just the opposite. While the thrills of this world diminish with time, the wonder of Christianity increases. Here Paul is contrasting the old covenant with the new covenant. The old law represents the best that man can do, but it is temporary. The New Testament gospel, by contrast, is eternal. It has an ever-increasing significance.

We hear, "The longer I serve Him, the sweeter He grows." That's not just a sentiment of a song—it's an accurate depiction of the growing Christian. Christianity gets better with age. I've never heard anybody repent of being a Christian on his deathbed. I don't want to leave the impression that being a Christian is one continuous emotional high—it is not. There are struggles, failures, and temptations. There are occasional moments of despair. Like a maturing marriage, if you stay through those difficult times, you will discover that the longer you serve Him, the sweeter He grows.

That's the reason you make a decision to commit your life completely to Jesus Christ. The world offers you temporary thrills followed by boredom, emptiness, misery, and death. Christ offers you commitment, followed by increasing joy, purpose, and eternal life. Jesus said, "I have come that they may have life, and have it to the full" (John 10:10).

An Increasing Glory

"Now if the ministry that brought death [came with glory,] will not the ministry of the Spirit be even more glorious?" (2 Corinthians 3:7, 8). Verse 18 speaks of an "ever-increasing glory, which comes from the Lord."

Glory is a Biblical word, and we need to understand what it means. If you're learning football, you need to learn the definition of some terms like *touchback, safety, blitz,* and *encroachment,* or you're not going to appreciate the game. If you're studying music, you need to know some terms like *crescendo, tempo, legato,* and *pianissimo,* or you're not going to understand music. If you're learning about Christianity, you need to add some Biblical words to your vocabulary.

Glory is used ten times in this section. It means "honor" or "tribute." In its simplest definition, we say, "He takes all the glory," or we sing, "To God be the glory." In a deeper sense, glory is "richness of character reflected in a radiant countenance." The Bible sometimes uses the word to describe God's visible presence, as in Isaiah 60:2, "The Lord rises upon you and his *glory* appears over you." There is a brightness, a majesty about God's character that is so powerful it radiates from His being—so much so that the Bible says that no one can look on the face of God and live. (See Exodus 33:20.) When God made His presence visible to people, it was His glory, the brightness of His character, that they saw. When Jesus was transfigured on the mountain, His inner character was revealed. "His face shone like the sun, and his clothes became as white as the light" (Matthew 17:2).

Did you ever see a person who has just fallen in love? He or she just seems to be aglow. People ask, "What happened?" God is so abundant in love that there's a radiance about Him that dazzles the eye—His glory.

As Christians, we should have an ever-increasing glory. As time passes, we should be developing a richness of character because we belong to

God. As we mature in Christ, we ought to have an ever-increasing sense of self-worth, because of the One to whom we belong. That should be reflected in our countenance and in our personality as we come closer and closer to Him.

To illustrate this point, Paul used the example of Moses. Moses spent forty days on Mount Sinai receiving the Ten Commandments. When he came back down from the mountain, according to Exodus 34, his face was aglow. He reflected the glory of God. In fact, Moses' face was so radiant that his brother Aaron was afraid to come near him. Then, "when Moses finished speaking to them, he put a veil over his face" (Exodus 34:33).

I used to think that Moses put a veil over his face because it was too bright. This passage says the reason he put the veil over his face was that the glory was diminishing with time, and he didn't want the people to see that God's glory was fading in his life. Who wants to follow a leader who has a diminishing glory?

Paul points out that just the opposite happens with a genuine Christian. Our glory doesn't fade, it intensifies.

Our glory intensifies because it is internal and not external. The Old Testament was written on tablets of stone, but the New Testament is written on the heart. Arthur Godfrey used to tell a story about a piano that was out of tune. He complained to a stage worker about it. The stage worker said, "That piano can't be out of tune. We just gave it a new coat of paint yesterday." People cannot be changed by externals. We need more than just an improved environment. We need tuning from within. The old covenant was external, written on stone. It grew cold. But the new covenant is written on the heart by the Spirit, and it increases. Moses reflected the glory of God. We can radiate the glory of God from within, because when we become Christians the Holy Spirit comes to dwell within us. The more the Holy Spirit gains control of our life, the more glory will increase.

The second reason our glory doesn't fade is that it is a cure and not just a diagnosis. The ministry of the old covenant brought death and condemned men (2 Corinthians 3:7, 8), but the Spirit gives life. The Old Testament law was good, but it was just a diagnosis of the problem. People were sinners and needed a Savior. The new covenant brought more than a diagnosis — it brought a cure. Jesus died for our sins. The more that message sinks in, the more glorious it is within.

Let's say that you become sick. Every day you get weaker and weaker. You lose weight and go to doctor after doctor, but no one can find out what is wrong with you. Finally, a doctor says he has found your problem.

You feel relieved until he says, "It's leukemia." Then you'd be devastated. Knowing the disease doesn't help if there's no cure.

Now suppose your doctor goes on to say, "I've got great news—they just found a cure for leukemia yesterday; you can start taking the medicine tomorrow and you'll begin to get better." You would be elated. The more you thought about that new hope, the more glorious it would become in your life.

The Old Testament diagnosed that we have a terminal illness—sin. The New Testament prescribes an immediate cure, Jesus Christ. "Therefore, since we have such a hope, we are very bold" (2 Corinthians 3:12). We can't conceal the exuberance of knowing that we've been cured.

The third reason this new covenant of glory intensifies is that it brings righteousness, not frustration. "If the ministry that condemns men is glorious, how much more glorious is the ministry that brings righteousness!" (2 Corinthians 3:9). The Old Testament told people how they ought to live, but no one except Jesus Christ could obey it. Sometimes the harder people tried, the more frustrated they became. Paul wrote, "I would not have known what sin was except through the law. For I would not have known what coveting really was if the law had not said, 'Do not covet.' But sin, seizing the opportunity afforded by the commandment, produced in me every kind of covetous desire." Rather than curing sin, the Old Testament just intensified it. "The very commandment that was intended to bring life actually brought death." Then he added, "What a wretched man I am! Who will rescue me from this body of death?" (Romans 7:7, 8, 10, 24).

A preacher in Arkansas announced that he had listed every known sin. According to his count, there were 153 sins in the world. He got letters from all over the country asking for that list. People must have thought they were missing something! Just telling people that something is wrong isn't going to prevent them from doing it. Sometimes it instills a desire for a new way to sin.

But the new covenant brings the power to become righteous. "We . . . are being transformed into his likeness with ever-increasing glory, which comes from the Lord, who is the Spirit" (2 Corinthians 3:18). The change does not come instantly—we are being transformed. It's a gradual transformation. That word translated *transformed*, is the same word used for "transfigured" in Jesus' experience. It comes from within and results in external change. When you become a Christian, God begins to work righteousness within you.

"I'm not what I ought to be, and I'm not what I'm going to be. But, thank God, I'm not what I was," says the song. When we feel that God is working righteousness in us through time, that brings glory. Paul says, "We do not lose heart. Though outwardly we are wasting away, yet inwardly we are being renewed day by day" (2 Corinthians 4:16). That's glory.

An Increased Understanding

"Their minds were made dull," Paul said of those living under the old covenant, "for to this day the same veil remains when the old covenant is read" (2 Corinthians 3:14). People who do not know Jesus Christ are spiritually blind. Their minds are dull. They may be very intelligent. They may be well educated. They may be richly experienced in the world. But if they don't trust Jesus Christ as Savior and believe the absolutes of Scripture, the older they get, the more foolish they become.

One intelligent man, a computer expert, owned two clocks. One clock was completely broken and the other clock lost one second a week. He calculated that the broken clock was exactly right twice a day, while the other one was exactly right only once every ten years. So he put the broken clock up on the wall and threw the other one out!

Every one of us can cite illustrations of brilliant people who arrive at the zaniest conclusions. J. Vernon McGee calls them "pseudo-psycho-ceramics." Sophisticated crackpots.

A woman in our city went to a well-educated counselor for advice. This woman was distraught because her husband had cheated on her a number of times. Her psychiatrist told her she was too rigid in her convictions. He advised her to go out and have her own affair to get even, and then she would feel justified. Now that's stupid! That compounds guilt, it violates the conscience, and it misunderstands the principles in Scripture of forgiveness and obedience. But if a counselor doesn't know the Lord, a veil is over his face. He loses sight of spiritual truth and common sense.

The front page of *USA Today* had an article entitled, "Big City Schools, Big Trouble." It talked about how in high school there's a problem with rape, assault, drugs, and murder. Inside the same paper was another article, "Paddlings Attacked as Child Abuse." It told how nine states have made illegal any kind of corporal punishment in the public school, and more states are considering doing the same thing. Now isn't that ironic? On one hand, we are having increasing problems in school, and on the other hand, we are taking away any leverage that the schoolteachers have. The Bible says, "Folly is bound up in the heart of a child, but the rod of discipline will drive it far from him" (Proverbs 22:15). It's not talking about child abuse, but the need to discipline children and to teach them that disobedience brings pain.

Apart from Christ, people have veils over their faces. They lose perspective of the truth.

> The wrath of God is being revealed from heaven against all the godlessness and wickedness of men who suppress the truth by their wickedness. . . . For although they knew God, they neither glorified him as God nor gave thanks to him, but their thinking became futile and their foolish hearts were darkened. Although they claimed to be wise, they became fools (Romans 1:18, 21, 22).

When people don't know the Lord, they are blinded to the truth. The further we drift from God, the more dull our minds become.

More and more high schools in America are giving out condoms free of charge. They are calling the units that dispense them "health clinics." The administrators argue that, since young people are going to be sexually active, and since disease is such a threat, we should help them have safe sex. That is not a wise argument. Young people are taking drugs, too, but we don't distribute clean needles in school. We have a slogan: "Just Say No." Newspapers report that drug use was actually declining in large part due to the program that encouraged young people to "just say no." What is needed is not endorsement for promiscuity in school, but encouragement for purity and self-discipline.

Eagle Forum, a Christian organization, has a program that teaches young people to think about the consequences of promiscuity and to understand that abstinence until marriage is in their own best interest. In one of their workshops, the young people write out slogans that can be used as bumper stickers, like the drug program's "Just Say No." Here are some of the slogans that were submitted by teenagers:

"Sex is like driving—you need a license for both."

"The safest birth control is self-control."

"Control your urgin'; be a virgin."

"Don't be a louse; wait for your spouse."

"Are you prepared to push a carriage? Probably not, so save sex for marriage."

I doubt you're going to see many of those slogans on bumper stickers throughout America. The reason is, as we drift further away from God, our minds become dull. There's a veil over our faces; we don't see spiritual truth, and we lose common sense.

Paul pointed out that there is one way to truth—to surrender to Jesus Christ. "Whenever anyone turns to the Lord, the veil is taken away" (2 Corinthians 3:16).

A grade school boy once asked, "Do you know what Goliath said when he got hit in the head with David's rock? He said, 'Nothing like this ever entered my mind before.'"

When a person surrenders to Jesus Christ as Lord, it hits him like a rock. "I've never seen it this way before," he says. "I'm not here by accident. I'm here because God created me and designed me to be here. I am not self-sufficient. I am weak and sinful, and I need a Savior." We start realizing that we can't just do our own thing, that Jesus Christ is the absolute standard of right and wrong. We begin to see that life is more than the next drink, the next buck, and the next thrill. It has eternal consequences. What matters is our relationship with God and our relationships with other people.

Once I've yielded to Jesus as Lord, the Bible starts making sense. It's spiritual food; I can't get enough of it. It is truth. The first step to understanding the Bible isn't intellectual, but spiritual. Paul didn't say the veil is lifted when you study history or philosophy or when you compare world religions. He said the veil is taken away when you turn to the Lord.

The first step to wisdom and common sense is to surrender to Jesus Christ as Lord. If you stubbornly, proudly refuse to yield to the Lord as the absolute truth, there will always be a veil over your face, and you will not see. But when you humbly say, "I don't have all the answers; I'll trust in Christ as the source of truth," the answers begin to be clear. There's an old saying: "Seeing is believing." In a sense, just the opposite is true. Believing is seeing. Spiritual things have to be spiritually discerned.

An Increasing Freedom

"Where the Spirit of the Lord is, there is freedom" (2 Corinthians 3:17). The sinful pleasures of this world bring slavery. We've all seen people become slaves to drugs or alcohol, but that can happen with any sin. Every sin is potentially addictive.

A man who weighed 1,000 pounds was featured in the newspaper a while back. He had not been out of his bedroom for fifteen years because he was too wide to get through the door. He had become a slave to gluttony, trapped in his own room by his sin. People can become slaves to lust, greed, or fear. "Don't you know that when you offer yourselves to someone to obey him as slaves, you are slaves to the one whom you obey—whether you are slaves to sin, which leads to death, or to obedience, which leads to righteousness?" (Romans 6:16). The Old Testament brought slavery of another kind, a slavery to guilt. God had given man a list of rules to obey, and He warned him if he sinned he would die. But man didn't keep the rules. He just felt guilty and became a slave to guilt.

Richard Hofler, in his book, *Will Daylight Come,* tells of a boy who went to his grandparents' farm for the summer. Jimmy built himself a slingshot and practiced shooting it, but he couldn't hit the broad side of a barn.

One day his grandmother's pet duck was in the backyard. On a whim, he aimed at the duck, shot at it, and lo and behold, he hit the duck in the head and killed it. He panicked, dragged the duck behind the barn, and buried it under some straw.

His sister Sally came to him and said, "I saw what you did with that duck." He begged her not to tell.

That evening, Grandmother asked Sally to do the dishes, but Sally said, "No, I think Jimmy would like to do the dishes tonight, wouldn't you, Jimmy?" And she whispered to him, "Remember the duck."

Jimmy did the dishes.

Later that night, Grandmother asked Sally to carry some clothes upstairs for her. Sally said, "No, I think Jimmy would like to carry the clothes upstairs, wouldn't you, Jimmy?"

Jimmy carried the clothes upstairs.

For a day and a half, Jimmy was Sally's slave, until finally he could take it no longer. In tears he went to his grandmother. He said, "Grandmother, I've got to tell you what I did. I didn't mean to, but I hit the duck with my slingshot and killed it."

Grandmother said, "Jimmy, I was watching out the kitchen window, and I saw what you did, but I love you and I wanted to hear you say that you were sorry. It's all right; you're forgiven." And Jimmy was free.

Sin makes us slaves to the dictates of this world. It makes our conscience hurt. It limits our effectiveness. But the good news of the New Testament is that Christ came, He saw what we did, and He will forgive us and release us from our sin if we confess it to Him. The longer you are a Christian, the longer you experience that freedom.

A lot of people have the misconception that being a Christian is a rigid, restrictive life. One reason they hesitate to make a commitment is the fear that they will be restricted by a set of rules. They're afraid they will shrivel up and be repressed and miserable. But just the opposite is true. The longer you are a Christian, the freer you become. The longer you serve Him, the sweeter He grows.

Jesus did say, "Broad is the road that leads to destruction, and many enter through it" (Matthew 7:13). When you walk with the world, it's a broad road to begin with. There's a lot of freedom; you can do your own thing. A lot of people are on the road with you. But the longer you travel that road, the narrower it becomes and the more restricted you are, until at the end you become a slave. Ask the aging prostitute or the drug addict. There aren't many friends along their path; there's not much freedom. And at the end, that road opens into the dungeon and the pit of Hell.

Jesus said, "Small is the gate and narrow the road that leads to life, and only a few find it" (Matthew 7:14). It's narrow because, when you start out, there's only one way, through Jesus Christ. But the longer you serve Him, the broader it becomes and the more friends you have, until eventually you open into the expanse and the freedom of Heaven.

Some Christians don't understand that. Jesus said that all of the laws can be reduced to two: love God with all your heart and love your neighbor as yourself. (See Matthew 22:36-40.) But some Christians and some churches have lists of extra-Biblical rules: Don't drink caffeine drinks, don't eat rum cake, don't go to movies, don't go to games on Sunday, don't play golf for a Coke, don't listen to rock music, don't observe Christmas, don't play the piano when you sing, don't clap in church, don't sell records in the vestibule, don't use anything but the King James version of the Bible. The longer you are a part of a fellowship like that, the more restricted you are and the more enslaved you are by the rules.

A Christian needs to be disciplined, and there are some absolutes, but don't add a bunch of extra-Biblical rules. Don't be repressed by groups that are always trying to give you a list of regulations.

> Since you died with Christ to the basic principles of this world, why, as though you still belonged to it, do you submit to its rules: "Do not handle! Do not taste! Do not touch!"? These are all destined to perish with use, because they are based on human commands and teachings. Such regulations indeed have an appearance of wisdom, with their self-imposed worship, their false humility and their harsh treatment of the body, but they lack any value in restraining sensual indulgence (Colossians 2:20-23).

"The letter kills, but the Spirit gives life" (2 Corinthians 3:6). "Where the Spirit of the Lord is, there is freedom" (2 Corinthians 3:17). The world's life-style loses its appeal the older you get. Christ offers a life that increases in glory, understanding, and liberty. The longer you serve Him, the sweeter He grows.

David Borden was an heir to the Borden Milk Company. He went to Yale, graduated with honors, and stood in line to inherit all that fame and wealth. But David Borden became a Christian and surrendered his life to Jesus Christ. He became a missionary to the Muslims. His friends thought he had flipped. He studied for the mission field and went to Egypt. He was in Egypt only a few weeks when he contracted a serious disease from which he died.

People might say, "What a waste. What a stupid decision. How foolish."

David Borden didn't think so. Before he died, he wrote in the flyleaf of his Bible, "No reserve, no retreat, no regret."

Who could measure the kind of influence that one life is going to have on the Muslim community or in motivating another missionary to go to the mission field?

Another missionary, Jim Elliot, said, "He is no fool who exchanges that which he cannot keep for that which he can never lose."

Decisions need to be made about life that is really life. I hope you can say with David Borden, "No reserve, no retreat, no regret." You'll discover that, the longer you serve Him, the sweeter He grows.

Don't Lose Heart

2 Corinthians 4:1-18

THE NEW YORK CITY TRANSIT COMPANY was missing a bus and a driver a few years ago. For over a week, authorities searched with no success. Finally, ten days after they had disappeared, the bus and driver were found – in Miami, Florida.

"I'd had it with the cold weather, the passengers, and my family," the driver said. "One day after the last passenger got off, I thought, 'I wonder what would happen if I just took off driving.'" So that's what he did until he got to Florida, where he enjoyed the sun and the surf for over a week.

Haven't we all felt like that driver on occasion? Maybe your marriage looks hopeless. You're frustrated because no matter what you try, it doesn't seem to improve. You think, "What would happen if I just took off?" Maybe it's your task of parenting. You try to discipline and teach, but you find your children resisting and rebelling, and you feel like just throwing up your hands and saying, "It doesn't work. I might as well just let them go." Maybe you have responsibilities at work and your job seems futile. You go through the motions every day, but it has lost all its appeal. Why not just take off and never come back?

There are all kinds of reasons that people get disillusioned and quit. Bills mount up, health fails, people disappoint, energy wanes, criticisms hurt. Maybe you feel like quitting the Christian life today. You started out with high hopes, but it's not working out as you imagined. You have yielded to temptation again and again. There have been troubles, and you begin to think, "Why bother? Why not just drop out of the church, indulge in the sinful pleasures of this world, and live for myself?" Or maybe you've had a responsibility in the church that you have performed year after year to the point of drudgery, and now you've reached the point of wondering, "What's the use?"

The worst defeat in college football came in 1916 when Georgia Tech defeated tiny Cumberland College of Kentucky 222 to 0. Cumberland never even made a first down. The much smaller Cumberland players were being mauled. Halfway through the first half one of the Cumberland backs fumbled the ball. As it rolled toward his teammate, he yelled, "Pick it up. Pick up the ball!"

The man yelled back, "You pick it up! You dropped it."

We know how he felt. Sometimes our situation looks so hopeless we quit trying. We're just tired of getting knocked down again and again. But the Bible encourages us never to quit in the Christian life. "Let us not become weary in doing good, for at the proper time we will reap a harvest if we do not give up" (Galatians 6:9).

The people I've come to appreciate most over the years are not the flashy people or the gifted people, but the people who just don't quit. They are there at their posts year after year. They're dependable. They're tenacious. They are the people who make the wheels turn in the church or in any organization. The apostle Paul was that kind of person. Twice he said in this fourth chapter of 2 Corinthians, "We do not lose heart." In this age of burnout and disloyalty, we need to rediscover Paul's secret.

Remember Your Responsibility

Duty has become a nasty four-letter word. It used to be a good word, an honorable word, but we've come to hate it in our culture.

"I quit going to church because I didn't want to go just out of *duty*."

"I quit putting in the extra time at work. I didn't enjoy it any more, and I didn't want to keep doing it just because I was *obligated*."

"I'm not going to stay in this marriage out of a sense of *duty*."

"I quit giving just because I felt that it was my *duty*. I don't want to give because I'm *obligated*."

One reason there is so much irresponsibility today is that we have convinced ourselves that all of life is supposed to be pleasant. We've all seen that bumper sticker that reads, "If it feels good, do it," and we know that that's wrong. The problem is, we think that the opposite is true: if it doesn't feel good, we should quit doing it. We think any time we go contrary to the way we *feel*, we're being cheated or we're acting hypocritical.

That's not true. Much of life is fulfilling responsibility: showing up on time whether you feel like it or not; doing your job even if it isn't what you want to do; disciplining your children even though you'd rather just let them go; performing quality work even when you're tired. Life is not all fun and games. Everybody's enthusiasm runs out on occasion. The real test of your maturity is to keep going at times when you've lost the joy, but you do it out of a sense of duty. Cavitt Roberts said, "Character is the ability to stay with a resolution long after the mood in which the resolution was made has left."

Most of the time, I come to work in the morning because I can't wait to get there, but there are times when I come out of a sense of responsibility.

Most of the time, I come to church on Sunday morning because I am eager to preach and to worship, but there are a few times—not very many—that I come more out of a sense of duty. Sometimes I would rather pull the covers up over my shoulders and call the associate minister and tell him he's on today. I don't feel like singing, I don't feel like shaking hands and smiling, and I don't feel like preaching. But I come out of a sense of duty. There are a few occasions when I feel like getting up in the pulpit and looking back at the people the way they look at me. "Just *try* to reach me!" their blank expressions seem to say, and sometimes I don't feel like trying. But I do because it's my duty.

Ecclesiastes 12:13 says, "Fear God and keep his commandments, for this is the whole duty of man." I come to church because the Bible commands me, "Let us not give up meeting together" (Hebrews 10:25). I come and smile and shake hands sometimes because the Bible commands me, "Be kind . . . to one another" (Ephesians 4:32). I sing because the Bible commands me, "Sing the glory of [God's] name; make his praise glorious!" (Psalm 66:2). I preach because the Bible commands me, "Preach the Word . . . in season and out of season [when you feel like it and when you don't]" (2 Timothy 4:2).

Where did we ever get the idea that enthusiasm for a task returns when we quit? I find that, when I go through those motions out of a sense of duty, many times my spirit begins to pick up again. We have the idea that, if we're tired of something, we've got to back off for a year so that we can be rejuvenated.

There are times when people really have been over-committed and need a vacation. But a lot of talk about "burnout" is a cop out for irresponsibility. We need to develop a sense of duty, a commitment to keep going regardless of feeling.

> I slept and dreamed that life was beauty.
> I woke and found that life was duty.

Paul said, "Since through God's mercy we have this ministry, we do not lose heart" (2 Corinthians 4:1). He realized that he had a responsibility greater than his own personal feelings. He had a ministry to carry the gospel to as many people as possible. I think there were probably times when Paul did not feel like going to prison. There may have been times it did not feel good to be flogged. It probably wasn't always fun to be ridiculed and rejected and shipwrecked. But he refused to quit because he had a duty. He had a ministry to take the gospel to the world.

Paul acknowledged that he had this ministry "through God's mercy." He remembered how he had received his salvation. He deserved death because he had persecuted the Christians. But God in His mercy had sent Jesus Christ to die in Paul's place.

I doubt that Jesus went to the cross because it felt good. In fact, in Gethsemane Jesus sweat drops of blood and pleaded with the Father, "If it be possible, let this cup pass from me" (Matthew 26:39, KJV). But Jesus went to the cross because it was His responsibility. It was certainly contrary to His immediate desires, but Jesus had a sense of duty because of His concern for man. Paul said, "Remembering God's mercy, and God's sacrifice for me, I cannot lose heart because I have this ministry."

In 1957, Oscar Mills, a twenty-seven-year-old Indiana State Trooper was chasing a speeder when he lost control of his car and was seriously injured in a horrible accident. His wife and children were called to his side in the hospital. Mills was unconscious, in a deep coma. The hours turned to days and the days to weeks—and then to years. Finally, more than eight years later, Mills died without ever having regained consciousness.

Do you know where his wife was when he died? The same place she had been nearly every one of the previous 3,055 days: at her husband's side. There had been no communication, no affection, and no sign of hope. She was there out of love, commitment, and duty. And we're not surprised. When she remembered how much Mills had loved her in the past, how could she be anywhere else?

That kind of duty is honorable. It's the kind of commitment we should feel when we remember how much Christ has sacrificed for us. When we remember God's mercy, how much He has done for us, how can we be anywhere else when His loved ones gather together? I feel an obligation to be present at such gatherings. Most of the time, I come out of joy. Sometimes it's more from a sense of responsibility. But I don't lose heart.

If you are a parent, one of the best lessons you can teach your children is a sense of responsibility. Insist that they do their chores even if they're tired. Teach them to go to school even if they have a little headache. Make them write thank-you notes for gifts they received at Christmas even though they'd rather not and they get writer's cramp. Make them go to Sunday school and church even if they don't feel like going. I am grateful for parents who made me go to church. We went Sunday morning, Sunday night, and Wednesday night. We didn't ask, "Are we going or aren't we?" just, "What time are we leaving?" I think I was out of college before I ever saw the end of *The Wizard of Oz.* We'd start watching it on Sunday afternoon, and then we'd have to leave and go to church.

I hear parents saying today, "I don't want to force my children to go to church because I don't want them to have it crammed down their throats so that they resent it later." I believe that, for every person who says, "I don't go to church today because my parents made me go," there are twenty who are still in church because their parents made them go.

One Sunday morning we awakened and found twenty inches of snow on the ground. We thought, "Nobody in his right mind would pile six children in the car and try to go fifteen miles to church on a day like this." Then my father piled all of us in the car and we took off. A half mile from home we got stuck; we couldn't go forward or backward. So we trudged back home through the snow while my brother and I exchanged knowing glances. We thought this was one time we wouldn't have to go to church. We'd go out to the barn and shoot basketball. Not so. We sat down in the living room, and my sister plunked out some choruses on the piano. My father was not a preacher, but he got out the Bible and read it and made comments. My mother went into the kitchen and got some grape Kool-Aid and saltine crackers, and we had Communion as a family in our living room.

To this day, that's the most memorable church service I've ever been in. I'll never forget that lesson. "We have this ministry." We have this responsibility. We have this treasure that is greater than ourselves, and it is our duty to remember the mercy of God and not to lose heart. Paul didn't quit because he remembered his responsibility.

Maintain Your Authenticity

If you're going to be a faithful person, you must be for real. You can pretend for only so long. There's nothing more exhausting than being insincere. Even worse than being "worn out" is being "found out."

A butcher had only one chicken left in his freezer just before closing time. A woman came in and said, "I want a three-pound chicken." He got the chicken and put it on the scales. As the scale registered two and a half pounds, she said, "Well, I really have to have one that is three pounds."

The butcher said, "Wait right here." He went back to the freezer and stuffed a lot of ice cubes in the stomach of that chicken. He came back out and put it on the scale, and it weighed three pounds.

"Oh," she said, "I've changed my mind. I'll take both of those chickens!"

If you try to be something you're not, you'll either exhaust yourself or you'll be discovered. Either way, you won't finish the course. You'll have to quit. If you're not going to lose heart, you must make a commitment to authenticity. Be yourself; be for real. Paul said, "We have renounced secret and shameful ways; we do not use deception, nor do we distort the word of God" (2 Corinthians 4:2).

There are two reasons people distort the Word of God. One is for profit. I watched a TV evangelist the other day. He was telling people he'd had a vision from God, and no matter how poor they were, they ought to send him their money (although he doesn't make any public account of where the money goes). He says it's "seed money," and that God says He will give you a bountiful harvest if you sow the seed.

He's distorting the Word of God! He's taking Scripture out of context. It's incredible that anybody would send him money, but they do. But he will not last; he may get rich, but eventually he will quit or be exposed.

The second reason they distort the Word of God is pride. They are too proud of their intellectual pursuits to submit humbly to the truths of Scripture. The general assembly of a denomination met in our city not long ago and defeated a resolution stating that "homosexuality is one of the sins listed in the Bible and is an unacceptable lifestyle for Christians." The assembly also deferred a hotly debated resolution concerning salvation in Jesus Christ for additional study. This debated resolution would have affirmed the basic truth that Jesus Christ is the only Savior, but opponents said it might "damage interfaith and ecumenical relationships." Jesus plainly said, "I am the way and the truth and the life. No one comes to the Father except through me" (John 14:6). But human pride rejects Jesus and crowns itself as authority.

Sitting in the pews of that denomination are many dedicated Christian people who are troubled by these events. That denomination wonders why it is losing members, why its people are losing heart. The simple fact is they have distorted the Word of God. Human pride has suppressed the Bible.

Paul said he did not distort God's Word, even if it hurt peoples' feelings. "On the contrary, by setting forth the truth plainly we commend ourselves to every man's conscience in the sight of God" (2 Corinthians 4:2). Some people may not have liked what he said, but it was his job to tell the truth as clearly as he could tell it.

Truth is seldom vague. It should be obvious to others, regardless of your endeavor, that you are not hiding anything, that you're dependable, that you're for real.

"We have this treasure in jars of clay to show that this all-surpassing power is from God and not from us," Paul continued (2 Corinthians 4:7). In that day, it was customary to hide valuable treasure in very unimpressive jars so that it wouldn't be suspect. We are like those clay jars. We're not very impressive. We may have cracks and imperfections. But it's not the vessel, it's the content that is important. Inside these unimpressive jars of clay we have this treasure of the Word of God. We don't claim to be perfect, but Christ is. We don't preach ourselves; we preach Christ.

Wayne Smith has been the minister of Southland Christian Church in Lexington for over thirty years. There are many reasons for his "staying power," but one of the reasons is that he's authentic. He's for real. I listened to a tape of Wayne's preaching the other day, and, in the middle of the sermon, he apparently looked at his watch and said, "Dag nabbitt, I've run out of time." You don't say *dag nabbitt* in the pulpit, but Wayne does. The people say, "Well, that's Wayne!" They've said that for more than thirty years, and they know that he is the same person in the pulpit that he is in the pew. That's one of the essentials of a long ministry.

"We have this treasure in jars of clay," Paul said. We're not trying to deceive you; we're not hiding secrets. We don't preach ourselves; we preach Christ. We're authentic. We don't lose heart.

Combat the Adversary

"The god of this age has blinded the minds of unbelievers, so that they cannot see the light of the gospel" (2 Corinthians 4:4). If you are a competitor, you know that there are times you don't quit simply because you want to overcome the adversary. Your team plays its best against your archrival because you don't want to give that team the satisfaction of gloating over your defeat. You refuse to quit because you can't stand the thought of your opponent's winning.

All through the Bible, we are told there is a supernatural evil force who is ruthlessly seeking to defeat you. Sometimes he's called Satan, the devil, the prince of darkness, or the prince of the power of the air. Here he is called "the god of this age." That's in contrast with the God of eternity. The god of this age is the archenemy of God, and he is seeking to defeat God's people. "Be self-controlled and alert. Your enemy the devil prowls around like a roaring lion looking for someone to devour" (1 Peter 5:8).

He seeks to defeat you and me in two ways. First he distorts the truth through false teachers so that the gospel is confusing. Second, he blinds the minds of unbelievers so that they cannot see the light of the gospel. He gets people so caught up in pride and pleasure that they are spiritually blind.

It is incredible how close people can be to the truth and still not see it. An article in *Newsweek* magazine,[11] "Search for Adam and Eve," told how geneticists claim to have found our common ancestor, a woman who lived two hundred thousand years ago. They are calling her Eve, but reluctantly, because that name "evokes too many wrong images, like the weak-willed figure in Genesis," which they consider a myth. It's incredible how close they are coming to the truth, but they cannot see it.

> Eve has provoked a scientific controversy, bitter by even the standards of anthropologists. Their feuds normally begin when someone's grand theory of our lineage is contradicted by the unearthing of a few stones or bones. This time, however, the argument involves a new breed of anthropologist who . . . looked at an international assortment of genes and picked up a trail of DNA that led them to a single woman from whom we all descended. Most evidence indicates it was either in Africa or Asia. A veteran excavator, Richard Leakey, declared in 1977 there is no single center where modern man was born, but now Stephen J. Gould, the Harvard paleontologist said, "It makes us realize that all human beings, despite differences in external appearance, are really members of a single entity that's had a very recent origin in one place. There's a kind of biological brotherhood that is more profound than we ever realized.

The more man discovers, the closer he comes to the truth. As Richard des Ruisseaux wrote some time ago, "The scientist scales the mountain of knowledge, only to discover when he reaches the peak that the theologian has been sitting there waiting for him all along."

The *Newsweek* article continues:

> "What bothers many of the paleontologists," said Fred Smith of the University of Tennessee, "is the perception that this new data from DNA are so precise and scientific and that we paleontologists are just a bunch of bumbling old fools. If you listen to the geneticists you realize that they are as divided about their genetic data as we are about the bones. We may be bumbling fools, but we're not any more bumbling than they are."

[11]"Search for Adam and Eve," *Newsweek* (January 11, 1988). Copyright 1988, Newsweek, Inc. All rights reserved. Reprinted by permission.

Scientists from both sides admit they are "bumbling fools," but meanwhile we've eliminated the creation story from our textbooks and put in evolution as factual. Isn't it incredible that men can be so near to the truth, and yet the adversary has blinded their eyes to Jesus Christ? Some people are so loaded down with sin that they're always learning but never able to acknowledge the truth. "These men oppose the truth — men of depraved minds, who, as far as the faith is concerned, are rejected" (2 Timothy 3:8).

Develop a Resiliency

Paul had the capacity to bounce back after his setbacks. "We are hard pressed on every side, but not crushed," he said (2 Corinthians 4:8). Paul knew stress. He knew the pressures of travel schedules and personnel who disappointed him and money problems, but he didn't allow the pressure to grind him down and crush him.

"[We are] perplexed," he continued, "but not in despair." *The Living Bible* paraphrases that, "We are perplexed because we don't know why things happen as they do, but we don't give up and quit." Paul didn't have all the answers; he didn't always understand God, but he refused to yield to doubt and despair.

"[We are] persecuted, but not abandoned" (2 Corinthians 4:9). Paul's enemies had ridiculed, beaten, stoned, and imprisoned him; he had been neglected by his friends, but he was confident that God had not abandoned him.

I talked with a man whose wife died several months ago. I said, "How are you coping with being alone?"

"I'm lonely, but I'm not really alone," he said.

Paul would have liked that. He knew that God had not abandoned him even though he was persecuted.

Paul said he was "struck down, but not destroyed." Paul was stoned at Lystra, dragged outside the city, and left for dead. The Bible says the disciples gathered around him and Paul miraculously got up. I would have said, "That's it! I'm taking early retirement. I hear God calling me to be a sports announcer or something." But Paul "got up and went back into the city. The next day he and Barnabas left for Derbe," where he "preached the good news in that city and won a large number of disciples" (Acts 14:20, 21). *The Living Bible* says, "We get knocked down, but we get up again and keep going." That is a resilient spirit.

Dale Carnegie used to tell that the manufacturers of automobile tires originally tried to make a tire that would resist the shocks of the road. It was a tire that was so brittle it would be cut to pieces. Then they started making tires that would give a little and absorb the shocks, and that style of tire is still with us today. They are enduring because they are resilient. Every Christian's life has some bumps and some potholes. Jesus said, "In this world you will have trouble" (John 16:33).

A woman who was baptized at our church immediately had a series of setbacks. After she got out of the baptistery, she had a terrible sinus headache that got so bad that afternoon they had to take her to the hospital. She was dismissed the next day, and she came to church, where she fell down the steps after Sunday school. That week, her son was in an automobile accident, and she began to wonder if she had made a mistake. But every life has setbacks. You go along smoothly for a while, and then a spell of sickness hits you. You prosper for a few years and you feel secure, and then the bottom drops out. You attach yourself to someone with a deep affection, and then he disappoints you or death snatches him away.

The difference is how you react to the bumps in the road. You can either be resentful or you can be resilient. Resentful people are brittle; they break and they quit. But people with staying power are people who have a resiliency of spirit. They get back up when they are knocked down.

A Knoxville, Tennessee, newspaper once carried two articles about similar situations in which the main characters had opposite reactions. The first was a story of a boy who was jilted by his sweetheart, so he jumped off the Henley Bridge. He left a note behind that read, "To Whom It May Concern: I'm going to jump off this bridge because my people are all against me, and the only one I ever loved is mad at me, and I think this is the only way out." So he jumped. The other was a brief editorial comment about a young Air Force corporal who, when his girlfriend jilted him, wrote out of his heartache a country song. The tune became a hit and netted him $20,000. When your romance fails, don't jump off a bridge. Write a song and get rich! Make your disappointments pay!

That's the kind of spirit Paul had. "We always carry around in our body the death of Jesus" — people see these scars — "so that the life of Jesus may also be revealed in our body" (2 Corinthians 4:10). Paul did more than just *endure* his problems; he *employed* them. He used each one to promote the purposes of God. When God was honored, people listened.

When Paul was stoned and then went on to preach at Derbe, I think the people saw the bruises and the cuts, so they listened to him and there were many converts. Later, Paul was thrown into prison, and he converted the jailer. When he was dragged before kings, he turned the palace into a pulpit. When he was put into solitary confinement in prison, he turned the prison into an author's workshop, and he came out of the dungeon with a good share of the New Testament in his hands. He would be knocked down but never knocked out. Every disappointment was a door; every interruption, an opportunity; every frustration, a stimulation. Paul had a resiliency that would never quit, no matter how bad the situation looked.

You have to admire people who, when the situation looks bad, are able to make the most of it. In 1852, many California vineyard owners were going bankrupt because of a drought. All the grapes had just shriveled up on the vines. One vineyard owner picked them anyway, took them to the market, and advertised them as Peruvian delicacies. We've been eating raisins ever since! We all need that kind of resilient attitude, that kind of ingenuity. Every life is going to have trouble; everybody is going to get knocked down; but we've got to get back up and make the most of it.

J. Wallace Hamilton said, "Every man's life is a diary in which he means to write one story and he's forced to write another." Edison started out selling newspapers on a western railroad. He was fired from his job because he spilled acid in the baggage car and set it afire. That accident turned him to telegraphy and scientific research.

John Wesley wanted to be a missionary. He came to Georgia to preach to the Indians, but he was a miserable failure. Wesley went back to England a defeated man, but that turned him even more to the Lord, and he started a great revival in England that resulted in the Methodist Church.

Whistler, the artist, wanted to be a soldier, but he failed his chemistry exam at West Point and had to become an artist. He later wrote, "If silicon had been a gas, I would have been a major general."

Michael Jordan, a leading scorer and MVP in the NBA, was cut from his high-school basketball team when he was in the tenth grade.

Someone said resourceful men never make mistakes; their failures are always portals of new discoveries. Socrates once advised a young man to go ahead and be married. "You marry a good woman, you'll be happy; you marry a bad one, you can turn into a philosopher." Christians should look for something positive even out of defeat—whether it's sickness or criticism or suffering; make it pay a profit.

We may be knocked down, but we're not knocked out, and the difference is in that little three-letter word *but*. We usually use that word negatively to qualify good things:

"It's a beautiful day, *but* we need rain."

"It's good to see the church growing, *but* I wonder how much of it is for real."

"He's a fine person, *but* I'm not sure I trust him."

It's interesting to go through the New Testament and see how that word is used positively in the Scripture:

King Herod, who had intended to persecute the church and even had James killed, was struck down by the Lord for blasphemy. "But the word of God continued to increase and spread" (Acts 12:24).

"Peter was kept in prison, but the church was earnestly praying to God for him" (Acts 12:5).

"We are hard pressed on every side, but not crushed; perplexed, but not in despair; persecuted, but not abandoned; struck down, but not destroyed" (2 Corinthians 4:8, 9).

We could use some of that resilient faith today. We need to be able to say, "Hey, the world is bad; Satan seems to be winning some victories, *but* greater is He that is in us, than He that is in the world." (See 1 John 4:4.) "Sin abounds, *but* grace abounds all the more." (See Romans 5:20.)

Respond Unselfishly

Paul wouldn't lose heart because he was so convinced that he was helping other people. "Death is at work in us, but life is at work in you," he said (2 Corinthians 4:12). He endured for the benefit of others.

We parents will often do things out of love that we wouldn't do otherwise, things that we wouldn't do just for ourselves. My *ideal* Christmas day would be to sleep in until nine o'clock, get up and for two hours sit around the Christmas tree, casually open presents, talk and laugh, eat a late brunch, watch a little football, take a little nap, a little more football, a little more nap, eat dinner at about seven o'clock, and spend the whole day with the family.

You know how I spent one Christmas? My younger son had a job as a disc jockey at a Christian radio station. He was low man on the totem pole, so he had to work Christmas day. We got up at 6:00 A.M., opened the gifts, and I went with him down to the radio station. While he was on the air, I went into a side room and read. His mother and his older brother came down at about 10:30 with some stale doughnuts and frozen orange juice. That's the way we spent Christmas morning.

That may sound like a lousy day to you, but it wasn't. It was a wonderful day. I would do it again in a heartbeat, because I didn't want him to be there by himself. We'll do things for other people that we won't do for ourselves.

Paul felt that kind of unselfish love for his brethren who were lost. He says, "Death is at work in us, but life is at work in you" (2 Corinthians

4:12). I may have to put up with some hurt on occasion, but if it brings life to those I love, then it's worth it. Paul was so convinced his message was true and needed by others that he would not quit.

> It is written: "I believed; therefore I have spoken." With that same spirit of faith we also believe and therefore speak, because we know that the one who raised the Lord Jesus from the dead will also raise us with Jesus and present us with you in his presence (2 Corinthians 4:13, 14).

Paul was certain that God had raised Jesus from the dead. He was also certain that, if other people put their faith in Christ, they would be raised, too. So he just would not quit even though there was opposition.

Eighteen-month-old Jessica McClure fell into a Midland, Texas, well. The nation held its breath and prayed for fifty-eight hours as the rescuers tried to find a way to rescue her from twenty-two feet beneath the surface. She was lodged in a twelve-inch space. Hundreds of thousands of dollars were spent. Several went without sleep. Others crawled into a tiny shaft and risked their own lives to spare her, and they refused to quit until she was rescued. Paul felt that kind of desperation for his brethren. He knew that only Jesus could spare them from the disaster of sin. If it meant he had to go without sleep and brave the cold, shipwreck, beatings, poverty, and imprisonment, he would do it so that others could be spared. He would speak as long as he had breath.

"All this is for your benefit," he said, "so that the grace that is reaching more and more people may cause thanksgiving to overflow to the glory of God" (2 Corinthians 4:15). That sense of concern for other people should motivate a lot of us never to quit.

A teacher may say, "I'm weary," and take a vacation. But he gets back in there because he's concerned that his students need what he has to give.

A wife may say, "I've had it with my husband; I'm tired of this neglect. I'm going to quit." Then she remembers her family and the Lord, and she gets back in there.

A nurse may say, "I'm tired of low pay, demanding patients, and bad hours." Then she remembers her vow to serve.

A policeman may say, "I'm tired of abuse and ridicule and lack of appreciation. I'm just going to quit." Then he remembers the needs of the innocent and keeps going.

A Christian businessman may get discouraged because people are cheating and getting ahead, and he's tempted to quit. Then he remembers the testimony he has to others, and he won't quit.

You probably know this part of Longfellow's "Psalm of Life":

> Lives of great men all remind us
>> We can make our lives sublime,
> And, departing, leave behind us
>> Footprints on the sands of time.

But do you know the next stanza?

> Footprints, that perhaps another,
>> Sailing o'er life's solemn main,
> A forlorn and shipwrecked brother,
>> Seeing, shall take heart again.

Paul knew that he was making footprints that were going to lead to salvation for the people who were following him. So even though he got weary, he said, "I don't lose heart; I will not quit."

Focus on Eternity

"Therefore we do not lose heart. Though outwardly we are wasting away, yet inwardly we are being renewed day by day" (2 Corinthians 4:16). Outwardly, we're wasting away. We usually don't like to put it that bluntly, but it's true. Our bodies are wasting away. I signed up to play basketball in a thirty-five and over league. I didn't get to play one week, but I went down to watch, and I visited a little with the referees. They say they dread officiating games for that age group—they have more trouble with that age than any other. The reason is the guys used to be able to play and they think they still can, but now they're old and slow and they don't want to blame themselves, so they blame the referees.

Reflexes slow down; the elasticity goes; eyesight isn't as keen; memory fades. People used to say, "It's good to see you"; now they say, "You haven't aged a bit." I heard a representative for handicapped persons say, "There are three types of people in the world: those who were born with handicaps, those who have developed handicaps through injury or aging, and those who are temporarily living in healthy bodies." If you are living in a healthy body, understand that it is temporary. We're all wasting away. If your focus is on this life only, then the older you get, the more discouraged you will be, because no matter how well you try to eat, or how much you exercise or jog, you still get older. You sense that life is slipping by; there's nothing you can do. Eugene Christian wrote a book called *How to Live to Be One Hundred* — he died at sixty-nine.

Out of desperation people quit. They may not quit life, but they quit their jobs, they quit their marriages, they quit the straight life, they quit making sense, they chase after some fantasy of youth. Paul says, "Let's be honest: outwardly we're wasting away, but inwardly we're being renewed day by day. We don't quit because our focus isn't on this body, it's on the spirit. Instead of developing the body, we develop the soul." That's smart because this outer case we live in is going to dissolve altogether. The spirit inside is going to live forever, so we don't lose heart.

Dan Truex of our church is in his seventies. He had always been a strong and healthy man. But after he developed pains in his stomach, he was diagnosed as having stomach cancer. Before he was operated on I visited him in the hospital, and after we prayed together, he said, "I hope I get better, but if the Lord wants to take me, I'm ready."

That's the kind of spirit we should have. As we get older in the Lord, the more attractive, the more vibrant our spirit should be. "Though outwardly we are wasting away, yet inwardly we are being renewed day by day."

If you are a senior citizen, we younger Christians need you to set an example of a Christian spirit. Don't get crotchety; don't get childish; don't get overly sensitive. Paul wrote Titus,

> Teach the older men to be temperate, worthy of respect, self-controlled, and sound in faith, in love and in endurance. Likewise, teach the older women to be reverent in the way they live, not to be slanderers or addicted to much wine, but to teach what is good. Then they can train the younger women to love their husbands and children, to be self-controlled and pure....(Titus 2:2-5).

As the outward body wastes away, set an example of what it is to be renewed inwardly day by day.

"So we fix our eyes not on what is seen, but on what is unseen," Paul said. "For what is seen is temporary, but what is unseen is eternal" (2 Corinthians 4:18). We think of the physical world as the real world, the things we see and touch. That's the unreal world. We think of the spiritual world as the unreal world, the things we cannot see. That's the real world; that's the world that is going to last.

The Washington Monument, the Statue of Liberty, and the Los Angeles Coliseum will all be gone some day. This is the unreal world. The things of the spirit — the things of God — are the things that are going to last forever. When we get into the new dimension, then we'll be in the real world. If we're not going to lose heart, then we need to fix our eyes on what is unseen. That's our goal.

On a foggy July 4, in 1952, Florence Chadwick tried to swim twenty-one miles from Catalina Island to the coast of California. No woman had ever done it before. Millions watched on television. Her mother and trainer were alongside giving encouragement. There was another boat with men with guns to shoot any sharks that might come too near. Fifteen hours and fifty-five minutes later, she quit, only a half mile from shore. They helped her out of the water. She said she did not quit because it was cold, though it was. She didn't quit because she was tired, though she was. She said, "I quit because I just couldn't see the shore." Three months later, on a clear day, she came back and tried it again. She swam it in two hours less than any man had ever done.

It's so important that we keep our eyes on our goal of eternal life. Satan will try to blind us, to get us to focus on material values, to get us to focus on sensual pleasures. But fix your eyes on what is unseen, and don't quit. It just may be that you're almost home. That's why we need to sing about Heaven sometimes. We need to sing those old songs about "when the roll is called up yonder." We need to remind ourselves that "some glad morning . . . I'll fly away," and "this world is not my home, I'm just passing through." We need to sing about being "in the sweet by and by." Let's never get so sophisticated that we quit singing those songs because they give us heart. They focus our eyes on the goal. We may be almost there, so we don't quit.

Don Evans, a member of my church, was a forty-six-year-old county policeman with a great record. One morning, Don went out jogging, came back in, took a shower—and then died of a heart attack. How fragile life really is! The Bible says it's a vapor that appears for a little while and then vanishes away (James 4:14). Don's sudden death reminds us how important it is every day that we be faithful and that we don't quit because we might be almost home. It reminds us how critical it is that we make every day count.

"Be faithful, even to the point of death, and I will give you the crown of life" (Revelation 2:10). You're not normal if you don't get weary. You're not normal if you don't occasionally think of quitting. But "we do not lose heart. Though outwardly we are wasting away, yet inwardly we are being renewed day by day. . . . So we fix our eyes not on what is seen, but on what is unseen. For what is seen is temporary, but what is unseen is eternal" (2 Corinthians 4:16, 18).

Facing Death With Confidence

2 Corinthians 5:1-10

MY FAVORITE SECTION of Ripley's Believe It or Not Museum in Gatlinburg, Tennessee, is the part that has replicas of unique epitaphs. For example, there's a gravestone near Uniontown, Pennsylvania, that reads, "Here lies the body of Jonathan Blake. He stepped on the gas instead of the brake."

A cemetery in Cooperstown, New York, has an inscription that reads: "Here lies Susannah Ensign, Lord, she is thin." It was supposed to read, "Lord, she is thine," but the stonemason did not have enough room for the *e* in the *thine*.

Boot Hill Cemetery in Tombstone, Arizona, has an epitaph that reads: "Here lies Lester Moore; Four slugs from a .44; No Les, no Moore."

A bitter inscription at a cemetery near Girard, Pennsylvania, reads: "In loving memory of Ellen Shannon, age 26, who was accidentally burned March 21, 1870, by the explosion of a lamp filled with R. E. Danforth's non-explosive burning fluid." Evidently the family couldn't sue, but they were going to get even with R. E. Danforth one way or another.

There's a minister's tombstone that reads: "Gone to another meeting." I can understand that! Then there's the gravestone in Thurmont, Maryland, that reads: "Here lies an atheist, all dressed up and no place to go."

A New England tombstone carries this epitaph of a woman who evidently was a big talker: "Beneath this sod lies Arabella Young, who on the 26th of May began to hold her tongue."

My all-time favorite is one from a cemetery near Wetumpka, Alabama: "Solomon Peas. Peas is not here, only the Pod. Peas shelled out and went home to God."

We smile at those epitaphs, but death is a serious matter. Just a few years ago, death was not mentioned in polite society. One newspaper editor in California would not even permit the word *death* to be mentioned in his presence. But now we have gone to the opposite extreme. Books about life after life and out-of-the-body experiences become best-sellers. Shirley MacLaine's miniseries on television and her writings about reincarnation hold a certain fascination with the curious. Educators are saying that death has come out of the closet, and it's in the classroom. College classes on death and dying are among the most popular courses offered. Students are visiting morgues and making their own funeral arrangements. Think of all the disaster movies of recent years that picture people right on the brink of death for hours at a time. They were so successful because we're curious about how people will react when they think they're going to die. One writer called our present fascination with it "a voyeurism of death."

Both extremes, the nervous silence and the constant obsession, are indications that the fear of death still holds many people in its grip. The Hebrew writer describes the human family as "those who all their lives were held in slavery by their fear of death" (Hebrews 2:15). The fear of death holds many people in bondage. It's one of the few human dilemmas that cannot be resolved through technology.

We need to consider the subject of death from God's vantage point. The Bible calls it "the last enemy to be destroyed" (1 Corinthians 15:26). In the fifth chapter of 2 Corinthians, Paul told how that enemy will be defeated and what happens when we die. Four principles from this chapter will help us face death with confidence.

Our Present Existence Is Increasingly Difficult

The longer a Christian lives in our present world, the less attraction it has. Twice in this passage Paul compared our lives to a tent. He called the body "the earthly tent we live in" (2 Corinthians 5:1). I've never been big about camping out. My idea of roughing it is a motel with no remote control for the television, but on several occasions I've stayed in a tent by a lake with friends.

Two words describe living in a tent. One is the word *insecure*. A tent is not a very good fortress. You can't bolt the door against intruders. The canvas doesn't seem like good protection against wild animals. If you've ever spent the night in a tent in a storm with lightning and wind, you know that it can collapse easily. Paul was a tentmaker. When he compared this life to a tent, he knew it was not very secure.

This life is uncertain. It can be destroyed in a second. We try to develop security through insurance and the accumulation of goods and support groups and people, but no matter how much we have of this world's goods, we're still living in a tent that can be blown over easily. David said, "There is only a step between me and death" (1 Samuel 20:3). We teach our children to pray, "Now I lay me down to sleep; I pray the Lord my soul to keep; If I should die before I wake, I pray the Lord my soul to take" —we're that vulnerable.

The second word that describes living in a tent is the word *uncomfortable*. When I bed down for the night with a sleeping bag on the ground inside a tent, and it's humid, and the mosquitoes are biting, the ground gets harder the longer I'm there. As I lie there in darkness, I start to think about my queen-size bed, the air conditioning, and my wife at home. And then there's always somebody who breaks the silence and says, "This is the life, isn't it?"

"Yes," I respond. "This is what camping's all about."

The longer I toss and turn, the more uncomfortable it gets. After four or five days, everything smells like socks.

Spiritually, the longer we serve the Lord, the sweeter He grows. But physically speaking, the longer we're in this world the more uncomfortable it is. "While we are in this tent, we groan and are burdened," Paul says (2 Corinthians 5:4). Some of you know what it means to groan—you have experienced disease, sickness, disloyalty, death, financial disaster.

> The length of our days is seventy years—
>   or eighty, if we have the strength;
> yet their span is but trouble and sorrow,
>   for they quickly pass, and we fly away (Psalm 90:10).

In other words, the average life expectancy is seventy, but if you're strong, you could live to be eighty or more. But the years pass quickly, and they become increasingly troublesome and sorrowful as you get older.

"I think we're finally at a point where we've learned to see death with a sense of humor," Katherine Hepburn said. "I have to. When you're my age, it's as if you're a car—first a tire blows and you get that fixed and a headlight goes and you get that fixed. Then one day you drive into the shop and the man says, 'Sorry, Miss, they don't have this make any more.'"

We smile about that, but we know that life is increasingly uncomfortable. That's the reason Revelation says, "Blessed are the dead who die in the Lord . . . they will rest from their labor" (Revelation 14:13). The longer you live in this world, the less attraction it holds for you.

Understand What Happens When We Die

Information is always a good antidote for fear. If you're going to have major heart surgery, it helps when the doctor draws a diagram of a bypass so that you know exactly what is going to happen. Somehow that information reassures you. It's helpful to read God's Word and understand what is going to transpire when we die. This passage in 2 Corinthians, along with some other Scriptures, reveals that death initiates a series of events.

First, there is the departure of the spirit from the body. This tent, this body, is just the outer casing. Inside the body is a spirit that continues to live. You could cut off both my arms, and I would still be fully Bob Russell inside this tent. You could cut off both my legs, and I would still be fully Bob Russell in spirit inside this body. A doctor could take out my appendix, tonsils, gall bladder, kidney, and give me a heart transplant, and I would still be fully Bob Russell inside this case. But one day this tent is going to be destroyed, and my spirit will depart this body. Jesus said, "Do not be afraid of those who kill the body but cannot kill the soul" (Matthew 10:28).

When the hand is removed from a glove, the form of the hand remains in the limp glove, but the substance that gave it life is gone. And when one dies, the body retains the form, but the spirit that animated it has departed.

After the departure from the body comes the immediate presence with God. Paul said he "would prefer to be away from the body and at home with the Lord" (2 Corinthians 5:8). There is no intermediate stage where you go to be purged of your sins. If you are a Christian, all of your sins were taken care of at the cross. When Christians die, they go immediately to be with the Father. When Jesus died, He prayed, "Father, into your hands I commit my spirit" (Luke 23:46). When Stephen was stoned, he said, "I see heaven open and the Son of Man standing at the right hand of God. . . . Lord Jesus, receive my spirit" (Acts 7:56, 59). When Lazarus died, he was immediately comforted at Abraham's side; when the rich man died, he was immediately in torment in Hell (Luke 16:19-31).

When Mrs. D. P. Schaffer, my home preacher's wife, died, she lifted up her eyes, got out of her chair, and started walking. "I'm coming," she said, and she slumped down and died.

The great preacher, Lee Carter Maynard, was in his nineties when he died. His secretary sat by his bed and copied down his last words. He said, "I see it. It's beautiful. Do you see it?" And he died.

There are all kinds of reports of Christians, saying, "I see Jesus," "I see angels," or, "I see the Lord." I shared some of those quotes in a revival meeting some time ago. One woman told me afterward, "I want to tell you what my uncle said when he died. He was not a Christian—he was a very wicked man—and just before he died he got a horrible expression on his face and said, "I see a fiery pit!"

You see, I'm talking about what death is like for the *Christian*. David said, "Yea, though I walk through the valley of the shadow of death, I will fear no evil: for thou art with me" (Psalm 23:4, KJV).

As a boy, sometimes I would get a ride home after a Little League game. My driver would let me off on the highway and I'd walk the half-mile up the dirt road to where I lived. If we came home after dark, I sat in nervous silence in the car, because I dreaded that walk. For a little child, every bush is a bear and every movement is a robber. But if my father was sitting there at the end of the road in the car waiting for me, I rejoiced, and my fears were gone. I think that's what it's like to die. We dread it, but when we come to that moment, we find that the Lord Jesus and our Heavenly Father are there to take us home.

That will be followed by a new glorified body. "We will not be found naked," Paul said (2 Corinthians 5:3). We're not going to spend eternity as disembodied spirits floating around on a cloud. God is going to clothe us with new bodies, glorified bodies, but that will not happen until Jesus Christ returns and our bodies are resurrected. When we die, our spirits go immediately to be with God. We're alert, we retain our personalities, and we'll be joyful, but our eternal existence is not complete until the resurrection of our bodies.

> Brothers, we do not want you to be ignorant about those who fall asleep, or to grieve like the rest of men, who have no hope. We believe that Jesus died and rose again and so we believe that God will bring with Jesus those who have fallen asleep in him. According to the Lord's own word, we tell you that we who are still alive, who are left till the coming of the Lord, will certainly not precede those who have fallen asleep. For the Lord himself will come down from heaven, with a loud command, with the voice of the archangel and with the trumpet call of God, and the dead in Christ will rise first (1 Thessalonians 4:13-16).

The spirits of the dead are going to come with Jesus when He returns, and their dead bodies are going to be resurrected as new glorified bodies, and there will be a uniting of the spirits with their new bodies. That's why the return of Jesus Christ is such a glorious event as we all begin our new perfection in Christ together.

"After that, we who are still alive and are left will be caught up together with them in the clouds to meet the Lord in the air. And so we will be with the Lord forever. Therefore encourage each other with these words" (1 Thessalonians 4:17, 18). Old time Christians used to be buried facing the east. They believed the Lord was going to come from the east, and they wanted to be raised from the dead facing Him. Today, we worry about whether it's a sealed casket or a watertight crypt. I want one with a flip-top lid so I can just come out of there as fast as I can come out! If God was able to create Adam from the dust of the ground—from nothing—He won't have any trouble at the resurrection creating new glorified bodies. The Bible says, "We will all be changed—in a flash, in the twinkling of an eye" (1 Corinthians 15:51, 52).

Then comes the judgment. "We must all appear before the judgment seat of Christ, that each one may receive what is due him for the things done while in the body, whether good or bad" (2 Corinthians 5:10). The judgment of the non-Christian will be a judgment of sin. He will receive a punishment commensurate with his deeds. Even those things done in secret will be exposed. He will give account for every idle word he has spoken. But the judgment of the Christian will be to determine reward. Our sins have been washed away and forgiven by God. We're not going to have to be accountable for those. But there will be a greater reward for martyrs like Paul than there will be for softies like most of us. Our work "will be shown for what it is. . . . It will be revealed with fire, and the fire will test the quality of each man's work. If what he has built survives, he will receive his reward. If it is burned up, he will suffer loss; he himself will be saved, but only as one escaping through the flames" (1 Corinthians 3:13-15).

My judgment as a Christian will not be for my sin, but for my work. God will judge my preaching, for example. If my preaching was the best that I could do and it was with genuine motives, then I will receive a reward for it. But if my preaching was careless, or if it was just an ego trip, then I will lose the reward, though I myself will still be saved. That's the reason 2 Corinthians 5:9 says, "We make it our goal to please him."

That's what happens after we die: departure from the body and immediate presence with the Lord. Then, at the return of Christ, the body will be resurrected and we'll stand in judgment before God. After that comes perfect existence in eternity. Jesus said, "Do not let your hearts be troubled. Trust in God; trust also in me. In my Father's house are many rooms; if it were not so, I would have told you. I am going there to prepare a place for you. And if I go and prepare a place for you, I will come back and take you to be with me that you also may be where I am" (John 14:1-3).

Eagerly Anticipate Eternal Life

The longer we live as Christians, the more attraction Heaven should have for us. Vance Havner, a crusty old Baptist preacher, once said, "I am homesick for Heaven. It is the hope of dying that has kept me alive for this long." Paul must have felt the same way. He said, "We groan, longing to be clothed with our heavenly dwelling"; "We do not wish to be unclothed, but to be clothed with our heavenly dwelling"; "We . . . would prefer to be away from the body and at home with the Lord" (2 Corinthians 5:2, 4, 8).

And Paul knew what he was talking about when he said this. Later, in this same letter, he told how, years before, he had been "caught up to paradise" in a vision and "heard inexpressible things, things that man is not permitted to tell" (2 Corinthians 12:4).

The older we grow in the Christian life, and the more loved ones precede us to eternity, the more eagerly we ought to anticipate Heaven. I like this anonymous poet's description:

> The view of heaven that I sing
> 　is not of angels on the wing,
> white-robed with harps and golden crowns.
> 　I vision rather little towns
> with smogless skies and rivers clear
> 　and not an airplane that you can hear.
> No dust, no rust, no rats, no rot,
> 　no raucous rock, no potent pot,
> no growing old with weakened sight,
> 　no dentures slipping when you bite.
> No bombs, no guns, no courts, no jails,
> 　where all succeed and no one fails.
> No strikes, no layoffs, full employment,
> 　and everyone with job enjoyment.
> All tell the truth, state only facts,
> 　no wars, no debt, no income tax.
> According to this dream of mine,
> 　in heaven no one stands in line,
> and there are only smiling faces
> 　and lots and lots of parking places.

Four words that describe Heaven make me eager to be there. The first is the word *permanence*. There will be no hurry there. Paul said this world is like a tent; it can collapse, but God is going to give us a permanent dwelling place in Heaven.

The second is the word *perfection*. There will be no sin there to wound or scar. God is going to wipe away every tear from our eyes. There will be no pain or sorrow, no mourning or death. The former things will pass away.

Billy Graham wrote an excellent book on death and dying. He says that when his grandmother died, she sat straight up in bed and said, "I see Jesus. His hand is outstretched to me. And there's Ben, and he has two legs and two eyes." Then she died. Billy Graham said that his grandfather, Ben, had lost an eye and a leg at Gettysburg.

The third word is *people*. There will be no alienation; it will be a place of reunion. The Bible says we're going to sit down with Abraham, Isaac, and Jacob. If we know those people, then we're going to know each other, too.

I like to stand at the airport and watch people hug and embrace when they get off the plane and reunite with people they haven't seen for a long time. Can you imagine just standing and watching people the first day in Heaven? Won't it be great to see grandparents embrace their grandchildren, ministers reunited with their church members, and missionaries welcome their supporters? What a day that will be!

The final word is *praise*. There will be no barriers there to our relationship with Jesus Christ. Now we see through a glass darkly, but then we'll see Him face to face. Can you imagine singing, "Amazing grace! How sweet the sound," or "Jesus, we just want to thank You," when He is standing there in front of us?

> When we all get to Heaven,
>   What a day of rejoicing that will be!
> When we all see Jesus,
>   We'll sing and shout the victory.[12]

Be Confident in Your Salvation

Paul was confident. "We have a building from God, an eternal house in heaven," he said (2 Corinthians 5:1). We know this because God "has given us the Spirit as a deposit, guaranteeing what is to come" (2 Corinthians 5:5).

[12]Eliza E. Hewitt, "When We All Get to Heaven," 1898.

When I attend a conference or convention out of town, I generally make hotel reservations in advance. When I arrive, I know I have a room because I have a guarantee from the hotel. I have a piece of paper to prove it.

I know I have a room in Heaven, too. Jesus Christ has already paid the way at the cross. He's given me the Holy Spirit living within me as a deposit, guaranteeing that it is just a foretaste of what is to come.

"Therefore we are always confident and know that as long as we are at home in the body we are away from the Lord. We live by faith, not by sight" (2 Corinthians 5:6, 7). We can't see Heaven physically. We can't prove that it exists. But we are confident by faith in Jesus Christ that it is so. We are so confident, in fact, that we "would prefer to be away from the body and at home with the Lord" (2 Corinthians 5:8).

Some people are not confident of their salvation. They say, "I'm not sure that I'll go to Heaven when I die." They need to know two verses of Scripture. First, "If you confess with your mouth, 'Jesus is Lord,' and believe in your heart that God raised him from the dead, you will be saved" (Romans 10:9). Second, "Whoever believes and is baptized will be saved" (Mark 16:16). If you believe in Christ, all you have to do is confess Him publicly, surrender your life to Him, and be baptized into Him. You need not have any doubt about whether you are saved.

Other people aren't confident they are saved because they haven't lived a perfect life since they became Christians. They say, "I've sinned since the time I gave my life to the Lord. I don't feel confident anymore." We need to repent and to ask Him to forgive us, but please understand that Christ died for all of our sins on the cross. When we accepted Him as Savior, He adopted us into His family. He made us children of His Father.

My two sons have been good boys, but they haven't been perfect. When they first started to walk, they fell down a lot. When they first started to eat, they messed up a lot. They didn't get straight A's in school, and they've made some other mistakes, but I still want them to be my sons. I guess they could get so rebellious that they would turn their back on me and say, "Dad, we don't want to have anything to do with you anymore," but I count them as my children.

God is a much better father than I am. He loves us more than I love my children. He wants you to be saved. He wants to forgive you even though you've fallen short. He adopted you into His family and He has promised that if you surrender your life to Jesus as Lord, you will be saved. He doesn't lie. Claim His promise and be assured.

During a concert I attended some time back, Derrick Johnson of the Regeneration singing group told a story about his daughter, Debbie, that

I've never forgotten. When she was four years old, Debbie got lost in a crowded supermarket. After an anxious search, she was found only one aisle over from her mother, but she was petrified. For a long time after that, she was terrified of crowds.

Shortly thereafter they had a devotional about Heaven one night, and the little girl said, "Daddy, will there be a lot of people in Heaven?"

"Yes, there will be a lot of people in Heaven," he said. "So many that we can't even count them, the Bible says."

"How will I ever find you and Mommy when I get to Heaven?" she asked.

He knew that was a childish question, but he wanted to give her a good answer. "I'll tell you what—when you get to Heaven you just wait for us right inside the gate, and we'll all meet there as a family."

"Daddy," she said, "is there more than one gate in Heaven?"

He remembered that Revelation said that there are four walls and there are three gates in every wall. He said, "Yes, there are twelve."

She said, "Which gate?"

He said, "I tell you what, when you get to Heaven, you ask somebody which way is east. Then you just walk and walk until you come to the eastern wall, and then you find the middle gate in the eastern wall. Let's all meet as a family just inside the middle eastern gate."

That seemed to satisfy her, so he kissed her good-night. Then he said, "Now remember, we're going to meet just inside—"

"—the middle eastern gate," she interrupted.

Derrick Johnson said that, ever since that time, he and his daughter had hardly ever said good-bye to each other without one saying, "Meet you just inside," and the other saying, "the middle eastern gate."

At this point Johnson turned to a girl in the singing group and said, "Is that story true?"

She winked and said, "Yes, it is."

"How do you know?" he asked.

She said, "I was that little girl."

The congregation burst into applause because, until then, we didn't know that was his daughter. When the applause died down he looked at her and said, "Meet you just inside."

"The middle eastern gate," she said.

I didn't hear much of the next song. I was thinking about where I was going to meet my family some day, just inside the gate. We know by faith that to be absent from this body is to be present with the Lord forever.

What a day that will be! Don't miss it for the world.

Sharing Christ With Your Friends

2 Corinthians 5:11 — 6:2

SYRIAN KING BEN-HADAD and his army had surrounded the city of Samaria. He was permitting no food, no water, and no provisions to enter. It was already a time of famine, and the king was determined that he was going to starve the Samaritans into surrender. He nearly succeeded. Inside the city of Samaria the situation got so desperate that *The Living Bible* says a donkey's head sold for $50 and a pint of dove's dung brought $3. The Bible even tells of two women who were so hungry that they resorted to cannibalism in an effort to survive. (See 2 Kings 6:24-29.)

Meanwhile, four lepers were sitting at the city gate. One of them said, "Look, if we just sit here, we're going to starve to death. It's time for some action. Why don't we just walk into the enemy camp? They'll probably kill us, but so what? We're going to die anyway. On the other hand, maybe they'll take us captive and put us in a cell and feed us. Either way, we've got nothing to lose."

So they just walked into the enemy camp. But, to their amazement, they found the entire camp deserted. The Lord had caused a strange noise to surround the Syrians, and the soldiers panicked. They concluded it was the thunder of horses' hooves in the distance, and that the Hittite and the Egyptian armies were coming to rescue the Samaritans. In a panic, they fled and left behind all of their provisions.

The lepers walked into the camp with their hands up ready to surrender, but nobody was there. They walked into the mess hall and found food spread out on the table, and they began to gorge themselves until they were full. Then they went into individual tents and discovered clothing and gold and silver, which they began to stuff into their pockets.

Then the lepers said to each other, "Hey! This isn't right. This is wonderful news, and we aren't sharing it with anybody. Even if we wait until morning, some terrible punishment will fall on us. Let's go back to the city and tell the people what we've discovered."

They returned to Samaria and informed the people that the siege was over and there was plenty of food at the enemy camp. But the people of Samaria were hesitant to believe them. They concluded that the news was too good to be true—it must be a ploy by the enemy to ambush them. The lepers had a hard time convincing the people that the message was true. Finally, the people believed, stampeded out of the city, and took advantage of the food that God had provided for them. (See 2 Kings 7:3-16.)

That story contains a parable for many of us today. In the kingdom of God, we have found food for hungry souls. We have found riches for the poor in spirit. We worship week after week, being fed from the Word of God and renewed by the Spirit of God. It's refreshing and strengthening to be a Christian. But if we care anything about other people, we realize that it's wrong not to share the good news of Christ with others.

You may have family members or friends who are spiritually starving to death and don't know what to do. When you enthusiastically tell them what you have discovered in Christ, they think it's too good to be true; they suspect it's a trap to take away their money and their time. We need to develop some convincing ways to persuade them to come to Christ and be fed. We need to know how to convince others of their need of the gospel.

An Obvious Sincerity

If we're going to convince other people, they must see in us a transparency or a genuineness that cannot be denied. "Since, then, we know what it is to fear the Lord, we try to persuade men. What we are is plain to God, and I hope it is also plain to your conscience" (2 Corinthians 5:11). Paul says, "What I am is plain." There's always the temptation for us to try to cover up, to be deceptive, to pretend.

Reader's Digest carried a story about a woman who traveled fifty miles to visit a friend. When she went to the car to go home, she discovered she had locked her keys in the car. She didn't know what else to do, so she telephoned her husband long distance. He was exasperated with her, but he said, "You just stay there, and I'll drive out and bring my keys to you." The woman went back out to the car and found that actually one of the back doors was open. She raced back into the house and telephoned her husband, but he had already left.

"What are you going to do when your husband arrives?" her friend asked. "He's really going to be mad when he finds out that the trip was unnecessary."

She said, "I'm going to do what any red-blooded American wife would do!" And she went out and locked the door and slammed it shut!

It is hard to admit our imperfections, and it is doubly hard when they are repeated. Some Christians try to conceal their mistakes from the world. They think that the way to influence others is to leave the impression that they never fall and they have all the answers. So they go around with a pious attitude and a self-righteous expression. The result is a phoniness that turns people off. They lose credibility—they're not real.

Paul says, "I don't cover up. What I am is plain to God and it's plain to you." Paul was a great Christian, but he referred to himself as the chief of sinners. In fact, he admitted that "what I do is not the good I want to do; no, the evil I do not want to do—this I keep on doing. . . . What a wretched man I am!" (Romans 7:19, 24). But since Paul was such an authentic Christian, there was an attractiveness about him that was irresistible.

Admit to the people of the world that you're imperfect and you don't have all the answers, but you believe in a Christ who forgives sins and provides the answers in His Word.

Authenticity does not mean one should flaunt his sin. There ought still to be a sense of shame attached to sin, along with a desire to do what is right. And in this passage, we find some motivators for righteous living.

The highest motivation is in verse 14: "Christ's love compels us." It compels us to live rightly. When we think about what Jesus did for us on the cross, we can't help but say, "I've got to live for Him even if it means sacrifice." That word *compel* means "over master." Christ's love masters us. It makes us helpless to do anything else.

People have asked me why our church has four services on Sunday mornings. They say, "Why not be satisfied with having 6,000 people in worship and just say, 'Sorry, there's no room for more'?" I trust that our motive is Christ's love, which compels us. It's the same motive that forced Paul to travel and to preach the gospel even when he was under threats of persecution. We are motivated today to make sacrifices to share the gospel because of what Christ did for us on the cross. His love compels us to win people.

Another motivation to sincere living is concern for others. "We are not trying to commend ourselves to you again, but are giving you an opportunity to take pride in us, so that you can answer those who take pride in what is seen rather than in what is in the heart" (2 Corinthians 5:12). Paul said, "I'm trying to live a genuine Christian life so that you'll have some-body to look up to, someone who will teach you and inspire you."

William Barclay wrote, "A man's message will always be heard in con-text with his character." If we want to influence others, our testimony must be backed up by genuine lives. "Live such good lives among the pa-gans," Peter wrote, "that, though they accuse you of doing wrong, they may see your good deeds and glorify God" (1 Peter 2:12).

The first motivation for obedience to God is fear. "Since, then, we know what it is to fear the Lord" (2 Corinthians 5:11). Proverbs 1:7 says, "The fear of the Lord is the beginning of wisdom." The fear of the Lord is the last line of defense, too. Maybe if we don't do the right thing because we love Christ, and if we don't do the right thing because we love other people, we'll do the right thing because we fear the Lord.

I once could have watched an X-rated movie in a motel room hundreds of miles away from home. I'd like to be able to say I *never* saw a movie that I shouldn't have watched, but I can't say that. I had never seen an X-rated movie, though, and I was curious. This one was advertised as one that would make the blood race through your veins. Most men know what kind of temptation that stimulates. I trembled and I resisted, not because of love for Christ at that moment, but because of fear—fear of the conse-quences: of addiction, of losing my testimony, of getting caught, of not being able to be transparent anymore. "Be sure that your sin will find you out," says the Bible.

The word *fear* goes beyond the concept of terror, however. On a higher level, it is an awesome reverence, a genuine respect for God. William Barclay said, "It's not the fear of a dog that cowers awaiting a whipping. It's that reverence that keeps even a thoughtless man from doing things that would break the heart of someone he loves." It is the fear that keeps a man from desecrating a holy place. "Through the fear of the Lord a man avoids evil" (Proverbs 16:6).

When the world sees a genuine Christian life—no pretense, no sham, but a genuine effort—they'll be more likely to believe.

A Scriptural Conviction

It's been said that one man with conviction is worth ninety-nine with opinions. As Christians, we should be thoroughly convinced of the truth of the gospel. "We are convinced that one died for all," Paul said (2 Corinthians 5:14). When Jesus Christ died on the cross, God laid on Him the iniquity of us all. Jesus' death was not simply a martyr's death. It was a vicarious death, a substitute death. He died in our place. God laid on Him all of our sins. "God made him who had no sin to be sin for us" (2 Corinthians 5:21).

"We are convinced that one died for all, and therefore all died" (2 Corinthians 5:14). When Christ died on the cross, I died, my sins died. We sing, "Were you there when they crucified my Lord?" and we say, "Yes, I was there—I was dying with Him. He died for my sins."

"We died to sin; how can we live in it any longer?" Paul wrote in the book of Romans.

> Don't you know that all of us who were baptized into Christ Jesus were baptized into his death? We were therefore buried with him through baptism into death in order that, just as Christ was raised from the dead through the glory of the Father, we too may live a new life. If we have been united with him like this in his death, we will certainly also be united with him in his resurrection. For we know that our old self was crucified with him so that the body of sin might be done away with, that we should no longer be slaves to sin—because anyone who has died has been freed from sin (Romans 6:2-7).

Paul said, "He died for all, that those who live should no longer live for themselves but for him who died for them and was raised again" (2 Corinthians 5:15).

If you are really convinced about all of this—that when you accept Jesus Christ as Savior, your sins are forgiven and you're going to rise from the dead and live forever—then you've got to share it, and you're going to be persuasive because you believe it.

I complained to a young athlete about a pain in my shoulder. "I think I've got bursitis," I said. "For two years I've not been able to throw a softball or shoot a basketball, because when I lift my arm over my shoulder, it's like someone stabbing me with a knife."

He said, "I know exactly what you're talking about. I've felt that same pain, but I took a cortisone shot in my shoulder and within three days it felt like new."

This fellow was so convinced I decided to try it. I took a cortisone shot and the pain went away. I wouldn't have done that if I had just read an article from a medical journal, but here was a man who had the same experience, and he believed it—and that persuaded me.

That's what evangelism is! Have you had the pain of guilt removed? Do you have the hope of eternal life through Jesus Christ? If you are really convinced of these things, you've got to share it. We used to sing that song,

It's bubbling, it's bubbling, it's bubbling in my soul.

There's singing and laughing since Jesus made me whole.

Folks don't understand it, but I can't keep it quiet.

It's bubbling day and night.

A convinced Christian frequently appears a little weird to the world. On more than one occasion, Paul was considered a madman because of his intense convictions. When he shared his convictions about Christ to King Agrippa, Festus interrupted him and said, "You are out of your mind, Paul! Your great learning is driving you insane." Paul answered, "I am not insane. . . .What I am saying is true and reasonable" (Acts 26:24-26).

People thought the same thing about Jesus. Not only Jesus' enemies, but even His family thought He had gone overboard. When they heard about His zealous ministry, they said, "He is out of his mind" (Mark 3:21). But Jesus hadn't lost His mind; He was just zealous for the truth. He was convinced. If you become deeply convicted about Christianity, some of your friends may think you are out of your mind. "What's wrong with you, getting up so early on Sunday morning? What's wrong with you, giving away your money? What's wrong with you, giving up some of these pleasures of the world?"

The parents of a young woman in our church came to visit our services one Sunday. They lived out of town and they were concerned that maybe their daughter and son-in-law had become fanatics, coming to church every Sunday, giving their money, and talking about the Lord and His church all the time. Maybe they had become part of a cult or something!

So the parents came that morning with a skeptical attitude, coming to check us out. After services they stayed for forty-five minutes, meeting people and talking and laughing. They said, "You know, if we lived here, this is where we would go to church."

There is nothing as contagious as enthusiasm, and once you are genuinely convinced about who Jesus is and what He is doing for your life, it's just going to bubble over as you share it with others.

A Spiritual Perspective

The world measures people's worth by physical means. If a person is talented, the world says, "Boy, she's really something! She can play the piano"; or, "He's a great athlete—pay attention to him." If a person has money, he has worth. Even if he has inherited it, he's worth something in the world's eyes because he has purchasing power. Or perhaps a person has influence—"She's really important because she's the executive vice president of a company." "He's an advisor to the governor."

James Dobson suggests that our number-one criterion for determining worth in America today is appearance. If somebody is very attractive, we put him on the pedestal of worth. An article entitled "A Real Lift for Mr. Blackwell" told how the designer who created the "Ten Worst-Dressed List" received an award from the American Academy of Cosmetic Surgery for outstanding contributions to the field. In 1985, Blackwell told *People* magazine that his ears stood out like open taxi doors until he had surgery. He said, "Before my facelift, I looked like an aging Bassett hound on a drunk, but now, thanks to cosmetic surgery I have a reason to live—a whole new life. I have courage enough to have dreams and fantasies."

He's had a facelift—so what? He's still the same age, and he's still the same character inside. He's still getting older, and one day he's going to die. But that's an indication of the kind of value our world places on appearance. The world looks at externals.

"From now on we regard no one from a worldly point of view," Paul said. "Though we once regarded Christ in this way, we do so no longer" (2 Corinthians 5:16). Paul was ambitious as a young man. He was going to be a member of the Supreme Court, the Sanhedrin. Nothing was going to stop him. Then Jewish people began to turn to Jesus Christ in droves. Paul saw Jesus as a threat to his goals. He tried to stamp out Christianity. But Jesus appeared to him on the road to Damascus, and Paul had to invert his values. He said, "Whatever was to my profit I now consider loss for the sake of Christ" (Philippians 3:7). The things he had once counted as his goals, he then counted as rubbish for the cause of Christ. And he didn't look at Christ or at people the same way anymore.

If we are going to influence people for the Lord, we've got to begin to look at them with a spiritual perception. Don't look at the externals, look at the heart. Are they walking the narrow road that leads to life, or are they walking the broad road that leads to death?

Years ago, I witnessed a terrible fight in a college basketball game. During the brawl, one of the players grabbed a folding chair from the bench and attempted to hit the other team's players with it. The police came in and subdued him and took the player off the floor in handcuffs. I thought, "That is the most out-of-control human being I've ever seen. He ought to be locked up for life."

I was sitting next to a campus minister from that player's school—a fellow who was active in the Fellowship of Christian Athletes. He said, "That young man comes from the ghetto. He doesn't have much perspective about spiritual things, but I want to turn him on to the Lord so bad I can taste it."

What a contrast—I wanted him to be locked up and this spiritual man wanted to turn him on to the Lord. What a great perspective!

"If anyone is in Christ, he is a new creation; the old has gone, the new has come!" (2 Corinthians 5:17). There's no one who can't be changed if he will yield his heart to Jesus Christ. When we begin to see people through that perspective, it affects our attitude. We begin wanting to see the lost won.

If you are a parent, how do you see your children? What are your primary goals for your children—that they get rich, or marry somebody important, or bring you fame? Or is your primary goal for your children that they come to know the Lord Jesus Christ?

If you are a teacher, how do you see your students—in terms of academics only, or do you see the ones that need the Lord?

As an employer, how do you see the people who work for you—as assets or liabilities, or do you see them as people who are either saved or lost?

Warren Wiersbe, in his commentary on 2 Corinthians,[13] tells that during an especially controversial presidential election, a church officer came to Sunday-school class wearing a large button that promoted one of the political candidates. The minister stopped him in the hall and asked him if he would take off that button until he was out of church.

"Why take it off?" the church officer argued. "This man is a perfectly good candidate. Every Christian should vote for him."

The minister said, "Suppose the pin is seen by an unsaved man of the other party. Will it upset him and maybe keep him from hearing the Word and being saved?"

Solemnly, the man removed the pin and then smiled and said, "I guess I should remember that people aren't Republicans or Democrats, they're sinners who need a Savior. And that's more important than winning an election."

When we start seeing people as sinners who need Christ, we'll begin to persuade them.

An Appealing Urgency

"We implore you on Christ's behalf: Be reconciled to God," Paul said. "I tell you, now is the time of God's favor, now is the day of salvation" (2 Corinthians 5:20—6:2).

[13]Warren Wiersbe, *Be Encouraged* (Wheaton: Victor, 1984), pp. 55, 56.

There's a level of aggressiveness that is repugnant and repels, but I don't think that's our problem. I think most of us go to the opposite extreme. We have such a casual spirit about us that people might not even know we are Christians. They don't know what we're convinced about. We don't even look for an opportunity to say something.

Let's never leave the impression that it doesn't matter whether someone turns to Christ or not. Let's acknowledge that time is passing. Decisions are being made that affect lives and families and eternity.

Martin Niemöller was a Lutheran pastor who was imprisoned by the Nazis during World War II. He told of a horrible dream he had one night in the concentration camp. He heard the voice of God ask, "What's your excuse?" and a voice behind him answered, "No one ever told me about Jesus."

Niemöller awakened in a sweat. He recognized the voice of the responder as that of Adolf Hitler. Niemöller remembered that in the mid-thirties he had been seated at a banquet with Hitler right beside him for several hours, and they just made small talk the whole night. He thought maybe he would just befriend Hitler and talk about the Lord at some other, more convenient time, but the more convenient time never came.

You have no idea what a difference you might make in someone's life just by making a brief comment or extending an invitation to a worship service. Have you found food? It's not right that you keep it to yourself. It needs to be shared.

An anonymous poem passed on to me by a friend expresses the need well. It's called, "My Friend":

> My friend, I stand in judgment now,
> And feel that you're to blame somehow.
> On earth I walked with you day by day,
> And never did you point the way.
>
> You knew the Lord in truth and glory,
> But never did you tell the story.
> My knowledge then was very dim;
> You could have led me safe to Him.
>
> Though we lived together here on earth,
> You never told me of the second birth.
> And now I stand this day condemned,
> Because you failed to mention Him.

You taught me many things, that's true.
   I called you "friend," and trusted you.
But I learn now that it's too late,
   And you could have kept me from this fate.

We walked by day, and talked by night,
   And yet you showed me not the light.
You let me live and love and die;
   You knew I'd never live on high.

Yes, I called you "friend" in life
   And trusted you through joy and strife.
And yet, on coming to this dreadful end,
   I cannot, now, call you "My Friend."

The greatest phrase we will hear when we get to Heaven will be the words of Jesus: "Well done, good and faithful servant. Enter into the joy of your Lord."

The second greatest phrase, I think, will be a friend's words: "Thank you. I'm here because you invited me here."

Genuine Expressions of Love

2 Corinthians 6:3-13

WE NORMALLY THINK OF PAUL as a tough troubleshooter. We see him as a person who boldly testified for Christ and courageously confronted people who disagreed. But Paul was also a tender-hearted Christian who knew how to communicate affection. He wrote, "We are not withholding our affection from you, but you are withholding yours from us. As a fair exchange . . . open wide your hearts also" (2 Corinthians 6:12, 13). It takes a humble spirit to make yourself vulnerable like that and to say, "I love you and I need you to love me in return." That's what Paul did. He knew how important it was for the Corinthians to know he appreciated them. As psychologist William James said, "The deepest need in human nature is the craving to be appreciated."

Let's look at how Paul expressed his love. Then let's apply the principles in a practical way to our love for others.

Avoid That Which Offends

"We put no stumbling block in anyone's path, so that our ministry will not be discredited" (2 Corinthians 6:3). Barclay translates that, "Trying to put an obstacle in no man's way, for we do not wish the ministry to become a laughing stock for critics."

Paul was always concerned about how other people interpreted his actions. Since he loved God and he loved people, he didn't want to do anything that would damage his testimony about Christ. Paul did not have the attitude, "Well, I'm going to live as I please and the rest of you can like it or lump it." He was willing to eliminate from his life-style anything that

105

would be a stumbling block to other believers or anything that could be used against him by his critics.

Some Christians disagreed about whether it was okay to eat pork and other food that had been considered unclean according to the Old Testament. The Jews still abstained from these foods, but when they became Christians, they debated about whether it was all right to eat those things or not. Paul said,

> One man's faith allows him to eat everything, but another man, whose faith is weak, eats only vegetables. The man who eats everything must not look down on him who does not, and the man who does not eat everything must not condemn the man who does, for God has accepted him (Romans 14:2, 3).

The point is, there is liberty in the Christian life, so one can't be judgmental about those who disagree in matters of opinion. "One man considers one day more sacred than another; another man considers every day alike. Each one should be fully convinced in his own mind" (Romans 14:5). Some Jewish Christians were insisting the Old Testament feast days should be observed, but other Christians were saying no, we ought to abolish those altogether. It is rather like some Christians today who suggest we shouldn't celebrate Christmas or Easter because, after all, those aren't Biblical holidays. Paul said, "Look, it's just a matter of opinion. Don't make a big deal out of it."

> Therefore let us stop passing judgment on one another. Instead, make up your mind not to put any stumbling block or obstacle in your brother's way. As one who is in the Lord Jesus, I am fully convinced that no food is unclean in itself. But if anyone regards something as unclean, then for him it is unclean. If your brother is distressed because of what you eat, you are no longer acting in love. Do not by your eating destroy your brother for whom Christ died (Romans 14:13-15).

If we love people, we'll express it by eliminating things that are an obstacle to them in following Christ, or that will influence them in a negative way.

We're not married very long before we discover things about each other that are obstacles to love. Don't talk with your mouth full. Please don't wear those heavy woolen pajamas to bed. Don't pick at your toenails and leave the scraps on the floor; that's nasty. If you love your mate, you're willing to eliminate habits that offend. Ann Landers tells that one of the most unusual letters she ever received came from a woman who did not understand her husband. She wrote, "He burns the hair in his nose with a lighted match, and he thinks I'm crazy because I voted for Goldwater." When you live with somebody for a while, you find out you have some annoying idiosyncrasies. It may take you a while, but you make the necessary adjustments even if you think it seems silly. You do it so there is no obstacle in the path of love.

If we love people and seek to influence them for Christ, we have to be aware of things that can offend. They may not be Biblically prohibited, but they are a stumbling block to leading others to Christ. Sin is always an offense; in other areas you may be free as a Christian, but because of your love for people, you choose to abstain.

For example, it's okay for a Christian to work in the yard or wash his car on Sunday. The Old Testament had all kinds of prohibitions about working on the Sabbath, but in the New Testament we are free in Christ on the Lord's Day. But many people believe that Sunday should be a complete day of rest. If I mow my grass or wash my car on Sunday, some of my neighbors might say, "He's supposed to be a Christian; he's supposed to be a leader. And yet, look, he's working on Sunday." I would be an offense to them. So I just stay in and take a nap—you have to make sacrifices!

A Christian man asked me, "What's the difference between my going to the race track and spending up to my limit of $50 to have a good time, and your going on a golf trip and spending $50 to play golf?"

"Well, gambling is potentially addictive," I said.

"So is golf," he said.

I choose not to gamble because it can do harm to my witness. It can be a stumbling block. Many Christians and many pagans automatically associate gambling with sin, and it would do harm to my witness for Christ if I went out to the track and gambled. If my picture were in the paper because I won big in the Trifecta, many people would be disappointed in me and it might be a stumbling block to them.

Don't participate in an activity that is going to harm others. We have to be sensitive to younger or weaker Christians who are watching, who could be led astray. We have to be sensitive to unbelievers who are watching and may be influenced negatively.

I know that principle can be taken to extreme. You can't please everybody. Some people are going to be offended at minor matters of opinion, but we do need to be sensitive as to how our behavior is affecting a large number of people.

Years ago it was considered sinful for Christians to play pool, because the pool hall was a place of sin and gambling. But then a lot of people bought pool tables for their basements, and today we don't think anything about playing pool. It has nothing to do with the liberalizing of standards. It has everything to do with responsible use of our freedom and the understanding of what is a stumbling block. It has something to do with loving people.

One young Christian had a lot of charisma, especially in influencing young people. He wanted to be a youth sponsor at his church. One day at a ball game he was carrying his beer up the steps, and he ran into a couple of junior-high students from church. They stopped and talked and laughed, and he could tell that they looked up to him and admired him. As he sat down in his seat with that beer, he said to himself, "It would be awful if tonight, because those young people look up to me, they decide it's okay to drink and they go out and don't handle it and they violate their parents' wishes. I think I'll stop." That was the last beer he ever drank. He did not stop drinking beer because there's a verse in the Bible that says, "Thou shalt not drink one beer." He stopped because, in loving people, he didn't want to do anything that was going to put a stumbling block in somebody's path.

Be Faithful in Times of Adversity

In verses 4 and 5 Paul listed nine types of adversities that he endured for the sake of the gospel. Chrysostom called these Paul's blizzard of troubles. The first three are general trials that come to all of us—troubles, hardships, and distresses. They have to do with pressures we all experience. For example, the word *distress* means literally "too narrow a place." It means to be trapped in your circumstances. And every life has moments when we feel shut in, suffocating from responsibilities and pressures.

The next three are adversities that are inflicted by others: beatings, imprisonments, and riots. Clement of Rome tells us that Paul was in jail no less than seven times. He wasn't in jail because he disobeyed the law; he was in jail because he preached the gospel clearly. Today you probably won't be imprisoned or beaten for being a Christian, but you may be ridiculed. You may be isolated on occasion.

The last three adversities are self-inflicted—they're voluntary: hard work, sleepless nights, hunger. In Troas, Paul preached until midnight, until Eutychus fell out the window and Paul restored him. Then Paul went upstairs and preached until dawn. He preached all night long—he went without sleep because of his love for the gospel and his love for people. *Hunger* probably referred to times that he fasted and prayed. It is not easy to go without food, but Paul did so for the sake of prayer and concern for others. Paul endured because he loved people.

One of the best demonstrations of love is how you do when the going gets tough. It's easy to say, "Oh, how I love Jesus," when you have a good job and you have good health, when your family is together—but how do you endure when life starts falling apart? What happens when your new grandbaby is born with half its face covered with a purple birthmark and the doctor says, "Nothing we can do"? Do you still love the Lord? Do you endure under trials and distresses?

It's easy to love Christian people in the church when everything is going well and it's inspirational, but how do you do when the preacher leaves or when there is financial pressure? How do you do when your church is forced to make program changes that inconvenience your schedule?

It's easy to love your mate when you're young and your marriage is new and everybody is smiling and affectionate. But what happens when the make-up comes off and the romance fades, and the sewer backs up, and the kids cry out in the middle of the night?

Love endures adversity. First Corinthians 13 says love is patient, it always protects, it always trusts, it always hopes, it always perseveres. Love never fails. That's the reason, in the marriage ceremony, you took those vows that said, "In sickness and in health," "in good times and bad times," "in riches and in poverty."

Love endures in purity. One of the most tangible ways to express love for God or love for your mate is to keep yourself pure, even when it is difficult to do so. There may be times when the romance fades and you find somebody else initially more exciting. The best expression of love is just to hang in there when it's not easy to do so.

Be Thoughtful of Others' Needs

One of the reasons there are so many breakdowns in relationships today is that we are selfish people. There are two kinds of people who walk into a room—one says, "Here I am," and the other says, "There you are." Many people today are self-centered. This is the "me" generation—here I am.

My parents are about the most unselfish people I know. One reason is that my dad was one of eighteen children and my mother one of seven children. They had to learn to share. After they got married, they lived through the Depression with three children and two of my uncles living in the house. They had to learn to share.

Recently, my sister asked us to a family get-together at her house in Cincinnati. They were in a new house, so she gave directions. She said there was room for only two cars in the driveway, but we couldn't park on the street. If the driveway was full when we arrived, we were to drive half a block down the street, park at the schoolyard, and walk back to the house. When my family and I arrived, there were no cars in the driveway, so I pulled in. When we went inside, we discovered my parents were already there. They had parked down at the schoolyard and walked so those who came later wouldn't have to walk. So I went back out and moved my car down to the schoolyard — it's almost disgusting!

That kind of sacrifice and selflessness is foreign to most of us today. We limit the number of children in our families so we can give them everything they want from the time they're born. We want to please them so badly, we overindulge them and they know little of self-denial. When they get into a relationship that isn't focused entirely on them, they feel cheated. "My husband isn't meeting my needs like my daddy did. He thinks of himself too much, not me." "My wife doesn't care for me like my mother did. She complains when I ask her to do little chores." We claim to be so liberal in our thinking, but in reality we are so self-centered in attitude. People who get married thinking "my mate will meet my needs" are soon disillusioned.

There are three words in 2 Corinthians 6:6 that require thoughtfulness and unselfishness. The first is *understanding*. To understand the feelings of another requires time and sacrifice. Instead of thinking, "How do I feel?" we have to take time to listen and learn about the feelings of the other person. Before a couple gets married, a man lies awake thinking about what his girlfriend says. After they get married, he falls asleep before she's finished saying it. We're not going to understand others if we don't take time to listen and think unselfishly about their feelings.

The second word is *patience*. William Barclay defines the Greek word as "the ability to bear with people even when they are misguided and wrong, even when they are cruel and insulting." If you're self-centered, you're going to be impatient. You'll immediately retaliate when people are cruel or short. You'll lash back; you'll raise your voice; you'll be defensive. The unselfish person learns to be patient. His goal is not self-defense, but harmony in the relationship, expressing love even when it isn't easy.

I got up one Sunday morning, looked in my sock drawer, and I didn't have any socks. It was Valentine's Day — and no black socks. Now that was a time I could have been very impatient. I could have exploded and said, "Do you expect me to get in front of 4,000 people with no socks today? I gave you a flower—you can't even have my socks washed and in the drawer?" Or it could have been a time for me to be patient and to remember all those years that I have had socks on Sunday morning, and all those times sacrifices were made for me, and to restrain my tongue and say, "Thank you for the sermon illustration! I'm grateful."

The third unselfish word is *kindness*. One commentator describes it as "sweetness of temper that puts others at their ease and shrinks from giving pain." It's the opposite of severity. It's a quality that thinks more of others than itself. "Love is patient, love is kind. . . . It is not proud. It is not rude, it is not self-seeking, it is not easily angered, it keeps no record of wrongs" (1 Corinthians 13:4, 5). Love is kind.

Mary Brunson was driving her husband's new car and made a wrong turn and sideswiped another car. Tearfully, she fumbled through the glove compartment looking for the insurance papers. Attached to the insurance papers was a note with her name on it in her husband's handwriting: "Dear Mary, when you read these papers, remember it's you I love and not the car." That's kindness, thoughtfulness, patience, understanding, selflessness. That's expressing love in a genuine manner.

How can you do that? Maybe if you're honest you'll admit, "I'm not very thoughtful, I am self-centered, and I'm not easy to live with." Paul said we can do it in the Holy Spirit and in the power of God. If you'll ask the Lord Jesus into your life and allow Him to help you, He can transform your life. It will probably take a while, but the Bible says if we're in Christ, the old has gone, the new has come.

> Make every effort to add to your faith goodness; and to goodness, knowledge; and to knowledge, self-control; and to self-control, perseverance; and to perseverance, godliness; and to godliness, brotherly kindness; and to brotherly kindness, love. For if you possess these qualities in increasing measure, they will keep you from being ineffective and unproductive (2 Peter 1:5-8).

You have to make the effort to add to your virtues, but if you have them in increasing measure, they'll make you effective in communicating love.

Be Joyful Regardless of the Circumstances

Verses 8-10 comprise a series of paradoxes in the life of a leader. "Through glory and dishonor"—a leader has to accept both criticism and compliments. "Bad report and good report" — Paul's enemies hated him; his friends loved him. People reacted to Paul in extremes, either positively or negatively. There was no middle of the road. "Genuine, yet regarded as impostors" — some felt that Paul was the greatest apostle; others thought he was a hypocrite. "Known, yet regarded as unknown" — the Christians knew Paul, and the world tried to ignore him. "Dying, and yet we live on; beaten, and yet not killed; sorrowful, yet always rejoicing; poor, yet making many rich; having nothing, and yet possessing everything" (2 Corinthians 6:8-10).

"Sorrowful, yet always rejoicing." One of the best ways you can express love to your family is to be easy to live with. You've seen those little boards that some people hang in their kitchens — on one side they have a happy face and on the other side a sad face. You're supposed to display the side that shows what kind of mood you're in that day. Let me tell you what to do with that plaque — put the happy face outward and nail it to the wall! Life is a series of ups and downs. Just about the time you think everything is coming together the way you want it to, something bad happens. Life is a roller coaster. If your happiness is dictated by circumstances, you are going to be a bear to live with. You are going to have that sad face showing a lot. People close to you will have to walk on pins and needles because they are afraid that you're going to explode and lose your temper — or they'll have to work constantly to boost you up because you're vulnerable to depression. You won't be easy to live with. Your family will be ill at ease all the time.

Demonstrate some compassion and maturity by developing a consistency in your life. If you are waiting for everything to be ideal so that you can be consistently joyful, you're going to go through life like a yo-yo, and you're going to make people around you ill at ease. Say each day, "This is the day that the Lord has made; I'm going to rejoice and be glad in it."

Parks and Helen Parker are both completely blind. Helen Parker just learned that she has lung cancer that is inoperable, even though she has never smoked. I'd never met them, but they've listened to our radio program for some time and they invited me to come, so I went to their home to try to minister to them. They live in a modest home, but what a joyful, remarkable couple they are.

They said, "We wanted you to come because we wanted to tell you, Bob, thank you for your ministry to us. You're our pastor by radio." She gave me a book that she had written about her blindness.

"Can I show you something?" Parks asked me. He took me down to the basement. He makes a living by repairing cane-bottomed chairs. He showed me his excellent craftsmanship. Though he couldn't see, he could point to various sections of the basement and tell me how many chairs were there, to whom they belonged, and what he was going to do with them. He gets on the bus and goes downtown to pick up his cane and brings it back by himself!

"Before you leave," they said, "would you pray with us?" We joined hands in the living room and prayed, and Helen smiled and said, "Thank you. We're just trusting the Lord."

Then Parks asked me, "How much does the radio ministry cost?" I gave him a ball-park figure. He opened up his fist and handed me a wad of five $20 bills that he had earned repairing cane-bottomed chairs. I left their little place buoyed in spirit, thinking I'd like to go back and visit those people again. I had gone to boost them, but they boosted me.

I don't know what your problem is today, but you can rejoice even in sorrow. If you have Jesus Christ, you can have everything even though you have nothing. One of the best ways to express love is to learn to be joyful regardless of the circumstances. Are you?

Express Your Affection Vocally

Paul said, "We have spoken freely to you, Corinthians, and opened wide our hearts to you. We are not withholding our affection from you" (2 Corinthians 6:11, 12). Paul knew how to tell people that he loved them. He wasn't too proud to say, "You're important to me. I love you." He wasn't afraid to make himself vulnerable and open himself up to being hurt. They weren't reciprocating in their love, but he still expressed it. The more I listen to those who have lost loved ones, the more I'm impressed with the need for frequent verbal expressions of love. It takes a lot more than words to make a loving relationship, and words don't have to be spoken often for there to be love, but it's reassuring to hear people in the family say, "You're special to me, I love you, I'm proud of you, I really care about you."

That's difficult for many men and women, particularly those who have to battle pride or who have a guarded personality. We need to learn to swallow our pride and develop a capacity to look people in the eye and say, "I love you," because someday it will be too late. A woman in our church whose husband died in his sleep said to me, "I'm so thankful that the last words we said were what we always say before we go to bed—'I love you.'" If you've got something to say, say it now.

Some of you may be thinking, "I know someone who needs to read this." Your children, your spouse, your grandchildren—"I'm going to lend them this book, because they need to learn to express love to me." If that's your attitude, then *you're* the one who needs to hear this. People need three things to be fulfilled. We need something to do, something to hope for, and someone to love. We think we need someone to love us, but in reality we need someone to love. So instead of sitting around bemoaning the fact that no one is expressing love to you, you need to find ways to express it yourself.

Do you try to abstain from that which offends? Are you faithful in times of adversity? Are you understanding, patient, and kind even when it means sacrificing yourself? Are you consistently joyful? Do you regularly verbalize your love even when there is no reciprocation? If so, you'll find such a sense of joy and satisfaction from loving that you'll never get stuck sitting around waiting for someone to love you.

Mary Martin was about to perform her last act in her last performance in *South Pacific*. A minute before she went on stage, a stagehand gave her a note. A tear creased her face when she recognized the handwriting as that of Oscar Hammerstein, who at that moment lay dying of cancer. She read the note, not knowing that almost everybody in the room would later know what that note said. It simply read,

> A bell is no bell till you ring it,
>   A song is no song till you sing it,
> And love in your heart wasn't put there to stay,
>   Love isn't love till you give it away.[14]

That night she went out and performed *South Pacific* at a new level. One of the reporters later told her, "There was something different."

She said, "Tonight I gave it away."

Has God put any love in your heart? Find a way to express it and you'll find a new fulfillment in life.

---

[14]Quoted from "Sixteen Going on Seventeen," by Richard Rodgers and Oscar Hammerstein II. Copyright © 1959 by Richard Rodgers and Oscar Hammerstein II. Copyright renewed. International copyright secured. Williamson Music Company, owner of copyright and allied rights throughout the world. Used by permission.

Maintaining Moral Purity

2 Corinthians 6:14 – 7:1

For millions of committed Christians, the late '80s brought agonizing disillusionment. One after another, some of the country's most prominent Protestant televangelists revealed themselves as pious pretenders, driven by lust or avarice or unsaintly ego. Perhaps most distressing was the ammunition the scandals gave to the skeptical and scornful. While erstwhile believers in Jim Bakker, Jimmy Swaggart and Marvin Gorman winced at the exposés of dalliance and the unconvincing protestations of repentance, countless other Americans were laughing.

THOSE INSIGHTFUL COMMENTS did not first appear in some preacher's newsletter or in a religious journal. Instead, they were published in *Time* magazine.[15] But in spite of their secular source, they accurately describe the agony many of us in the church felt – and continue to feel – at the humiliation of prominent religious leaders. We grieve not only for the fallen leaders, but because, as a result of their failings, America is laughing at our Lord, at His church, and at the rest of us who minister in His name.

When a policeman is on the take, the entire police force is discredited a little. When a preacher falls, people call into question the integrity of the ministry in general. After a recent moral failure of a media minister, one of our ushers, who stands about six feet, four inches tall and weighs some 240 pounds, put his arm around me and said, "If you ever do that, I'm going to kill you." And I believe he would! You begin to wonder – is anybody for real?

[15]William A. Henry, III, "God and Money Part 9," *Time* (July 22, 1991), p. 28.

When a preacher falls, we are reminded as Christians not to put our trust in human leaders. Jesus Christ alone is perfect. But with every moral failure of a media preacher, the enemies of God are given additional cause to blaspheme and to ridicule.

My sister works in a factory. Though she is not an obnoxious Christian, she is a vocal one. For an entire month, every day after the Jimmy Bakker scandal, somebody would slip a newspaper clipping about Bakker in her lunch pail. Finally it stopped, but soon after, there was a clipping in her lunch pail every day about Jimmy Swaggart. Their actions have given the enemies of God an occasion to gloat and to blaspheme.

There is another reason I am disturbed by the failings of these public figures. It's not just my concern for the fallen individual; it's not just my concern for the credibility of the church and other ministers and myself. I am especially concerned because it reminds me of my own weaknesses.

Now, I've never been unfaithful to my wife, and I've never invited a prostitute into a sleazy motel. But even though I'm a preacher, I have to admit my thoughts are not always pure. I can't say I've always turned off the television set when I should have. The Bible says, "If you think you are standing firm, be careful that you don't fall!" (1 Corinthians 10:12). We're all tempted at times, we're all vulnerable, and we all need to be reminded to be alert lest we succumb to temptation. One man boasted, "I don't have any trouble with the devil; he never bothers me!"

"That's understandable," another responded. "Two people traveling down the road in the same direction seldom bump into each other!"

If you are trying to live for Jesus Christ, you are traveling in the opposite direction from the devil. You're going to meet him occasionally, and his temptations are going to be difficult to overcome. The Bible says he is "like a roaring lion looking for someone to devour" (1 Peter 5:8). How do we keep ourselves morally pure in the midst of a society that is morally bankrupt?

Avoid Close Ties With Unbelievers

"Do not be yoked together with unbelievers" (2 Corinthians 6:14). This idea goes all the way back to Deuteronomy 22:10, where God instructed the Hebrew farmers, "Do not plow with an ox and a donkey yoked together." An ox and a donkey were not to be hitched together because they were two entirely different animals. The ox was considered a clean animal and the donkey an unclean animal. They had different natures. The ox was generally hard working and cooperative, and the donkey was stubborn and feisty. The two together would drag each other down.

Certain things are fundamentally incompatible. They were never meant to be brought together. This principle applies to the Christian and the non-Christian. The purity of the Christian and the pollution of the pagan cannot run in double harness. When we become Christians, God gives us a new nature. "If anyone is in Christ, he is a new creation; the old has gone, the new has come!" (2 Corinthians 5:17). When you accepted Christ, you became a participant in the divine nature (2 Peter 1:4). You're to be different from the world. That's the reason God says, "Come out from them and be separate" (2 Corinthians 6:17).

If a farmer puts pigs and sheep in the same pasture, it's not very long before the sheep are in a flock all by themselves and the pigs are over in the mud by themselves. They have different natures and they don't mingle very much. When you become a Christian, God calls you to have a new nature, to be separate from the world. The very word *church* means "called out."

Some overzealous Christians have abused this doctrine and have turned separation into isolation. They won't go into any store or restaurant that sells liquor. They won't have television sets in their homes. They would never go to a church unless it was exactly like their own. Their circle of fellowship becomes so narrow that they can't even get along with themselves.

The Bible says that Christians are to be the salt of the earth. Salt has to penetrate the food to add flavor. We've got to be in the world but not of the world. Jesus prayed, "My prayer is not that you take them out of the world but that you protect them from the evil one" (John 17:15). We're to make contact without being contaminated.

There's a big difference between casual association and being unequally yoked. To be yoked means to be tied together in close relationships. It means to be partners together over a long period of time. Christians are commanded not to be equally bound together with pagans because invariably that will drag the believer down. "Bad company corrupts good character" (1 Corinthians 15:33).

If you are a young person and a genuine believer in Jesus Christ, don't marry somebody who does not believe. If you are a committed Christian, don't marry somebody who is a nominal Christian. Someone has said, "If you're a child of God and you marry a child of the devil, you're going to have trouble with your father-in-law." Satan will tempt you to be unequally yoked with somebody who is not a believer. If you sincerely want to have a Christian home, begin by dating a Christian.

Wayne Smith tells the story about a former University of Kentucky football player in Lexington who was engaged to marry a beautiful girl. She joined the church, but a month before they were to be married, she said to him, "I've got to be honest with you. I don't want to go to church all the time after we get married. I really don't enjoy going. That's not the way I was brought up. I'll go occasionally, but I don't want to be involved like you are."

That young man came into Wayne's office in tears. "I've broken off the engagement," he said. "My father taught me to love the Lord, and now he's died and gone to Heaven, and there's no girl gonna keep me from seeing my Lord and my father in Heaven someday."

"What fellowship can light have with darkness?" the apostle Paul asked. "What does a believer have in common with an unbeliever?" (2 Corinthians 6:14, 15). You might argue that we've got a lot in common with unbelievers: sports and travel and hobbies and people we like. But the Bible says that the Christian is to seek first the kingdom of God. When you marry a non-Christian, that which is most essential is at odds between you. It won't be long before you're at odds not just over church, but entertainment, how to raise the children, and all kinds of other problems.

Not being unequally yoked together also applies to business partnerships. Christian entrepreneurs sometimes enter into long-term agreements with non-Christians. After all, business is business, and they've got all the contingencies taken care of in the contract. But Paul asked, "What harmony is there between Christ and Belial?" (2 Corinthians 6:15). It's not long before your partner's personal habits, attitudes, and values begin to rub you the wrong way. Two people with different natures and value systems are inevitably going to clash. The old country preacher said, "You can't walk with God and run with the devil at the same time."

Not being unequally yoked applies to close friendships, too. You need to associate with people in the world in order to influence them, and you ought to have friends who are not Christians so that you can win them to Christ. But your closest friends should be people who share your convictions. A young woman told me that she had moved into an apartment with a girl who was not a Christian. They thought they had it worked out, but it wasn't long before the non-Christian girl began to bring her boyfriend in to spend the night, and there was trouble. "He who walks with the wise grows wise, but a companion of fools suffers harm" (Proverbs 13:20).

The apostle Paul asked, "What agreement is there between the temple of God and idols?" (2 Corinthians 6:16). We are temples of God; the Holy Spirit dwells within. The world worships the idols of money, sex, and power. If your closest friends are idol worshipers, how can you expect not to be influenced? This principle certainly applies to young people choosing a college fraternity or sorority. If you go to a non-Christian school and you join a party fraternity or sorority, you're making a long-term agreement with unbelievers. You can rationalize and say, "Well, everybody has to sow his wild oats," or, "It's not as bad as everybody pictures it," or, "I'm going to influence them." But invariably you'll be dragged down into the mud. And as Charles Swindoll says, "When you put on white gloves and work in the mud, the mud never gets glovey."

Paul asked, "What do righteousness and wickedness have in common?" You're to be distinctive, so don't be too closely tied to unbelievers.

Soberly Rehearse the Consequences of Immorality

A few years ago, a nineteen-year-old West German boy astounded the world when he flew a small airplane across the Russian border, across hundreds of miles of territory, and landed in Moscow, in Red Square. Of course, this was before German reunification and the other democratic reforms we have seen in Europe and the Soviet Union in the last few years. He was immediately arrested and imprisoned by the embarrassed Communist authorities. As he awaited his trial, a reporter from *Newsweek* magazine asked him if he ever thought about what was going to happen once he landed. He said, "You know, I didn't think about that very much; I was so caught up in the challenge of it."

A lot of people get involved in immorality and never seriously think about where it's going to lead. They get so caught up in the pleasure and the thrill they refuse to think seriously about the consequences. When it all blows up in their faces, they can't believe they've been so stupid.

A friend saw a wrecked car being towed away. The front end was smashed in. On the back was a bumper sticker that read, "Don't Bother Me; I'm Having a Sexual Fantasy." We need to understand that when we get involved in a fantasy, it invariably ends up in wrecked lives.

First in the theaters, and then on TV, the movie was watched by thousands. It was about a middle-aged man who got caught up in an exciting affair. When he realized how foolish he had been, he attempted to terminate the relationship, but the woman refused to let him go. She pursued him, blackmailed him, threatened him, and even tried to murder his wife. The movie was entitled, appropriately enough, *Fatal Attraction*. Sin is enticing, but it is lethal. "A man who strays from the path of understanding comes to rest in the company of the dead. He who loves pleasure will become poor" (Proverbs 21:16, 17). The price you pay always exceeds the value of the pleasure you enjoy. Satan is cheating you. He is laughing at you up his sleeve.

"Come out from them and be separate. . . . Touch no unclean thing, and I will receive you" (2 Corinthians 6:17). In the Old Testament, the Jews were told not to touch a dead body, a leper, or a festering wound. When they did, they were considered to be unclean, and they were separated from God. For a week, they couldn't worship in the public assemblies because they were unclean.

You may think that you can handle unclean things. Pornography, marijuana, pagan literature, flirtations at the office — you can handle them. You won't be affected. But eventually they defile. Slowly they alienate you from God. Your repeated exposure to these things begins to defile your mind. It makes you spiritually unclean. You sit in church and there are flashbacks. You try to concentrate on Scripture, but your mind wanders.

Randy Alcorn, in an article in *Leadership* magazine wrote:

> A battering ram may hit a fortress gate a thousand times, and no one time seems to have an effect, yet finally the gate caves in. Likewise, immorality is the cumulative product of small mental indulgences and miniscule compromises, the immediate consequences of which were, at the time, indiscernible. Our thought is the fabric of which we weave our character and our destiny.[16]

Stop and think about the consequences of sin: a wounded family, a loss of employment, exposure to disease, undermining one's credibility with Christians and influence with non-Christians, a sense of guilt and regret, and maybe even death. Is it worth it?

The Bible says, "Be sure that your sin will find you out" (Numbers 32:23). You may think you're shrewd, you know when to stop, you're just toying on the fringe. But it will eventually catch up to you — and it will amaze you how quickly it can happen.

A preacher in San Jose, California, related an experience that sobered him. He went to Argentina, thousands of miles from home, on a mission trip. He said one afternoon he was resting and reading a book by the pool when an attractive woman in a skimpy bikini came and lay down in the lounge chair next to him and began to flirt. He tried to ignore her, but all of a sudden she screamed and said, "Oh there's a bee on my bathing suit, there's a bee on my bathing suit!" He got up and took his book and just brushed it away and immediately, alone, headed for his room.

[16]Randy Alcorn, "Strategies to Keep From Falling," *Leadership* (Winter, 1988), p. 46.

The next day, when he got on the plane to go home, he was amazed to see that same girl was a stewardess on his flight back to San Francisco. The next Sunday at church, a man said, "I have a sister who's a stewardess, and she was just in Argentina, too. I've been trying to get her to come to church."

"Here I was, thousands of miles from home, thinking that nobody would know," the preacher said. "And it could have been that two or three weeks later that woman would have walked into church where I am the preacher."

I don't know how sin can possibly blind a person so badly that a nationally known evangelist would think that he could be involved with prostitutes in a town and not be recognized. But sin does that to us all. It blinds us to reality.

Open your eyes. Here is the reality: sin carries an exorbitant price tag. It's not worth it. The price you pay always exceeds the value of the pleasure that you enjoy.

Deliberately Involve Yourself in Positive Activity

"Let us purify ourselves from everything that contaminates body and spirit, perfecting holiness out of reverence for God" (2 Corinthians 7:1). Circle that two-word phrase, *perfecting holiness*. Wiersbe says, "Separation is not just a negative act of departure; it is a positive act of dedication."

Jesus told a parable about a man who had a demon in his house. He swept the demon out, but he didn't fill his house up with anything else. Seven demons worse than the first one came in and occupied the house because nature abhors a vacuum. He was worse off at the end than at the beginning. (See Luke 11:24-26.) You can't just say, "I'm not going to do those things." You have to fill your life with something that is going to counteract sin.

One thing you can do is develop a good relationship with your mate.

> Since there is so much immorality, each man should have his own wife, and each woman her own husband. The husband should fulfill his marital duty to his wife, and likewise the wife to her husband. The wife's body does not belong to her alone but also to her husband. In the same way, the husband's body does not belong to him alone but also to his wife. Do not deprive each other except by mutual consent and for a time, so that you may devote yourselves to prayer. Then come together again so that Satan will not tempt you because of your lack of self-control (1 Corinthians 7:2-5).

Make your own marriage so loving, so free of inhibitions, and so ful-filling that you'll not be as tempted elsewhere. One of the primary reasons that I've not been unfaithful is that I'm blessed with a very loving and af-fectionate wife. But even if that were not the case, I would still have the re-sponsibility to honor the vows that I made before God and my family and my friends to be faithful to this woman for better and worse "until death do us part."

During times of war there have been couples who were separated two or three years, and they loved each other enough to be faithful. There are people whose mates have been disabled in accidents, and they've been faithful. If you love the Lord more than anything else, you can be faithful whatever your situation. Work at your marriage relationship. Be alert to the red flags of poor communication, discontent, and infrequent intimacy. When your mate says, "Honey, we need to spend some time together," don't brush it off. Stop what you're doing and take time for each other.

How can you improve your marriage if you don't spend time together where you are under no pressure? My wife and I have discovered that we need to get out of the area code sometimes. Every few months, we just go away for three or four days, riding together in the car, and spending time alone. One time we spent two hours in an antique shop. Now, I don't like antique shops, but I like her. On the other hand, there were no interrup-tions and no telephones—and I like that, too.

Take advantage of tapes, books, and marriage-enrichment seminars. I have noticed that the couples least likely to attend a marriage-enrichment seminar are the ones who need it the most. Christ loved the church as His bride and gave himself up for it. We need to be sacrificing for each other.

We can also fortify ourselves with regular Bible study. David said, "I have hidden your word in my heart that I might not sin against you" (Psalm 119:11). Every day we are badgered by the world's propaganda. The world tells us sex outside marriage is okay, that marriage is boring, that adultery is exciting and fornication is harmless—everybody who is normal does it. We have to be fortified with the Word of God or we're going to be impacted by that propaganda. A man picks up *Sports Illustrated*'s swimsuit issue, and he thinks, "My wife doesn't look like that; I must be deprived." In the soap operas, the woman's lover is always so tender and thoughtful; he says the nicest things, and the viewer thinks, "My husband doesn't have a romantic bone in his body. What a dullard he is. I feel cheated." If we don't have something counteracting that propa-ganda, we're going to be weakened like that gate that keeps getting hit by the battering ram.

The Bible presents sex in a realistic way. When it's within the bounds of marriage, it is holy. When it gets outside those boundaries, it's like a fire that consumes. Our world would have you believe there can be no fulfillment in life without sexual intimacy. The Bible presents it as one of the privileges of life, but realistically there is more to life than that. Jesus was single, and He was pure. Paul was not married, and still he was holy. There's more to life than sex. Read the Biblical accounts of David's falling, of Samson's messing up, of Solomon's being overindulgent, and it will make you aware of your own vulnerability.

Then read the story of Joseph. I love that story. He was sold into slavery by his brothers. He became a slave in Egypt, and later the head of Potiphar's house. Everything was going well. Then, when Potiphar was gone, Potiphar's wife tried to seduce him. She grabbed him by the coat and said, "Come lie with me." If anybody had an excuse, it was Joseph. If he had taken a modern psychology class, he could have said, "My brothers hated me. My father was overindulgent with me. My mother died giving birth to my brother Benjamin when I was a little boy. Here I am a young, virile, single man in my mid-twenties, having never known a woman's love; and the moral values of this culture are so bad, everybody's doing it. God has let me down, too. I guess I'll go ahead."

Baloney! Joseph said, "I can't do this thing and sin against my God." He turned and fled, and God ultimately blessed him. Joseph perfected holiness out of reverence to God.

Make yourself accountable to a close friend. "Confess your sins to each other and pray for each other so that you may be healed. The prayer of a righteous man is powerful and effective" (James 5:16). If you've got a problem and you can't overcome it, find a close friend of the same sex and say, "I want your help." One man was severely tempted to have an affair. He knew he was going to have breakfast with a close friend the next day, so he telephoned the friend and said, "Please pray for me, and when I see you tomorrow, ask me what I did today." He didn't want to tell his friend that he'd just had an affair, and he was strengthened just by making himself accountable to a friend.

Fill your idle time with positive activity. David got in trouble when he was supposed to be in battle but he lounged on the house top instead. If you don't have a positive activity to fill your idle time, you're asking for trouble.

Finally, practice forgiveness for yourself and others. We sometimes leave the impression that misappropriated sex is the one sin God can't tolerate or forgive. It is one of the worst. "Flee from sexual immorality. All other sins a man commits are outside his body, but he who sins sexually sins against his own body" (1 Corinthians 6:18). Sexual sins are grievous in God's sight because they hurt so many people. But even though they dishonor God, He can still forgive. His grace is sufficient.

Remember the woman caught in adultery (John 8:1-11). The Pharisees threw her at Jesus' feet and said, "The law says she should be stoned. What do you say?" They were trying to trap Him. If He had said, "Go ahead and stone her," He would lose His reputation for being loving, and if He had said, "Let her go," He wouldn't be obeying the law.

Jesus did something we don't read about His doing at any other time. He stooped down and wrote something on the ground. We don't know what He wrote. Some people think He was writing the names of women some of the Pharisees had been with. He said, "Let him who is without sin among you cast the first stone."

The Bible says they began to leave, one by one, beginning with the oldest. The older we are, the more we are aware of our own failures. After they all left, Jesus stood and said to the woman, "Has no one condemned you?"

She said, "No one, Lord."

He said, "Neither do I condemn you. Go and sin no more."

If you are involved right now in the wrong kind of relationship, I urge you to repent, receive the forgiveness of God, thank Him that you've got out, and go and sin no more. Or maybe there's somebody you need to forgive—maybe it's a mate or a son-in-law, or maybe it's a parent. You've been holding past indiscretions against him for a long time. Maybe you've never committed the *same* sin, but your life isn't without sin. Jesus said, "When you pray, say, 'Forgive us our debts, as we also have forgiven our debtors'" (Matthew 6:12).

It's been said that we are most like beasts when we kill; we are most like man when we judge; and we are most like God when we forgive.

The Cycle of Encouragement

2 Corinthians 7:2-16

EVERYBODY NEEDS ENCOURAGEMENT. When a little baby first begins to walk, normal parents encourage every step. The little baby delights in hearing, "Way to go!" "Oh, that's a big girl!" "That's really good!" Those positive words elicit squeals of delight and increased effort on the part of the child.

That desire for encouragement continues as the child grows older. When our children get good grades in school, we post the papers on the refrigerator. When they make the pep band or the cheerleading squad, we tell them how proud we are of them. We put their trophies on the shelf so that we can brag because we know that encouragement motivates them to keep on stretching. The role of encouragement in athletics can be seen clearly by the home court advantage. Why is a team much more likely to win at home than it is on the road? Familiarity with surroundings and breaks in officiating are factors, but the main reason the home team wins is encouragement from the fans. There's something about people rooting for you that brings out your best.

When I played basketball in high school for the Conneaut Valley Indians, our cheerleaders would do a cheer just before the game began that just sent chills down my spine. Each wearing a feather in her hair, they would sit on the floor and pretend to beat a drum in tom-tom fashion. Then they would chant, "Boom boom boom boom! Boom boom boom boom! Send them to their doom doom doom doom!" It puts goose bumps on my arms even today just to think about it!

But stop and think why we have cheerleaders at ball games, why fan support is so important. It's because we respond to encouragement from others. That need is not limited to athletes, and it doesn't stop with high school or college. It continues all through life for everyone. If you go to someone's hospital room, you see get-well cards lined up on the shelf. Those words of encouragement are incentives to restoration of health. Many people have a drawer full of encouraging notes written to them over the years. When they get discouraged, they open up that drawer and read over those notes to boost themselves up again.

Older people probably need encouragement more than anybody. People who once had important titles and who once were sought for counsel now sometimes feel unneeded. I was struggling with a sermon text one week. I couldn't come up with an outline. So I called Olin Hay in Florida, a retired, respected minister in his mid-seventies, and I asked him to take a look at it. The next day he called back with some really meaningful insights for me.

Later I told his wife that I had been really hesitant to call. She said, "Oh, please do that again! That really made his day. He stayed up half the night and was so encouraged that you needed him."

From the time we're born until the time we're old, we all respond to encouragement. That's the reason the Bible instructs us as Christian people to be sources of encouragement to one another. "Encourage one another daily, as long as it is called Today, so that none of you may be hardened by sin's deceitfulness" (Hebrews 3:13). "Let us consider how we may spur one another on toward love and good deeds. Let us not give up meeting together, as some are in the habit of doing, but let us encourage one another—and all the more as you see the Day approaching" (Hebrews 10:24, 25). The closer we get to the day of the coming of the Lord Jesus Christ, the worse the world conditions are going to be and the more we're going to need to spur one another on to be faithful to Him.

Warren Wiersbe has suggested that this chapter is kind of a cycle of encouragement. Paul encouraged the church, Titus encouraged Paul, and the church encouraged Titus. All of us can learn to be encouragers. Maybe we can't learn to be musicians or to teach if those are not our gifts, but I think we can all learn to be incentives for holy living.

Paul Encouraged the Corinthians

The church needed this encouragement because Paul had previously rebuked them for their sin. He had been concerned that his rebuke may have been too harsh (cf. 2 Corinthians 7:8), but by the time he wrote he knew the rebuke had been heeded and the erring Corinthians had repented.

"Better is open rebuke than hidden love. Wounds from a friend can be trusted, but an enemy multiplies kisses" (Proverbs 27:5, 6). Encouragement is meaningless if it is just shallow flattery. It must be an honest appraisal of strength. It must emanate from one who is courageous enough to confront weakness.

Have you ever had a friend who constantly told you how great you looked—"that's just a perfect outfit; that's just your color"—and said it so often it lost its meaning? When you go to buy a new suit, with every jacket you put on, does the salesperson say, "Oh, that's a perfect fit, just the one you ought to buy; that's just your color"? Eventually they lose credibility. "Whoever flatters his neighbor is spreading a net for his feet" (Proverbs 29:5). A parent who always praises and never disciplines is going to lose influence with a child. A coach who does nothing but praise creates an overconfident, lazy team.

A minister is to "rebuke" as well as to "encourage—with great patience and careful instruction" (2 Timothy 4:2). Titus 2:15 tells the minister to "encourage and rebuke with all authority." A real encourager doesn't go around telling everyone that everything is nice all the time. An encourager is honest. He knows words of encouragement don't mean much if the listener doesn't know that he will tell the truth if it's not good.

Rick Houp was a student at the Cincinnati Bible College. He sang for the Come Alive Singers, a music group that traveled the country representing the school. Charlie Stiles was their director, and Rick found him a tough taskmaster. All summer long, he was on Rick's case, warning him about his ego and his selfishness. Then, one Sunday night, it was Rick's turn to preach. When he finished, he looked down at Charlie sitting in the front row. Charlie gave him a thumbs-up signal and a little smile. Rick Houp says he remembered that little gesture of encouragement for years. It meant more than a thousand words of flattery because he knew it came from somebody who was telling him the truth.

Paul's encouragement of the church was not flattery. He would rebuke them when they needed it. But when he expressed approval, he did it in three ways.

First, he expressed it by a life of integrity. "We have wronged no one, we have corrupted no one, we have exploited no one" (2 Corinthians 7:2). Those are great words for a preacher because it's really tempting, when you're a preacher, to take advantage of people and exploit people. You don't mean to, but sometimes it just happens.

One Sunday I told my congregation that I looked in my sock drawer and there weren't any black socks there for me. The following week I got fifteen pairs of socks from people in the church. Now I didn't mean to exploit them, I didn't mean to take advantage of them, but I was tempted to tell them the next Sunday that I had a little hole in my shirt . . . and that my car hadn't been running very well, either!

I don't have anything to do with the finances in my church. I'm given a generous salary, and the elders handle the finances. But Paul handled the finances himself. He was traveling from church to church collecting money for the poor in Jerusalem. His enemies accused him of defrauding people. They suggested he was a con man who was keeping money for himself. Paul said that wasn't true. He didn't take money wrongfully or exploit people. He was going to take it back to the poor in Jerusalem just as he said he would. It's rare to have such an honest man; it's an encouragement.

He also encouraged them by his sacrificial spirit. "You have such a place in our hearts that [I] would live or die with you" (2 Corinthians 7:3). Paul was an inspiration because he was willing to go through adversity for other people. He said his body had no rest (2 Corinthians 7:5). He was constantly harassed. But he endured those difficulties because he cared for people.

It's been said some people call in sick, and others crawl in sick. The people who crawl in sick are the ones who inspire and encourage us. Lou Gehrig frequently played baseball with at least one broken finger. His courage and self-sacrifice inspired his teammates to give their best. Paul had conflicts and adversity and illness, but he kept going, and he was an encouragement to people. He said, "I'd live or die for you."

Another way Paul encouraged the Corinthians was by affirmation. He expressed his confidence in them. "I have great confidence in you," he said. "I take great pride in you. I am greatly encouraged [by you]" (2 Corinthians 7:4). Those words were not hollow flattery by someone trying to manipulate them; they were from a man who had rebuked them earlier. The fact that Paul could affirm them in spite of their problems boosted them up.

People in educational circles have been talking a lot about "positive reinforcement" in recent years. Rather than grinding their students down all the time by telling them what they are doing wrong, teachers are being encouraged to find out what they are doing right and to praise them. In most cases, this will inspire better behavior by the students. One teacher told me they have a slogan: "Catch 'em being good." It's a good slogan for teachers, parents, managers, church leaders, and anyone else who works with people.

That's what Paul did. He caught the Corinthians doing something right and said, "You're doing well. I'm proud of you."

Titus Encouraged Paul

Paul needed encouragement, too. He said, "When we came into Macedonia, this body of ours had no rest, but we were harassed at every turn — conflicts on the outside, fears within" (2 Corinthians 7:5). You normally don't think of Paul as being afraid, but he was. He didn't like being beaten. He worried about the churches he'd started, whether they would survive or collapse. Paul sometimes even worried about his own staying power. He struggled with exhaustion, opposition, and apprehension. He needed encouragement.

Sometimes, even the people who appear to be the most confident and the most spiritual need encouragement. Stephen Brown says we ought to pray for the strong because they are weak. Years ago there was a feature on *Sixty Minutes* about the day that President Abraham Lincoln was shot. It listed the items found in his pockets when he was killed: a pocket knife, some Confederate money, and — in his wallet — a yellowed newspaper clipping that he had been saving for some time. It had been opened and reopened so many times that the edges of it were frayed. It was an editorial by a British writer named Bright, who said that, though Lincoln was criticized by most Americans, he thought Lincoln would go down as one of America's greatest Presidents. Lincoln saved that clipping and read it over and over. Can't you just see him over in the corner of the living quarters of the White House some night after a hard day, under an oil lamp rereading that clipping that reminded him that somebody believed in him?

The President needs it. Your supervisor at work needs it. Your Sunday-school teacher and your preacher need it. And if those people need it, how much more the people who are insecure or the people who are really struggling in life!

A parent gave me a handwritten card that one of our Sunday-school teachers had sent to their daughter in the third grade.

Dear Stephanie,

I am so glad you have been coming to my Sunday-school class. You are such a nice person and pretty, too. I hope you're having fun and you're enjoying learning with us. If you ever need me for anything, please feel free to call. I'll be praying for you.

How thoughtful that was for a Sunday-school teacher to take time to encourage a nine-year-old girl! That card was a great incentive to return to class and to continue to learn. Let us encourage one another daily so that we won't be hardened by sin's deceitfulness.

God met Paul's need for encouragement by sending Titus to him with great news. "God, who comforts the downcast, comforted us by the coming of Titus, and not only by his coming but also by the comfort you had given him" (2 Corinthians 7:6, 7). Paul was encouraged not just by the arrival of his companion, but by the good news that Titus had to share, that the Corinthians had repented. "He told us about your longing for me, your deep sorrow, your ardent concern for me, so that my joy was greater than ever" (2 Corinthians 7:7).

The one thing that thrills most Christian leaders more than anything else is a changed life, a repentant spirit. I love to see people come forward at the invitation. I love to see people reading the Bible. The thing that thrills me more than anything else is to see people whose lives have been changed by Jesus Christ. When I see couples sitting together learning to love each other, and I know that years ago they were on the verge of divorce, that's encouraging. People whisper to me, "It's been six months since I've smoked a joint," or, "It's been a year since I've had a drink." That's inspirational to me. When I see people who were once proud and arrogant, but now are humble and have a servant's heart, that's encouraging.

"Now I am happy, not because you were made sorry, but because your sorrow led you to repentance. For you became sorrowful as God intended" (2 Corinthians 7:9). There is a big difference between godly sorrow and worldly sorrow. This is a relevant point when we think of the reaction of people to their sins. When Gary Hart says, "I'm sorry," is he really sorry? When Jimmy Bakker and Jimmy Swaggart say, "I'm sorry," are they really sorry? Do we just forgive them and trust them? If your mate sins against you and then says, "I'm sorry," do you immediately trust your mate again? How do you know whether it's for real? If a teenager rebels and you confront him, and he says, "I'm sorry," do you trust him again?

There's a godly sorrow that leads to life and a worldly sorrow that leads to death. One is legitimate, the other is phony. There are four differences between godly repentance and worldly sorrow.

First, godly sorrow is remorseful over sin. Worldly sorrow regrets being caught. A lot of people are not sorry for what they did; they're just sorry they were found out. They're angry at the person who blew the whistle on them or angry at the way they got caught. "What are you doing in my stuff?" they say. Or, "You have no business investigating my private life!"

Second, godly sorrow is evidenced by a penitent attitude. Worldly sorrow continues to display a resentful spirit. A person who is really sorry will be like David in the Old Testament. He will admit the facts and say, "I'm sorry; I have sinned." But if it is worldly sorrow, he will sneer, "Who are you to judge me? Let him who is without sin cast the first stone. There's no way I'll go back to church now that everybody knows about it."

Third, godly sorrow results in changed behavior. Worldly sorrow results in repetition of the sin if it's possible not to get caught. I've always been close to my older sister, Rosanne. When I was a senior in high school, Rosanne graduated from Cincinnati Bible College. She graduated with honors, and she was going to receive several awards. But on the day she was graduating, I was supposed to play a baseball game. When my parents were preparing to leave to drive several hundred miles to my sister's graduation, I faced the choice of going to her graduation and encouraging her or staying home and playing baseball.

I made the selfish choice. I stayed home. As soon as my parents drove out of the driveway, I knew that I was wrong and I began to cry. I knew my parents were stopping at my cousin's to pick up my aunt, so I called them there and I told my mother, sobbing, "Please tell Rosanne I'm sorry for what I did."

My mother said an awful thing. She said, "I understand. We'll come back for you."

I said, "Tell Rosanne I'm not that sorry."

It's a worldly sorrow if you just regret that you hurt somebody but you're not willing to change. William Barclay says this about worldly sorrow:

> If it got the chance to do the same thing again and if it thought it could escape the consequences, it certainly would do it. It does not at all hate the sin, it only regrets that its sin got it into trouble. But true repentance, a godly sorrow, is repentance which has come to see the wrongness of the thing it did. It is not just the consequences of the thing which it regrets; it hates the thing itself. . . . [and] is determined to never do it again, and . . . has dedicated the rest of its life to atone, by God's grace, for what it has done.[17]

Fourth, godly sorrow leads to salvation; worldly sorrow leads to death.

> See what this godly sorrow has produced in you: what earnestness, what eagerness to clear yourselves, what indignation, what alarm, what longing,

[17]William Barclay, *The Letters to the Corinthians* (Philadelphia: Westminster, 1954), p. 253.

what concern, what readiness to see justice done. At every point you have
proved yourselves to be innocent in this matter. . . . By all this we are encouraged (2 Corinthians 7:11, 13).

The difference is illustrated in the lives of Judas and Peter. Both men vi-
olated the Lord's will and denied Christ. Both of them were sorry. But
Judas had a worldly sorrow. He was too proud to change and he killed
himself. Peter had a godly sorrow that led to repentance. He changed his
life, asked the Lord to forgive him, and was reinstated.

Paul was encouraged by the Corinthians' godly sorrow that led to life.

The Corinthians Encouraged Titus

Paul encouraged the church, Titus encouraged Paul, and the
Corinthians encouraged Titus. "In addition to our own encouragement,
we were especially delighted to see how happy Titus was, because his
spirit has been refreshed by all of you" (2 Corinthians 7:13). It's not easy to
be the bearer of bad news. Titus had the responsibility to deliver a stern
letter to the church. He couldn't just drop it in the mailbox and run; he had
to stay around as Paul's representative and see what the people would
say. So Titus needed some encouragement, too, and the church provided
it. They put his mind at ease."I had boasted to him about you," Paul said,
"and you have not embarrassed me" (2 Corinthians 7:14).

Have you ever bragged about somebody over and over to a friend, and
then when the two got together you were a little nervous for fear your
friend wouldn't like him and you'd be embarrassed? Almost every week,
somebody calls me and says, "I've been bragging about our church to so-
and-so for a long time, and they're finally coming this Sunday. What's
going on?" I know what they mean. They want to make sure the music is
good and the sermon is not going to be boring and the speaker system is
going to work—and they are not going to be embarrassed. They don't
want to have to say to their friend, "I'm sorry. It's not usually like that. It's
usually better."

My first year in Christian work, I was a youth minister. I also played on
the church's softball team, and one night we had a heartbreaking defeat.
Evidently I was pouting about it, because one of my kids came up to me
and said, "I've got a friend I want you to meet, and I've been bragging
about you to him for a long time. So straighten up, OK?"

Paul had bragged to Titus about the Corinthian church. He told Titus,
"This is a stern letter, but they'll receive it well because they are good

people." He didn't get an answer for a long time and he began to worry. But when Titus came he said, "I had boasted to him about you, and you have not embarrassed me. But just as everything we said to you was true, so our boasting about you to Titus has proved to be true as well" (2 Corinthians 7:14). You can hear Paul breathing a sigh of relief because it all worked out. "His affection for you is all the greater when he remembers that you were all obedient, receiving him with fear and trembling. I am glad I can have complete confidence in you" (2 Corinthians 7:15, 16).

When a Christian has made a bad mistake and he genuinely repents, we have a responsibility not only to forgive him, but to encourage him as well. I hear people say things like, "Well, you know, twenty-five years ago they got a divorce," or, "She got pregnant before she was married," or, "He was pretty rowdy in high school and college." When repentance is demonstrated to the point of a penitent spirit and a changed life, then we are to forgive, encourage, and trust. The Corinthians had messed up, but Paul said, "I've got confidence in you." That had to be encouraging.

One of my favorite moments in NCAA basketball came from a tournament game between Georgetown and North Carolina. The score was tied, and there was only about twelve seconds to go. Freddie Brown of Georgetown had the ball and, out of the corner of his eye, he saw a player he thought was a teammate. He threw him the ball, but it was a player from North Carolina, who took it down to the other end and scored. Georgetown lost the game. During the post-game activity, the cameras focused on coach John Thompson of Georgetown, a six-foot-ten-inch hulk of a man, who grabbed Freddie Brown and embraced him in a big bear hug. In the moment of his horrible mistake, the coach was trying to encourage him. It's been said that "a word of encouragement during a failure is worth more than a whole book of praise after success."

Encouragement is desperately needed by everybody, so express it. People around you may appear poised and confident, but everybody has insecurities; everybody needs words of encouragement. You don't have to be talented to be an encourager, just unselfish. Speak a word; write a note. You may never know how much of a boost you have been.

Encouragement must be honest to be effective, so balance it. "He who rebukes a man will in the end gain more favor than he who has a flattering tongue" (Proverbs 28:23). Make sure you tell the truth.

A plaque in our kitchen reads,

"How much do you love me?" I asked Jesus, and Jesus spread out His arms and said, "This much," and He went to the cross and died for me.

Jesus Christ is the ultimate encourager, so receive Him. Every one of us has made horrible mistakes; we've all sinned. But Jesus came to embrace us. "To all who received him, to those who believed in his name, he gave the right to become children of God" (John 1:12).

The Importance of Giving

2 Corinthians 8:1-15

IT HAD BEEN A HARD WINTER in the Rockies. The snow piled deeper and deeper. The temperature dropped below zero and stayed there. The rivers froze over. People were suffering. The Red Cross used helicopters to fly in supplies.

After a long, hard day, as they were returning to their base, the rescue team in a helicopter saw a cabin nearly submerged in the snow. A thin wisp of smoke came from the chimney. The men figured those people in that cabin were probably critically short of food, fuel, and medicine. Because of the trees they had to set down about a mile from the cabin. They put their heavy emergency equipment on their backs, trudged through waist-deep snow, and reached the cabin exhausted, panting, and perspiring. They pounded on the door and a thin, gaunt mountain woman finally answered.

The lead man panted, "Ma'am, we're from the Red Cross."

She was silent for a moment, and then she said, "It's been a hard, long winter, Sonny. I just don't think we can give anything this year!"

We have become accustomed to people's relentless asking for money. The salesman who pounds on our door, the computer recording on the other end of the phone, the appeal letter in the mail, the offering meditation at church, and the Girl Scout who meets us at the mall are out to take our money. We brace ourselves to say no. When somebody approaches claiming to want to help us, we're suspicious. There has to be an ulterior motive.

The apostle Paul was traveling all over the world taking up a collection for poor Christians in Jerusalem. Usually the mother church supports the mission church, but in that day it was just the opposite. The Jerusalem church had sent out missionaries, but it had become a very poor congregation. There was famine in Judea, so the economy was down. On top of that, Christians were being persecuted, and many of them had lost their jobs. As a result, a great number of them were just barely staying alive. So Paul went from church to church urging the Christians to give generously to support those who were in need in Jerusalem.

Paul's instructions here to the Corinthian church about giving generously still apply today. Think about what he says and seriously evaluate your attitude toward your possessions.

The Corinthian Problem: Materialism

Paul said, "Just as you excel in everything . . . see that you also excel in this grace of giving" (2 Corinthians 8:7). He went on to say, "Last year you were the first not only to give but also to have the desire to do so. Now finish the work, so that your eager willingness to do it may be matched by your completion of it" (2 Corinthians 8:10, 11). That is a kind way of telling them that they weren't doing very well when it came to giving. They excelled in everything else. Their intentions were good, but somehow greed had shriveled up their intentions.

I think the three greatest temptations facing modern Christians are sex, greed, and ego. Those three temptations have always been Satan's fiercest weapons. They are also called the "lust of the flesh," the "lust of the eyes," and the "pride of life" (1 John 2:16, KJV). When Satan tempted Eve in the garden of Eden, she looked at the fruit and saw it was desirous to possess—it was pleasing to the eye—it looked good to taste to satisfy her appetite, and she thought that it would make her wise. Satan comes to us with those same temptations.

Everyone has his own specific weakness, a temptation that is especially hard to resist. What is a weakness for one person may be no problem for another. But, in general, we all face the same temptations, and we're all vulnerable to each one of them. We all need to think seriously about our attitude toward our possessions. Jesus said, "Be on your guard against all kinds of greed; a man's life does not consist in the abundance of his possessions" (Luke 12:15). Paul said, "The love of money is a root of all kinds of evil" (1 Timothy 6:10).

Most churches today do not excel in giving. Studies show that most Christians give only about three percent of their income to the church and other charitable causes. And the higher the income, the lower the giving percentage! In fact, one writer has calculated that, in most churches, if everyone quit his job and went on welfare—and then tithed his new income (that is, gave ten percent to the church)—the church's income would soar! We just don't excel in giving.

What would happen if we changed that? Just imagine, if we did excel in giving, what spectacular things we could do. What your church could do! What the churches on a national scope could do!

We could start new churches. A church in Georgia has started ten new churches in India over the last decade. We could start with churches in areas that were needed in our country, maybe in Massachusetts and New York. And we could finance those new churches.

We could complete a first-class crisis pregnancy center in every major city. We could develop ministries to families with mentally retarded children, persons with hearing impairments, battered wives, a ministry to the dying.

WHAS radio and television has a repair truck that just roams the city of Louisville during rush hour; they stop and help people with car problems. Wouldn't it be great if churches had repair trucks with Christian mechanics roaming our cities during the rush hour? What a great *practical* way to show people that the church knows how to tackle real problems.

Unfortunately, two dominant philosophies in this world are influencing us all. One is the yuppie philosophy of self-indulgence. This view is that your money is to be spent completely on yourself. The more wealth you have, then the more you can spend on clothing and vacations and privileges for yourself. After all, you've earned it! Jesus told of a rich man who lived in luxury every day. He ignored the poor man who begged for some scraps from his table. That's the yuppie philosophy.

We're surrounded by people who tell you, if you give it away, you're a sucker. You've earned it—keep it for yourself! The Bible says just the opposite: "If anyone has material possessions and sees his brother in need but has no pity on him, how can the love of God be in him?" (1 John 3:17). Let's not love just with words, but with deeds.

Most Americans were appalled at the extravagance of President and Mrs. Marcos in the Philippines. She had 2000 pairs of shoes while many people in her country went barefoot. But, except in such extreme cases, self-indulgence is difficult to define. What was extravagant to you yesterday may not be extravagant today. What is indulgent to you may not be to me.

When I learned that a woman in our church had thirty pairs of shoes, I started teasing her about her extravagance. "That's a different pair of shoes for every day of the month!" I said.

"How many pairs of shoes do you have?" she asked.

"Two," I said, "and I feel kind of guilty about that sometimes."

She said, "Do you have a pair of softball cleats?"

"Well, yes I do."

"Then you've got three. Do you play golf? Do you have golf shoes?"

"Yes, I do."

"Then you've got four. How many pairs of tennis shoes do you have?"

"I've got low cuts and high tops," I said.

She said, "You've got six. Do you have a pair of shoes you wash your car in?"

"Well, yes. . . ."

"That's seven."

All of a sudden I realized that seven didn't really seem like too many. It's really difficult to determine what's extravagant. But we must ask ourselves, "How much is enough?" And our standard must be something more objective than what we happen to have at the moment. We must draw the line at some reasonable point and realize we are being selfish if we cross that line!

The second philosophy impacting people today is socialism. That philosophy says that it's wrong to own more than anyone else, so all property should be owned by the state so it can be shared equally. This is the opposite of materialism, but it's the reverse side of the same coin. Like materialism, it begins with the premise that life consists of one's possessions, and one cannot be happy if he doesn't have as much as his neighbor. It is neither practical nor Scriptural. Jesus taught us to share with those who are in need of food, shelter, or clothing, but He did not command us that everything had to be distributed equally. Jesus was poor, but He owned a seamless robe that was of enough value that people gambled for it. He stayed at the home of Mary, Martha, and Lazarus. They were apparently wealthy people who had a large enough home to accommodate Jesus and some of the disciples. Remember, Mary poured out an alabaster jar of perfume that was worth a year's wages she had saved (cf. John 12:1-8). She had accumulated some wealth.

The Bible commands us to give as we have been prospered (1 Corinthians 16:2). That means we haven't all been prospered the same. Yet a number of American Christians have been so impacted by the philosophy of socialism that they feel guilty about what they have, even though they give generously. "My parents worked harder than I and they never had it this good. I don't deserve it," they say apologetically. The Bible says that, if we give generously, God will "open the floodgates of heaven" and pour out a blessing so great we will not be able to receive it. (See Malachi 3:10.) When we give generously, as God gives, we ought to be grateful, not guilty.

"Our desire is not that others might be relieved while you are hard pressed, but that there might be equality" (2 Corinthians 8:13). Paul was not saying there had to be equal distribution of material wealth. He was saying, "Look, the people in Jerusalem shared the gospel with you. You are indebted to them spiritually. Since they have been generous with you spiritually, repay that debt by sharing some of your abundance materially. Then there will be equality."

The Biblical attitude toward possessions is not self-indulgence or socialism, but stewardship. Make your money honestly, spend it wisely, and give it generously. If we're going to combat the philosophy of the world, we must learn to give generously.

The Macedonian Example—Generosity

"We want you to know about the grace that God has given the Macedonian churches" (2 Corinthians 8:1). They were poor, yet they were generous. "Out of the most severe trial, their overflowing joy and their extreme poverty welled up in rich generosity. For I testify that they gave as much as they were able, and even beyond their ability" (2 Corinthians 8:2, 3). Sometimes, when people are poor, they become resentful and miserly. They feel no obligation to give at all. They have all kinds of rationalizations why they're not going to give right now. "When I make my first million, I'll have a lot to give," or, "Certainly, God doesn't expect me to give when I can't pay my bills—I'd go bankrupt and be thrown in jail, and that would be a bad testimony." But these Macedonians responded to the need of the poor in Jerusalem. Even though they were poor, they gave.

That tells me everybody ought to be giving something. You're never so poor that you're not responsible for giving. At the feast of Purim in the Old Testament, a regulation commanded that however poor a man was he had to find someone poorer than himself and give him a gift. God was training them that everybody was to give. Now if poor Christians are generous with their resources, how much more should those of us who are rich be generous—and I think just about all of us are rich. If you have an average income in America, you're in the upper five percent of the economy of the world.

"Command those who are rich in this present world not to be arrogant," Paul wrote to Timothy. Don't act like you're superior because you have things. ". . . nor to put their hope in wealth, which is so uncertain, but to put their hope in God, who richly provides us with everything for our enjoyment" (1 Timothy 6:17). What a phrase! God provides us with things so we can enjoy them. It is not wrong to take a vacation or to go out to eat. God provides those things. Be grateful. "Command them to do good, to be rich in good deeds, and to be generous and willing to share" (1 Timothy 6:18). If God has given to you abundantly, then you give abundantly. "In this way they will lay up treasure for themselves as a firm foundation for the coming age, so that they may take hold of the life that is truly life" (1 Timothy 6:19).

We're to give generously. How much is generous? What standard determines generosity? Give "according to your means," Paul said. "For if the willingness is there, the gift is acceptable according to what one has, not according to what he does not have" (2 Corinthians 8:11, 12). Giving twenty dollars in the church offering is generous for some, but it's miserly for others because God does not evaluate the gift according to its amount, but according to one's ability. In the Old Testament days, God had a standard fee for the Jewish people. They had to give ten percent of their possessions to God. In the New Testament, God says we're under grace, not law, and you should give what you've been prospered to give.

When our first child was born, we were blessed to have a baby-sitter who lived right next door. I always felt sorry for people who had to drive their baby-sitters all over town. Patty Johnson was not only a good baby-sitter, she was a hard worker. She would fold clothes and do dishes, and she charged only fifty cents an hour. We gladly paid that. A few years later, our second child was born. I said, "Patty, now that your responsibilities have doubled, how much are you going to charge?"

She said, "Oh, Mr. Russell, you just give what you want to give."

Do you think she expected more or less than fifty cents an hour?

In the Old Testament, God commanded the Jews to give ten percent. In the New Testament, He's given us much more. He's given us Christ, the Holy Spirit, and the fellowship of the church. He's let us live in the richest country in the world. He says to us, "Now, you just give as you have prospered."

I've been a tither since my first job when I was just fourteen years old, so it's been relatively easy for me. It's not really been a sacrifice. I have the goal of becoming a double tither, but even that's nothing to boast about. I know of a preacher in California who gives forty percent of his income. When John Wesley first started to preach, he made only twenty-eight pounds, and he gave two pounds. Years later, however, when he was making ninety pounds, he kept only twenty-eight for himself and gave the rest of it away.

These Macedonian Christians were poor, yet they gave more than was expected. They gave "beyond their ability." They sacrificed, and yet they were joyful. "Their overflowing joy and their extreme poverty welled up in rich generosity" (2 Corinthians 8:2). Now the yuppie philosophy would program you to believe that, if you give it away, you're going to be miserable. The word *stingy* comes originally from the word *sting*. We think it stings to give; the very idea pains us. Just the opposite is true. The more you give, the more joy you have within. Jesus promised, "It is more blessed to give than to receive" (Acts 20:35). Here is a formula that doesn't work in a computer, but it works in life. Poverty plus adversity plus generosity equals joy.

Back in 1983 the leadership of our congregation knew that we needed to relocate. We were overcrowded. A twenty-two-acre plot of ground was available, so the board voted to purchase it. The down payment for the land was $215,000. After we voted to purchase it, we began discussing how we were going to get the money. Ron Geary, one of our elders, said, "Here's what we'll do. Next month when we come back for our regular meeting, let's just take up a cash offering among elders, deacons, and preachers. We'll give the entire down payment — $215,000 — in cash, tell the congregation what we've done, and let that be an encouragement to them to have a million-dollar offering in the fall so we can have seed money for a new building. I've done some calculating. There are fifty-five elders, deacons, and preachers here, so that boils down to $3,500 per man next month. Any questions?"

There were a few timid questions, and we voted it through. We walked out of that meeting saying, "What did we just do?" Most of us are not wealthy. We're tithers and we're already sacrificing. The board chairman began to receive some phone calls from board members who said, "I'm a schoolteacher. I don't make that kind of money," or, "My business wasn't that great this year," or, "We just bought a new house." But we stayed with the commitment we had made. As never before, we had to think seriously about what was first in our lives. Do we really love the Lord and the church enough to sacrifice? Or were we just mouthing words? I began to hear reports of people canceling Florida vacations and selling second cars. I know of several who went out and borrowed as much as $10,000 to give to that offering.

When we came in to next month's meeting, the tension was thick. We knew we had put our necks on the line, and we weren't sure what others were doing. One man came in with dark sunglasses, a cane, and a tin cup. He wanted everybody to know he had really made a sacrifice! We took up the offering, and it wasn't $215,000—it was $255,000 cash in one month's time! When that was announced, a spirit of joy just flooded the room. Sophisticated guys exchanged high fives and embraced and wept. In the silence after our prayer of thanks, somebody said, "I'll be outside polishing shoes."

"What shoes?" someone else said.

If you would have walked into that room at that moment, you might have concluded that everybody had just received a $10,000 bonus. But just the opposite was true—we had really made sacrifices. We had just given it away because it's more blessed to give than to receive. Today, I don't know of anybody who was in that room who wouldn't say that God has blessed him in the years since. I thought I had made a great sacrifice that night and didn't know if I'd recover, but since then my wife and I have moved into a new house and have been blessed beyond measure.

The Macedonians also gave *voluntarily*. Paul had told them about the need of the Jerusalem church, but he gave no arbitrary figure and made no assessment of the church people. "Entirely on their own, they urgently pleaded with us for the privilege of sharing in this service to the saints" (2 Corinthians 8:3, 4). Churches have all kinds of gimmicks to raise money, but God's method is for you just to give what He's laid on your heart to give.

Conrad Tittle, an author on gifts and taxes, tells about a fellow named Harold who pledged $1,000 to his church's building fund. In the church paper that week it came out that he had pledged $10,000. He called the church and said, "I didn't make a $10,000 pledge. It was only $1,000."

"We're sorry," they said. "We'll print a retraction next week and say that you only pledged a thousand."

He didn't want that, so reluctantly he pledged the rest of it—$9,000 more. When the building was finished, everybody who had pledged $10,000 could have his favorite Scripture verse below the stained glass window. He chose, "I was a stranger and you took me in."

"Each man should give what he has decided in his heart to give, not reluctantly or under compulsion, for God loves a cheerful giver" (2 Corinthians 9:7). I would rather the church give cheerfully and give less than to give begrudgingly and give more.

The Macedonians gave of their money, and yet they first gave of themselves. They gave *personally*. "They gave themselves first to the Lord and then to us in keeping with God's will" (2 Corinthians 8:5). I know a number of people who are willing to give their money, but they don't want to give their time. They'll give their money, but they don't want to have to be involved or to change their lives. God does not want your handout, He wants your hand. He doesn't want a tithe, he wants the tither. The Macedonians first gave themselves to the Lord.

A track coach told his pole vaulter, "Son, just throw your heart over the pole and the rest of you will follow." When you seek first the kingdom of God, your pocketbook follows.

When an American businessman and a lawyer were touring Korea, they saw a boy pulling a plow as his father guided the handles. The businessman said, "That must be a very poor family."

"Yes," the lawyer answered, "that's the family of Choy Ni. They're Christians. Their church had a building fund recently, and they sold their ox and gave the proceeds to the church, and now the boy is pulling the plow."

"What a sacrifice," the businessman said.

"Well, they didn't call it that," the lawyer said. "They were just thankful they had an ox to sell."

The businessman came back to America and doubled his pledge and went to his preacher and said, "Would you give me some plow work? I don't know that I've ever really given anything that cost me that much."

The Christian Motivation—Jesus

They first gave of themselves. Why would they do that? Why do some of us give sacrificially week after week? "You know the grace of our Lord Jesus Christ, that though he was rich, yet for your sakes he became poor, so that you through his poverty might become rich" (2 Corinthians 8:9).

Without a doubt the gift of Jesus' life was the most costly gift ever given. The Bible tells us that He was equal with God. He was God in Heaven. He owned the whole universe and yet He gave it all up to become a little baby. He went from a throne to a manger—and then to a cross! Not only did He become a baby, but He became a child of peasant parents. He had nowhere to lay His head. Not only did He become a man, but He became a condemned man. Not only a condemned man, but a man destined to die the most excruciating death known to man, even the death of the cross. He "made himself nothing," the Bible says (Philippians 2:7).

We're rich in *forgiveness*! "What can wash away our sins? Nothing but the blood of Jesus." What would people pay to know that all their past was forgiven?

We're rich in *fellowship*. What would people be willing to pay for the kind of relationships we're developing in the church?

We're rich in *hope*. What does it profit a man if he gains the whole world but loses his own soul? What would a man give in exchange for his life? What would a millionaire on his death bed give for the promise of life eternal? He'd give it all!

Since we've become so rich because of Christ's sacrifice, we in turn should give back to Him.

> When I survey the wondrous cross,
> On which the Prince of glory died,
> My richest gain I count but loss,
> And pour contempt on all my pride.
>
> Forbid it, Lord, that I should boast,
> Save in the death of Christ, my God;
> All the vain things that charm me most,
> I sacrifice them to His blood.
>
> See, from His head, His hands, His feet,
> Sorrow and love flow mingled down;
> Did e'er such love and sorrow meet,
> Or thorns compose so rich a crown?
>
> Were the whole realm of nature mine,
> That were a present far too small;
> Love so amazing, so divine,
> Demands my soul, my life, my all.[18]

If you've never given your life to Jesus Christ, you're poor, because you're going to die and leave it all behind. Only through the poverty of Jesus Christ can we become rich.

---

[18]Isaac Watts, "When I Survey the Wondrous Cross," 1707.

Common Sense Administration

2 Corinthians 8:16-24

D O YOU KNOW what is the most difficult part of the ministry? If you asked one hundred preachers, "What part of your responsibility do you least enjoy?" not many of them would say funerals or weddings or counseling. I think ninety of them would say the least enjoyable part of the ministry is administration. Most of us don't enjoy organizing staff, planning programs, developing job descriptions, or evaluating effectiveness. All the committee meetings and paperwork necessary for effective administration are not pleasant.

One reason we don't enjoy it is that we're not trained for it. Of the training I received for the ministry, only one course was on church administration, and now I've discovered that it's probably one-third of what I do.

Another reason we despise administrative work is that we don't anticipate it. When I thought about going into the ministry, I anticipated preaching in a church of maybe 150 people. I did not expect to oversee a staff of more than twenty ministers, each of whom had hundreds of volunteers under him. I didn't anticipate interviewing people for secretarial or staff positions. I didn't anticipate administrative committee meetings about adding paid help in the nursery, or food service or kindergarten problems.

All of a sudden, I discovered that administration was a critical part of my job, and I'm not particularly gifted in that area. I think I'm improving through experience, by being observant, and by taking seminars, but I suspect that my experience is not so different from many others. Maybe you started out to be a teacher, and now you're the head of a department, or you're a principal, or you're on the county board of education. Maybe you started out in sales and now you've become the sales manager and you're responsible for motivating people under you. Or you worked in a factory and now you are the foreman, or you were a nurse and now you're the supervisor of a nursing staff.

Whatever our position, just about all of us find ourselves in the role of administrator at one time or another. And most of us feel a little intimidated about that, a little less than competent. We read books and we attend seminars, but we know we need improvement.

It may surprise you to know that some of the most practical advice about administration is in the Bible. The Bible is an amazing book. There are lofty theological thoughts that stimulate the mind to the limit. Then there is practical, down-to-earth counsel about the most mundane, everyday matters. Since every word of Scripture is inspired by God, we need to learn the practical as well as the theological. The Bible says, "Whatever you do, do it all for the glory of God" (1 Corinthians 10:31). Whatever your everyday function is, you ought to be the most effective you can possibly be to glorify Christ in your life.

William Barclay said, "This same Paul who could write like a lyric poet and think like a theologian, could, when it was necessary, act with the meticulous accuracy of a chartered accountant." In 2 Corinthians 8, Paul discussed how he intended to administrate the offering he had been receiving for the poor people in Jerusalem. He'd collected quite a sum of money, and he didn't just stuff it in his pocket, saying, "Trust me." He was responsible in the administration of those funds.

Paul was a big enough man to do the little things and the practical things extremely well. Let's look at what made him an effective administrator.

A Willingness to Delegate Responsibility

Paul delegated part of the responsibility of collecting and administrating this offering to Titus, his associate. (See 2 Corinthians 8:16.) Paul did not try to do everything himself. The first step in effective administration is a willingness to delegate responsibility to other people.

That is not easy if you're a humble person, because you feel uncomfortable telling other people what to do. It seems egotistical. You expect them to say, "Who are you to tell me what to do? Do it yourself." Paul was humble, yet he gave directives to Titus because he knew it would result in more effective communication of the gospel—and that was his goal.

It is also hard to delegate if you're a conscientious person, because you're not sure that it will be done right. When Martha Layne Collins first became Governor of Kentucky, she appointed herself as Secretary of Education. She was an educator, and she had some very definite ideas about how the system should be improved. There's always a temptation to say, "I can do it better myself. I'm not sure it's going to be done right if I don't do it."

It's also hard to delegate if you are an egotistical person, because delegating means other people are going to get the glory. When I first came to Southeast Christian Church, I called on every person in the hospital almost every day. When they got out of the hospital, people would say, "Brother Bob, you were really good to me in the hospital." Now that's been delegated to other people on the staff, and when people get out of the hospital, they say, "The church was really good to me when I was in the hospital." That's probably better because it doesn't focus on me, but it's a little harder for me to swallow because I want people to think I'm good to them and I care about them.

Bill Weedman preaches in our children's church. He's a policeman and an effective communicator. He loves the kids and they love him. I went through the chapel one Sunday afternoon recently and saw three grade-school children playing church. I overheard one of them say, "I'll be Bill Weedman," and another one said, "No! I'll be Bill Weedman," and a third said, "No. I want to be Bill Weedman." Not one of them said, "I want to be Bob Russell." I'm not sure they even knew who I was!

To delegate is to allow someone else to get the glory; to let somebody else get the attention. There's an old saying, "It's amazing how much can be accomplished if you don't care who gets the credit." Because we want the glory, we keep on doing things ourselves, and soon we are overcommitted or burned out. Boyle's Law says, "If uncontrolled, work flows to the competent person until he submerges." Too often, the reward for doing your job well is that you get more work! People may say thank you or give you a little raise, but you get more and more responsibility until you submerge under it or until you're ineffective. That's why J. Oswald Sanders says, "Self-imposed tasks that others do better ought to be relinquished. Even if they don't do it as well, it ought to be relinquished. That's the test of the perfectionist. It's hard but it's necessary."

Moses had just led the children of Israel out of the slavery of Egypt. He was in the wilderness, shepherding about a million people, but Moses hadn't yet learned to delegate. Every day, people would bring their petty problems to Moses. They would stand in line and wait their turn as he sat on the seat of judgment from dawn until dusk, dealing with every problem they brought him.

Then Moses got a visit from his father-in-law. It's not easy to take advice from your father-in-law, but Moses had that kind of visit. "When his father-in-law saw all that Moses was doing for the people, he said, 'What is this you are doing for the people? Why do you alone sit as judge, while all these people stand around you from morning till evening?'" (Exodus 18:14). He asked two questions; one was about priorities, and the other was about personnel. What are you doing for the people and why are you doing it by yourself?

"Moses answered him, 'Because the people come to me to seek God's will. Whenever they have a dispute, it is brought to me, and I decide between the parties and inform them of God's decrees and laws'" (Exodus 18:15, 16). In other words, "They need me, Jethro—I'm the only one who can decide. Nobody else can do it."

"Moses' father-in-law replied, 'What you are doing is not good. You and these people who come to you will only wear yourselves out. The work is too heavy for you; you cannot handle it alone'" (Exodus 18:17, 18). The people were tired of standing in line, and there were too many of them for Moses to serve them well.

> Listen now to me and I will give you some advice. . . . [Doesn't that sound like a father-in-law?] You must be the people's representative before God and bring their disputes to him. Teach them the decrees and laws, and show them the way to live and the duties they are to perform. But select capable men from all the people—men who fear God, trustworthy men who hate dishonest gain—and appoint them as officials over thousands, hundreds, fifties, and tens (Exodus 18:19-21).

Jethro suggested that Moses should focus on his public ministry and appoint people to take care of the lesser tasks and bring only the most important issues to him.

This really speaks to rising young executives and all of us who keep taking on more and more burdens, more and more responsibilities. It warns us that, eventually, we'll break under that load and begin to neglect our families and the church. We won't have any time for recreation. Life will not be enjoyable if we don't learn to delegate, if we don't determine what our priorities are and who can help us. That's one of the toughest decisions for me in the ministry—to give up things that I enjoy doing but don't have time to do any longer.

John MacArthur preaches at a church in California that has about 8,000 people in attendance. Someone asked him, "How do you say no to all the requests that people make, demanding your time?"

"I had to make a decision how I was going to tell my people that I loved them," he said. "I could try to call them on the phone and say, 'I care about you,' or I could try to visit every one in their homes over a number of years and say 'I love you,' but I've decided to tell my people that I love them by dedicating myself to a sacrificial study of the Word of God, so that when they came to church on Sunday morning, I'd have something good to feed them."

The Bible says, "Moses listened to his father-in-law and did everything he said" (Exodus 18:24). I'm sure that some people complained that Moses was getting too big for his britches; he was unapproachable; he was seeing only the important people. But Moses coped with the pressure. Forty years later, he was still their leader because he had learned to delegate.

Maybe you need to learn that in your position, too. Paul did, and he was an effective administrator.

Selection of Qualified Personnel

This is probably the most important and difficult part of administration. The right people will do the job even if the administrator is weak. The wrong people will mess it up regardless of how skillful the oversight.

Paul selected Titus. Titus had four characteristics that made him effective. These are the four characteristics good administrators today look for in people they hire.

First, Titus had a *cooperative spirit*. He had "the same concern I have for you," and he "welcomed our appeal" (2 Corinthians 8:16, 17). Titus and Paul shared the same goals, the same dreams. They weren't at odds in their objectives. We're often tempted to choose people on talent or training alone, and that can be a tragic mistake. There has to be a oneness of purpose in the organization. A freewheeling maverick can create unrest among the others regardless of how talented he is. A backbiter can be divisive no matter how well educated.

Joe Gibbs, the coach of the former Super Bowl champion Washington Redskins, said that he chooses the personnel for his team by putting dedication above talent. The personnel he selects must be team players. In the language of the Bible, they must have a servant's heart.

Titus' second characteristic was his *compassion for people*. He had "the same concern I have for you." Everybody from the custodian to the chairman of the board ought to know how to relate to people. A person can be a genius with computers or an encyclopedia of knowledge, but if he alienates people, he will create more problems than he solves every time.

One church hired a genius for a music director. He knew everything about music. He had written songs. He had led orchestras. But in a year's time, the choir was down to half its number because he could not relate to people. He was sarcastic and condescending, and he permitted no style of music except the style he preferred. The church eventually had to let him go, and it almost split over the situation. Even though he was talented, he couldn't relate to people. "Above all, love each other deeply, because love covers over a multitude of sins" (1 Peter 4:8).

A third characteristic that made Titus valuable was a *healthy ambition*. "He is coming to you with much enthusiasm and on his own initiative" (2 Corinthians 8:17). Can you believe that? He came on his own initiative. Titus was a self-starter, a hard worker! He looked for ways to help.

It seems rare today for anybody to look for work. A couple of men at our church go out on their own every Sunday and stand underneath the portico and open up car doors, welcome people, and help the older ladies inside. Nobody told them to do that—they were just looking for some way to contribute. That's rare; most people today are looking for a way to get out of work. Nobody wants more responsibility. Everybody wants the easy way out.

An ad in the newspaper read, "Wanted to exchange: An exercise bike for a scale that weighs up to 350 pounds." It's a lot easier to increase the scale than it is to exercise. It's a lot easier to look for a way out of responsibility than to accept it. If you find in your business somebody who has initiative, somebody who looks for things to do, hire him! Pay him well, encourage him, and overlook some of his mistakes, because he's worth his weight in gold.

The fourth characteristic that Paul looked for was a *positive track record*. Paul knew the importance of good recommendations.

> We are sending along with him the brother who is praised by all the churches for his service to the gospel. What is more, he was chosen by the churches to accompany us. . . . In addition, we are sending with them our brother who has often proved to us in many ways that he is zealous (2 Corinthians 8:18, 19, 22).

A con artist can talk a good game in an interview, and an egotist can prepare an impressive resumé, but character is revealed, not in words, but in daily productivity. Ask the tough questions of people who know the prospective employee well. Does he come in on time every day? Does she miss many days because of sickness? Does he tell the truth? Does he follow up on details? Does she get along well with people? Does she know how to follow as well as lead? Those details reveal character and habits that stay with an individual regardless of how slick his resumé or how good his interview.

A Sensitivity for the Opinions of Others

"We want to avoid any criticism of the way we administer this liberal gift," Paul wrote (2 Corinthians 8:20). It is easy for an administrator, especially one who delegates, to lose touch with people. One can become isolated and not see the big picture. He may develop tunnel vision and see only financial problems or personnel problems and forget that he's there to serve people.

Don't you hate to go to a restaurant where the waitress acts as if you're an interruption? She wouldn't have a job if you weren't there! Or you take your new car into the service department, and the service manager acts as if he's doing you a favor to correct a problem that should have been fixed before the car ever left the showroom! What's worse is to come to a church where people act as if you're in their way, when that's the reason the church exists—to evangelize.

I heard Tom Peters speak on "The Power of Excellence." We are losing influence in America, he said, because we've quit serving people. We've lost sensitivity to consumers' needs. We've quit trying to be excellent in our dealings with people. He said that, fifteen years ago, nine out of the ten largest banks in the world were American banks. Now seven out of ten are Japanese banks, and only two are American. Why? Because we've lost our sensitivity to the consumers' needs. We don't care about excellence anymore.

He pointed to A. Ray Smith of the Louisville Redbirds as an example of excellence based on sensitivity for people. Smith drew over a million fans to Cardinal Stadium in one year—that's a minor league franchise—when many major league franchises weren't drawing nearly as many. How did he do that? By being sensitive to people.

Peters said, "You go to a major league park with your family, and it would cost you $60.00 by the time you pay $10.00 for parking, $8.00 for tickets, and $1.50 each for hot dogs. Then you sit in the upper deck and watch nine prima donnas on the field who don't hustle and who wouldn't sign an autograph unless they were tackled. But A. Ray Smith drew a million because he lowered prices—tickets are only $2.00, and parking just $1.00. He improved the food—you can get hot dogs for less than a dollar—he steam cleaned all the seats and hand wipes them every day. He cleaned up the area for the fans, painted the walls, cleaned up the rest rooms, and they even have an area in the rest room where a mother can change the diaper of her little child! No other ball park in America has a Diaper Dugout. Can you believe that?" Because of Smith's commitment to excellence and his sensitivity for people, the Redbirds drew over a million fans.

Paul was a successful missionary for a long time because he maintained a sensitivity for what people were thinking. "We want to avoid any criticism of the way we administer this liberal gift. For we are taking pains to do what is right, not only in the eyes of the Lord but also in the eyes of men" (2 Corinthians 8:20, 21). It is foolish pride that disregards the opinions of people. Paul knew what people thought. They saw him taking up a collection. He knew that behind his back they were asking, "How do we know Paul is going to take that to Jerusalem? How do we know he isn't padding his own pocket? How much is he using for expenses? I'd like to know that."

Paul didn't flippantly say, "Trust me." He gave detailed information to people as to what was going to happen. He said, "Titus is going to go with me, and we're going to take that brother you selected, a man with an impeccable reputation, and we're going to deliver this gift together." The money in the church needs to be handled carefully and respectfully so that we avoid criticism.

Three preachers were talking about what they did with the offering. One of them said, "I take the offering plate and I draw a little circle around it. Then I just take the money and throw it up in the air, and what comes down inside the circle I keep for myself, and what comes down outside the circle I give to the Lord."

Another said, "That's pretty much the way we do it, too. I draw a little circle and throw it up, but what comes down inside the circle I give to the Lord and what comes down outside the circle I keep for myself."

The third preacher said, "We do it pretty much the same way. I throw the money up and I tell the Lord to keep what He wants and what comes back down is mine!"

Beware of the freelance Christian worker who is accountable to no one but himself. We're all appalled at the extravagance of some television evangelists, but it's our own fault. Generous giving is not foolish giving. We need to support ministries that are accountable. It doesn't matter how truthful the person's face is or how heart-rending his appeal. It doesn't matter how many hungry people or handicapped people are shown in the ad. Before you give, make sure that the ministry keeps accurate records, that they are audited, and that you know where the money goes. When people set their own salaries and are accountable to no one but a board they appointed themselves — perhaps even with their own family members on it — that's too much temptation for even the most spiritual to handle.

A few years ago, the finance committee at our church appointed several bankers and financial administrators to re-examine every step in handling our money, from the time we receive the offering to the time it is spent. We wanted to handle our money carefully, so we would not be subject to criticism. We try to be good stewards of God's money and sensitive to the feelings of people.

Sensitivity for people goes beyond financial accountability. It includes moral accountability, too. With the scandals that are undermining Christians' credibility everywhere, we Christians need to be cautious. People are watching. They're looking for grounds for suspicion. "But among you there must not be even a hint of sexual immorality, or of any kind of impurity, or of greed, because these are improper for God's holy people" (Ephesians 5:3). Billy Graham follows a principle he established early in his ministry. He will not go out to eat or even ride in a car with a woman unless he is accompanied by his wife. Now that may seem rigid to some, and it may have created some awkward situations. But Billy Graham's ministry has credibility today that has not been shaken even by the highly publicized scandals that destroyed some others and tarnished the respect of most.

Paul said, "Don't let there be even a hint of immorality." Some people are anxious to criticize; they're looking for a way to find fault. They will twist some innocent situation if they have to. Try to avoid criticism in the way you handle your finances and the way you handle your moral life. Integrity is an essential component of effective administration.

The greatest administrator who ever lived was Jesus Christ. He delegated the responsibility of spreading the gospel to twelve men. They weren't particularly well-educated or skillful, but they had a oneness of purpose. They were self-starters. Jesus was always sensitive to the needs of people. He said, "Take this gospel to the world, and I will be with you always, even unto the end of the age."

Getting the Most for Your Money

2 Corinthians 9:1-15

MODERN FINANCIAL EXPERTS are eager to give you all kinds of advice on how to get the most for your money.

Some are saying you should invest in oil because prices are down and they're bound to escalate. Others say no, a treasury bill is the only thing that's safe, because it's secured by the government. Others insist it's best to invest in real estate because "they aren't making any more land, you know!"

But the more you read the so-called experts, the more you become convinced that none of them has all the answers. One multi-millionaire defined an economist this way: "An economist is somebody who thinks he knows more about money than us that has it."

Some people do not attend church services because, they say, "All they ever talk about at church is money." Even some Christians will complain after a sermon on stewardship and say, "When I go to church I don't want to hear anything about money." Those people would be uncomfortable with the preaching of Jesus Christ, because over half of Jesus' teachings had to do with our attitude toward possessions. He knew that God's greatest rival was money. He made it clear that one's relationship to God was closely tied to his attitude toward possessions.

It's not surprising that Paul also had a great deal to say to his readers about their attitude toward possessions. In 2 Corinthians 8, he encouraged them to follow the example of the liberal-giving Macedonians. And in chapter 9, he gave a series of instructions and incentives on how they could make the most of their money. The principles in this chapter are still valid for us today.

155

Instructions

The key word in God's counsel is the word *give*. Each person should give. A wise old Christian man told a group of young people, "If you will, from the beginning of your marriage, give ten percent away, save ten percent, and live on the rest, you will wind up being very well off." That's some of the simplest but the wisest counsel you could ever receive. Give ten percent away, save ten percent, and live on the rest.

The world's advice is "save, invest, and indulge yourself," but the first instruction from God is to give it away. Admittedly, worldly advisors suggest that it's good to give, also. The difference is when. The world tells you to earn, and then give of your abundance. The Bible instructs you to give first and then live off the abundance. In the Old Testament, that was called the principle of the "firstfruits." The first of the harvest belonged to God. The first of the spoils of the battle belonged to God. The people gave to God first, then trusted God to provide the rest.

The difference is one of faith. When we give away the firstfruits, we demonstrate we're trusting God to provide. It takes no faith to give God the leftovers. It's just leaving an appearance of generosity.

A man had a wife whose cat irritated him constantly. He hated that cat. He hated having cat hairs all over his coat, stumbling over the cat in the dark, and being kept awake by the cat's squealing in the night. So when his wife went to visit her mother, he drowned the cat. When his wife came back he said, "I guess the cat has just disappeared."

She was distraught and despondent; she pleaded with him to find some way to have that cat returned, so he put out a $1,000 reward.

A friend of his said, "That's the most ridiculous thing I've ever heard to offer a $1,000 reward for a cat you don't even like."

"When you know what I know," he said, with a twinkle in his eye, "you can afford to take the risk."

Some people give the appearance of generosity when they are not generous at all. But God wants more than pretense. Whatever you give, He wants you to give the firstfruits. He wants you to give in a way that demonstrates your faith. But He wants you to give.

God's instructions on how we're to give can be summed up with three adverbs. The first is the word *generously*. "Whoever sows sparingly will also reap sparingly, and whoever sows generously will also reap generously" (2 Corinthians 9:6).

I'm not trying here to motivate you to give more to the church. It's good if you do, but the goal of this chapter is to encourage you to be a generous person in every area of your life. Generosity is not just giving a percentage of your income on Sunday morning. It's an attitude of the heart that is demonstrated every day. For example, Jesus said, "If someone wants to sue you and take your tunic, let him have your cloak as well" (Matthew 5:40). In other words, don't see how little you can do to get by. Don't always be the last one to reach for your wallet when you're out to eat with a group. Look for an opportunity to share. Count it a privilege.

I think we Christian people ought to be generous tippers in restaurants. Christian employers ought to have a reputation for being liberal with salaries and bonuses to loyal workers. We ought to be the first to respond with financial help when a neighbor or Christian family gets hit with tragedy. We ought to be liberal with missionaries who are needy. If God has blessed you with a car, be willing to share it. If He has blessed you with extra furniture, and you have more than you need, don't just stick it in the attic and let it rot up there—give it to somebody who can use it. If He's blessed you with expertise in an area that is needed, be quick to volunteer your service free of charge sometimes. I know one man who volunteered to pay the college tuition for a young woman in his church who couldn't have gone to college otherwise. In our church, a group of doctors volunteered to furnish and equip a first aid room. Other people pay for sermon tapes to be sent to missionaries, college students, or families who move away. We are to be generous people.

Christians ought also to give *quickly*. Apparently, the Corinthians were reluctant to give. They had made promises, but they had not fulfilled them. So Paul wrote them to encourage them to follow through with their pledge. "There is no need for me to write to you about this service to the saints," he wrote (2 Corinthians 9:1). That's like when a wife says to her husband, "Now I know I don't have to remind you about our upcoming anniversary." She *does* have to remind him! Paul said, "I don't have to remind you, but I'm going to."

"I know your eagerness to help...." In other words, he was pleased with their good intentions. "I have been boasting about it to the Macedonians" (2 Corinthians 9:2). You've made a good pledge, but you haven't sent any money yet. "I am sending the brothers in order that our boasting about you in this matter should not prove hollow, but that you may be ready, as I said you would be. . . . Finish the arrangements for the generous gift you had promised" (2 Corinthians 9:3, 5).

Christian people should be the first to give. We shouldn't have to be prodded and begged all the time. Everybody on a church softball team is supposed to pay a franchise fee. Coaches tell me some people must be reminded every week and encouraged. They'll bring it next week, they say.

Our church has a tape ministry; we send out sermon tapes to people who ask for them. But our volunteers sometimes must send out repeated reminder notices to subscribers who will not pay. Kindergarten directors and Christian school personnel must almost threaten to refuse to admit some children to class because their parents get so far behind in the tuition. Surprisingly, the last to pay aren't usually the poor, but those with resources available. They think it's clever to wait until the last moment. They're able to get a little more return on their money if they keep it in savings. We ought to be the first to give because God gave so quickly to us.

What would have happened if certain people hadn't given when they did? What if Mary had waited a week to pour the precious alabaster box of perfume on the feet of Jesus? What if the man who owned the colt used for the triumphal entry said, "I'm going to wait until I've ridden that colt myself a few times before I lend it to anybody"? What if the owner of the house where Jesus and His disciples ate the Last Supper had said, "I think I'll host Jesus another time — after the holiday rush is over"? All those events transpired in the final week of Jesus' life. If any one of those people had delayed for a week, he or she would have missed the opportunity to give to the Lord. We need to learn to give while the opportunity is there. A Latin proverb reads, "He gives twice who gives quickly."

A third word that summarizes God's instruction is the word *cheerfully*. "Each man should give what he has decided in his heart to give, not reluctantly or under compulsion, for God loves a cheerful giver" (2 Corinthians 9:7). The word *cheerful*, in the Greek, is the source of our word *hilarious*. God loves a hilarious giver.

Suppose it's your anniversary, and your mate throws a brown paper sack on your lap and says, "Well, there's your anniversary present! I didn't want to give it; it cost too much money; but I knew you would gripe if I didn't. So there it is." That gift doesn't mean very much to you. If it does, you've been badly neglected!

On the other hand, if your mate buys you a thoughtful gift and wraps it up and writes down a little note and says, "You deserve so much more than this. When I have the resources, someday I'm going to give you a lot more" — that gift means a lot.

If you give with a grudging spirit, it doesn't mean anything. But if you give, saying, "Lord, I wish I could do more. This is such a meager amount, but it's my way of saying, "Thank You; I'll do more when I can'" — that's a gift that is properly received because it's properly given. Listen to this passage in James: "If any of you lacks wisdom, he should ask God, who gives generously to all without finding fault, and it will be given to him" (James 1:5). God gives generously without finding fault. I like that. God is a cheerful giver to us.

When my college alma mater was in financial trouble, I accepted the challenge to raise $100,000 on its behalf. I called a number of alumni and friends of the school and asked them to give. Many of them gave, some of them generously, but very few gave without finding fault. They used the opportunity to criticize the school. "Why don't they get rid of this professor?" "Why don't they get rid of that financial advisor?" "Why don't the trustees build a new chapel?" Rare was the individual who said, "I love the school. I know it's in trouble, and I'm glad to give. I'll do the best I can."

When we ask God for wisdom, He doesn't say, "Well, I'll give it to you, but you know, you missed church three weeks ago. I heard that bad word you said yesterday. And you've not given very generously to Me." He gives generously without finding fault. That's the way we ought to give.

When a Girl Scout comes around wanting you to buy Girl Scout cookies, don't say, "Oh, you again. Every time I turn around somebody wants me to buy something. I guess I will, but you know you charge too much for those cookies and they're not always very good. Well, here you are." That little girl feels rotten. When they come around, say, "Oh, it's Girl Scout cookie time! That's great. I love those cookies. You mean they're only $5.00 for three cookies? Give me some more!" They're on cloud nine. (My wife doesn't let me answer the door anymore!)

I know you have to say no to some appeals. You can't give to everyone to whom you'd like to give. But if you're going to say yes, do so cheerfully, not grudgingly, and if you have to say no, do that politely, too. Just say, "I'd love to help you and I know you've got a worthy cause, but things are too tight right now. When I can, I'll be sure to help you."

Learn to give generously, quickly, and cheerfully because that's the way God has given to us.

Incentives

One motivation is that *giving is a wise investment.* "Whoever sows sparingly will also reap sparingly, and whoever sows generously will also reap generously" (2 Corinthians 9:6). A farmer who sows ten bushels of wheat doesn't begrudge one kernel of grain because he knows it's going to be multiplied at the harvest. When we give to the Lord's work, He promises it's going to be returned to us many times over. "You will be made rich in every way" (2 Corinthians 9:11). Other Scripture verses say the same thing:

Give, and it will be given to you (Luke 6:38).

A generous man will prosper; he who refreshes others will himself be refreshed (Proverbs 11:25).

He who is kind to the poor lends to the Lord, and he will reward him for what he has done (Proverbs 19:17).

"Bring the whole tithe into the storehouse, that there may be food in my house. Test me in this," says the Lord Almighty, "and see if I will not throw open the floodgates of heaven and pour out so much blessing that you will not have room enough for it" (Malachi 3:10).

Paul says, "Give, and you'll be made rich in every way." I hesitate even to point that verse out because it has been so abused by the "health-and-wealth gospel" preachers. There are preachers who tell you that, if you will give to their cause, God will make you rich financially; you'll drive a BMW, you'll take vacations in Bermuda every two months, and you'll have a million-dollar home. That is not what Paul said. We're not promised that we're going to be made rich financially.

Whenever you read that "you will be made rich in every way," remember at least two qualifiers. First, God's riches are not always material. You will be made rich in *every* way. Probably material blessings are near the bottom of the list of God's priorities. Maybe God wants you to be rich in faith, character, family, humility, patience, friends, and sensitivity. He has promised to supply your need and make you rich in a lot of different ways. He may determine that, if He made you rich financially, you wouldn't be rich in family anymore, so He gives you the best riches. God's riches aren't always material.

The second qualifier is God's rewards are not always immediate. The farmer who sows seed doesn't reap a harvest immediately. He has to wait. A Christian who gives generously shouldn't expect to win the *Reader's Digest* Sweepstakes the next day. In fact, much of the reward may not occur until eternity.

Jesus told a rich young ruler, "Go, sell everything you have and give to the poor." The man turned away, because he had great riches and he wouldn't do it. "How hard it is for the rich to enter the kingdom of God!" Jesus said. (See Mark 10:17-23.)

In the discussion that followed, Peter said to Jesus, "We have left everything to follow you!"

"I tell you the truth," Jesus replied, "no one who has left home or brothers or sisters or mother or father or children or fields for me and the gospel will fail to receive a hundred times as much in this present age (homes, brothers, sisters, mothers, children, and fields—and with them, persecutions) and in the age to come, eternal life. But many who are first will be last, and the last first" (Mark 10:29-31).

If you sacrifice anything, He'll give it back a hundred fold. If you earn 10% on your money—do you think that's a good investment? A hundred fold is 10,000% interest on your money! God keeps accurate records. He is no person's debtor. If you sacrifice for Him, He promises He will pay you back a hundred fold. Sometimes the reward is delayed—perhaps until eternity. But God will repay, and some who are last on earth will be first in Heaven.

Peter was showing a new arrival around Heaven when they saw his good friend drive by in a Mercedes.

"Boy, this is wonderful!" said the new guy.

Then they came to a Honda motorcycle parked at the curb. Peter said, "Here's your transportation. You may go anywhere you like on this."

"Wait a minute!" the man said. "My friend gets a Mercedes and I get a Honda?"

"Well, you see, your friend was generous during his life. But I'm afraid you didn't give very much while you were on the earth. We just didn't have much to work with."

The man drove off in a huff, but a week later he came back all smiles. "Are you happier now?" asked Peter.

"Yes," he said. "I just saw my boss go by on roller skates!"

I don't know if it works that way or not, but God promises that there will be rewards, and not all of God's rewards are immediate. Some of them are going to be in Heaven, and if people don't get those rewards here on earth, some of the ones who are last are going to be first.

God says, "If you give, I'll reward you in this age and in the age to come." If you're struggling financially right now, don't get angry at God. Don't resent others. Be confident that God will supply your need, and He will reward you generously. He will make you rich in every way. He doesn't make a promise He doesn't fulfill.

The riches God gives are not to be used selfishly. Look again at the second half of that promise in 2 Corinthians 9:11: "You will be made rich in every way *so that you can be generous on every occasion.*" You're to be a funnel. God pours it in the top and you're to pour it out the bottom. The faster you pour it out, the faster God promises He will pour it in. He dares you to try, to take the risk.

One man was very generous but also very prosperous. "How come you keep giving it away but you still have so much?" he was asked.

He said, "Well, I shovel it out and God shovels it in. His shovel is bigger than mine." It happens like that.

Another incentive for giving is that *you're meeting the needs of others.* "This service that you perform is . . . supplying the needs of God's people" (2 Corinthians 9:12). You need to give to people who need your help. You need to give to causes that are legitimate, that are spreading the gospel. Be cautious—but don't wait until you're 100% sure that you're not being had. You can always use that as an excuse for not giving. When you do give to meet needs, you get a sense of satisfaction.

We used to have a glass jar on our counter in the kitchen. At the end of the day we would take the change in our pocket and put it in the glass jar. After several months we would accumulate twenty-five or thirty dollars, and when we were desperate and needed some money, we would say, "Let's see how much we've got in this glass jar." We'd use it for something selfish.

Then somebody gave me a little bank for the Christian Church Foundation for the Handicapped. Now that can sits on our counter. On the outside is a picture of a handicapped child in the arms of Jesus. The money we put in goes to help meet the needs of handicapped people. Just little dimes and pennies at the end of the day. There's such a sense of satisfaction just from dropping in the change we're never going to miss and to know it's going to a deserving cause. We're giving to meet needs. There's satisfaction that comes with that.

A third incentive is that giving is a *testimony of your faith.*

> This service that you perform is not only supplying the needs of God's people but is also overflowing in many expressions of thanks to God. Because of the service by which you have proved yourselves, men will praise God for the obedience that accompanies your confession of the gospel of Christ (2 Corinthians 9:12, 13).

The people in the world may not be impressed with your verbal testimony. Anybody can talk a good game. But one thing that does impress the people in the world is when you give of your material possessions to do something for others, because you're speaking their language. They know that that's a sacrifice. When they drive by and they see a church building, they know somebody sacrificed. When outsiders hear that a church has given several thousand dollars to help a missionary cause, they take note. When people give food and clothing to needy families, people are impressed. One of our church families was burned out years ago. Our people responded with food, clothing, and furniture. People said, "Some of the people from Southeast Christian Church were there before the fire trucks!" What a great testimony of the church.

Four hundred of our women went to a two-day women's retreat in Frankfort, Kentucky, one year. The restaurant manager told my wife when it was over, "Your women were really impressive. We were crowded and the service was a little slow. They had to wait, but they were patient—and boy, they were good tippers, too." Isn't that a great testimony?

One of our families owns a bakery. They take the excess bakery goods and give them to the Home for the Innocents. On the outside of the box they write "Southeast Christian Church" or sometimes just "SECC." The man who delivers those bakery goods said the people don't know his name, but when he walked in the other day, somebody said, "Hey, that guy from Southeast Christian Church is here again." When people give, it's a testimony of their faith.

Whenever you give, it's good to give through an agency or the church, because then it becomes a testimony to God and not yourself. Jesus said, "Let your light shine before men, that they may see your good deeds and praise your Father in heaven" (Matthew 5:16).

One other incentive for giving is that *you're expressing your thanks to God* for His goodness to you. Paul says simply, "Thanks be to God for his indescribable gift!" (2 Corinthians 9:15).

God gave to us generously. His own Son, Jesus Christ, was the best that He had. He gave to us quickly. He didn't wait until we deserved it. The Bible says, "We love because he first loved us" (1 John 4:19). God gives to us cheerfully. The Bible says that Jesus endured the cross "for the joy set before Him" (Hebrews 12:2).

Did you ever do something really nice for somebody and really sacrifice for him, and then he didn't even bother to say thank you? You feel let down. Every time you give to somebody in the name of the Lord, that's a thank you note to God saying, "Thank You, Lord, for sending Jesus Christ to die for me. Thank You for being so generous to me."

The Bible says, "Freely you have received, freely give" (Matthew 10:8).

Coping With Criticism

2 Corinthians 10:1-18

WHILE SITTING IN A BARBER'S CHAIR, a salesman mentioned that he was excited about an upcoming trip to Rome. The barber was an Italian, but also a very critical man. "You'll be disappointed," he said. "Rome is overrated. The service in the hotels is horrible. The airlines have all kinds of trouble. You better stay home."

But the salesman insisted that he was going to Rome to close a big business deal and he hoped to see the Pope. The barber shook his head in disgust. "You'll be disappointed trying to do business in Italy. Nobody buys there — and you'll never get to see the Pope, because he only sees important people."

Two months later the salesman reappeared in the barber's shop. "How was your trip?" the barber asked.

"It was wonderful," said the salesman. "The flight was smooth, the service in the hotel was perfect, I made a big sale, and I got to see the Pope."

The barber was astonished. "What happened when you saw the Pope?"

The salesman said, "I knelt down and kissed his ring, and he patted me on the head and said, 'My son, who gave you such a lousy haircut?'"

We're all criticized on occasion. Ours has become a very critical society. We pay people to criticize music, art, politics, and athletics; if you're not critical in this society, you're considered to be naïve or maybe unsophisticated. I think a lot of American people, if they had been present at the feeding of the 5,000, would have criticized Jesus for not providing lemon for the fish or enough butter for the bread. Bible-believing Christians are probably going to be criticized more and more as our pagan society becomes worse, so we need to be prepared for it.

165

We're all vulnerable, some more than others. If you are an insecure person, criticism can be devastating to you. With the slightest objection you might go to pieces or quit the project. If you belong to a normal family, you're going to be criticized. Rare is the family whose members don't sometimes speak disparagingly of each other.

J. Oswald Sanders, in his book on spiritual leadership, says, "No leader is exempt from criticism and his humility will nowhere be seen more clearly than in the manner in which he accepts it and reacts to it." If you are a leader, you will inevitably be criticized.

There is such a thing as constructive criticism. Sometimes a loved one criticizes us to encourage us to excellence or to guide us away from sin. If somebody has a loving word of constructive criticism, we need to appreciate and pay attention to that.

But most of the time, criticism is not constructive. It's not meant to build us up but to tear us down. Usually we don't hear of it directly, it's not factual, and it serves no positive purpose. Still, we need to respond in an appropriate manner, displaying grace and Christian love.

In 2 Corinthians 10, Paul responds to some accusations against his authority. We can learn much from Paul's reaction.

Accept Criticism as Normal

Criticism is an inevitable part of life, so we might as well anticipate it. Paul was one of the greatest men in history, yet he was frequently censured. He was criticized for his questionable past. After all, he had persecuted the Christians before his alleged conversion. He was criticized for his dubious authority. He claimed to be an apostle, but unlike the others, he was not one of the original twelve. How could he prove he had that special vision of Jesus on the road to Damascus? Paul was also accused of having materialistic motives. He said he was taking up an offering for the poor in Jerusalem, but how could people be sure Paul wasn't pocketing some of the money himself?

Apparently someone was challenging Paul's inconsistent personality. He repeated their criticism, "I . . . am 'timid' when face to face with you, but 'bold' when away!" (2 Corinthians 10:1). "Some say, 'His letters are weighty and forceful, but in person he is unimpressive and his speaking amounts to nothing'" (2 Corinthians 10:10). Have you read somebody's book or newspaper column, and you had a mental image of what that person looked like, but then when you saw him in person, you were astonished that he was so different from what you had imagined?

A woman came up to me and said, "I've heard you preach on the radio for a couple of years now, and I came to church today to see what you looked like."

"What do you think?" I asked.

"You don't look like you sound," she said.

I said, "What do I sound like?"

She said, "You sound like you've got black hair."

Paul seemed inconsistent to some Corinthians who had read his letter. It had nothing to do with Paul's consistency. It had everything to do with their mental image of him. Apparently Paul was not very impressive-looking. Tradition says that Paul was short, bald, and had a hooked nose. He may not have been a very good public speaker, at least as good as they anticipated that he should be, considering his reputation. I think in person Paul was a gentle, compassionate, understanding person, and some who were shallow would interpret that as weakness. So they sneered, "He sounds tough in his letters, but in reality he's nothing. Don't respect him. Don't fear Paul."

I think two factors made that criticism difficult to take. First, those criticisms were in areas where he was vulnerable. If he had been accused of lacking love for the Lord or lacking intelligence, he could easily have shrugged it off. But he did have a questionable past. He was embarrassed about the way he had persecuted the Christians. He was called to be an apostle in unique circumstances. He spoke of himself as one being called out of due season. He was taking up an offering, and though he was honest, it was hard to prove it. He was not impressive in person and shallow people would think that he lacked charisma and force. Criticism is harder to take when there is a dash of truth in it or when truth to the contrary is hard to prove.

Another factor that made this criticism difficult was that it came from Christian people. It's one thing when the world finds fault. You expect that. But when attacks come from fellow believers, it's much more difficult to take. You expect fellow Christians to be supportive.

I probably get three or four critical letters a week, partly because of the size of our church, and partly because of our radio ministry. Some of those letters are kind, but still critical. Others are downright nasty. The ones that come from people in the world really don't bother me much. The ones that come from members of other churches concern me, but I don't take them personally. The ones that really hurt are the ones that come from members of my own congregation because those are the people I love the most and whose support is most important to me.

Paul was under attack from people in the church he had established in Corinth. That had to be difficult, but I don't think Paul was surprised by it. He knew that Jesus, his Lord, was under constant criticism, and that most of the attacks against Jesus came from the religious leaders. The religious leaders accused Jesus of blasphemy. They accused Him of being demon-possessed. They accused Him of being an illegitimate child. They accused Him of being a drunk and a glutton. Jesus had said, "No servant is greater than his master. If they persecuted me, they will persecute you also" (John 15:20).

Because of its rapid growth, our church is occasionally criticized. People say, "It's got to be a cult to grow that fast," or, "They've got to be compromising the gospel and being liberal to appeal to that many people." Others say, "They've got to be appealing to people's old-fashioned moral virtues that are no longer up to date," or, "It's all built around one personality; it will come crashing down some day." I'm not surprised by that. Whenever you do something out of the ordinary, there's going to be some criticism. In fact, in the Sermon on the Mount, Jesus said, "Blessed are you when people insult you, persecute you and falsely say all kinds of evil against you because of me. Rejoice and be glad, because great is your reward in heaven" (Matthew 5:11, 12).

When someone becomes more committed in his Christian walk, he is often surprised that not everybody approves of it. Family members think he's gone overboard. "You think you're better than anybody else," they say, or, "You've renounced the religious heritage of your past!" It hurts that the people closest to a person don't understand and rejoice with such a positive change in his life. Maybe it's because they are threatened by it, or they resent the reminder of the void in their own lives. Peter wrote, "Dear friends, do not be surprised at the painful trial you are suffering, as though something strange were happening to you. But rejoice that you participate in the sufferings of Christ. . . . If you are insulted because of the name of Christ, you are blessed" (1 Peter 4:12-14).

I had lunch with Steve Chapman of Nashville just after I had received a really nasty letter, and I remarked about it.

"Oh, that's good," Steve said. "That gets the woe off your back."

I said, "What do you mean?"

He said, "It gets the woe off your back. Jesus said, 'Woe to you when all men speak well of you,' and all men aren't speaking well of you, so you've got that woe off your back. Rejoice!"

I'd never thought of it that way. Criticism is inevitable. Paul was criticized, Jesus was criticized, and so will we.

Refuse to Fight with Worldly Weapons

"For though we live in the world, we do not wage war as the world does. The weapons we fight with are not the weapons of the world" (2 Corinthians 10:3, 4). There is one word that describes the world's weaponry: *retaliation*.

The world fights injury with violence; arrest with hostages; criticism with sarcasm; deception with trickery. That's expected. Retaliation is a means of defending one's rights, proving one's self-worth.

Winston Churchill and Lady Astor had a running feud. "Sir Winston," Lady Astor once said, "I believe that you're drunk!"

Churchill said, "Lady Astor, I believe that you're ugly, but I'll be sober in the morning."

They were constantly attacking one another. Once, following a crude remark by Churchill, Lady Astor sneered, "Winston, if you were my husband, I'd put poison in your tea."

"If you were my wife, I would drink it," he answered.

When we retaliate we feel better. When we get cut on, we like to find some clever way to cut back. It appeals to our carnal nature. But Paul resisted that impulse. He said, "The weapons we fight with are not the weapons of the world." The Christian's weapons are love, prayer, the Bible, the Holy Spirit, patience; if you are a shallow person, you think that that is weak.

But Paul said, "By the meekness and gentleness of Christ, I appeal to you" (2 Corinthians 10:1). Meekness is not weakness. Meekness is strength under control. Meekness pictures a stallion that has been tamed—all that power is under control. Gentleness is not cowardice; it is restrained power. Paul had all authority as an apostle to bring these people to their knees. The world's solution would be, "If you have the authority, just pull rank." But Paul refused to use the worldly weapons. He refused to fight the way the world fights.

Tony Campolo tells of watching Martin Luther King and his followers kneel and pray on the bridge to Selma. The police came in wielding clubs and knocking heads. Campolo said that moment when the demonstrators did not retaliate and the camera showed their bloody faces, he knew that Martin Luther King had won. What looked like an immediate defeat for King ultimately sparked the conscience of the nation, and love won out over hatred. Non-violence was stronger than violence.

It takes tremendous self-control not to retaliate even against the smallest criticism. But Jesus said, "If someone strikes you on the right cheek, turn to him the other also" (Matthew 5:39). "Do not take revenge, my friends. . . . It is written: 'It is mine to avenge; I will repay,' says the Lord" (Romans 12:19). Don't fight with worldly weapons.

Respond Only When Necessary

I believe that, ninety-five percent of the time, criticism should just be ignored. When Nehemiah was rebuilding the walls of Jerusalem, there were some critics who didn't appreciate it. Two men, Sanballat and Tobiah, began to make cutting remarks. They said, "If even a fox climbed up on it, he would break down their wall" (Nehemiah 4:3). Five times they sent word up to Nehemiah saying, "Come on down and let's talk about this project. We don't approve of what you are doing." Nehemiah sent word back down, saying, "I am doing a great work and I can't come down." (See Nehemiah 6.)

When you respond to the critics, it takes time and energy away from what ought to be done. It gives the critic unwarranted credibility. So the best course of action is just to ignore the criticism. By not responding, you are saying, "I'm doing an important work, and I'm not going to stop."

But occasionally criticism needs to be answered. It could be undermining the credibility of a worthy project. It could be so damaging to the character of the leader that it needs to be stifled. Sometimes a simple answer can silence the critic, prove the innocence of the leader, and rally support.

Jesus usually ignored criticism, but occasionally He responded to it. Once, His critics said, "Jesus, you're casting out demons by the devil's power." Jesus replied, "The devil is not going to cast himself out. If a house is divided against itself, that house cannot stand. And if Satan opposes himself and is divided, he cannot stand" (cf. Mark 3:22-30). The critics were silenced.

Paul responded to the accusation that he had no authority with a little sanctified sarcasm of his own. He said, "We . . . will confine our boasting to the field God has assigned to us, a field that reaches even to you" (2 Corinthians 10:13). You Corinthians question whether I have authority from God? Who do you think started the Corinthian church? You wouldn't even be Christians if I hadn't reached out to you. If I'm not legitimate, what does that make you?

A reporter saw Billy Graham disembark the Queen Mary. Sarcastically, he said to Grady Wilson, a Graham associate, "When Jesus was on the earth, He rode into town on a lowly donkey. I can't imagine Jesus arriving from England on the Queen Mary."

Wilson quipped, "Find me a donkey that can swim the Atlantic Ocean and I'll buy it." Sometimes criticism needs to be answered, but most of the time, we're better off to ignore it.

Be Confident the Truth Will Prevail

> The weapons we fight with are not the weapons of the world. On the contrary, they have divine power to demolish strongholds. We demolish arguments and every pretension that sets itself up against the knowledge of God, and we take captive every thought to make it obedient to Christ (2 Corinthians 10:4, 5).

We're involved in a bitter spiritual war. Satan has strongholds. He has fortresses that seem impenetrable. He has a fortress of pornography. He has a citadel of drugs. He has a bastion of abortions. He has a stronghold of humanistic thought. The temptation is, when we begin to see those evils, to try to knock down his strongholds through human power.

"Let's bomb the abortion clinics!" someone says. "Let's burn the pornography shop!" shouts another. "Let's use false propoganda and nasty labels to force all the liberals in education out of office," suggests a third. These are natural means, and they are powerless against a supernatural foe. We will never win by following them. "For our struggle is not against flesh and blood, but against the rulers, against the authorities, against the powers of this dark world and against the spiritual forces of evil in the heavenly realms" (Ephesians 6:12). There is a satanic conspiracy to destroy mankind. If we try to fight the battle the way the world fights, we'll be like little gentle lambs going out against raging wolves.

In my first year of ministry, a church member who was a militant anti-Communist began to channel literature to me. I became concerned about the encroaching dangers of Communism in our country. He asked me to go with him to an anti-Communist society that he belonged to, and I went. Before the meeting began, the members were standing around drinking their cocktails, some of them getting pretty high. During the meeting, they cursed the lousy Communists and, when the meeting was over, I decided that I would not go back. For while I saw the danger of Communism, I concluded that it could not be resisted with human effort alone.

There is only one way to break Satan's stronghold. That is by consistently sharing the truth of the gospel. Paul said, "Don't wage war on the world's terms. You'll lose." The weapons we fight with are spiritual ideas, eternal values, and the truth of the gospel. That truth has the power to take captive every thought and make it obedient to Christ. On the surface, that may appear to be ineffective, but anyone who can think deeply knows it's our only hope.

During a two-hour conversation with a man who had been an undercover narcotics agent in Miami, I asked him what we can do to combat the infiltration of drugs into this country. "There's nothing we can do!" he said. "It's just too lucrative; it's too easy for two boats to meet out in the ocean a few miles off shore or a plane to land on a remote airstrip. We'll never stop it.

"Except," he said, "there is one hope. That is the gospel of Jesus Christ."

This man was not a preacher, but a converted narcotics agent who came to see the futility of human effort and the only hope of the gospel. He said, "We've got to convert people to Christ so they don't need drugs anymore. And we've got to convert the drug pushers, too." That's our only hope. The more you analyze our problems, the more you realize that's true.

Charles Colson in his book, *Who Speaks for God,* tells of the conversion of Jack Eckerd, the founder of Eckerd Drugstores. Shortly after his conversion, Eckerd removed all the pornographic magazines from his chain of drugstores and led a campaign to get other people to do the same. Just one man, changed by the power of the gospel, is demolishing a stronghold of Satan. Some people want the church to be always marching, always demonstrating, always signing petitions, always wielding its political power, but the most powerful thing we can do is consistently teach and preach the truth of the Bible. That truth is so powerful it shatters false ideas. It transforms lives. It crumbles Satan's strongholds.

Many years ago, Christians were stunned when a judge ruled that prayer and Bible reading were not permitted in public schools. Madalyn Murray O'Hair had sued the local school district, on behalf of her son, saying that these practices were an affront to his right not to believe in God. The judge agreed, and Christians have been trying to stop O'Hair ever since. Too often, however, we have used only human means. How many times has someone circulated a petition to stop her from removing Christian broadcasting, only to find out there was never any such threat in the first place? We are so quick to fight—and by human means—that we fail to check the facts.

But one event did more to silence Madalyn Murray O'Hair than all the petitions in the world. Her son Bill became a Christian. He became a preacher. He is now preaching the gospel of Christ. She has renounced him, of course, but he has disclosed her folly and broken her stronghold with his book, *My Life Without God.* The very person she used to remove prayer and Bible reading from the schools is now preaching the Bible.

The most powerful thing we can do as a church is keep teaching the Scripture. I honestly believe that Satan is more intimidated by one church consistently teaching the Bible than he is by 100,000 people demonstrating on the steps of the Capitol building in Washington every day.

The only thing that demolishes arguments and takes captive the enemy is the truth of the gospel. That's why Paul said, "I am not ashamed of the gospel, because it is the power of God for the salvation of everyone who believes" (Romans 1:16). That's why John said, "The one who is in you is greater than the one who is in the world" (1 John 4:4). Have confidence that the truth is going to prevail.

What is true in the spiritual realm is also true on a personal level. The truth has the power to endure. When you're criticized falsely, you have a tendency to say, "I've got to defend myself." The best response is just to stand consistently for truth and believe that it will prevail in the end.

Abraham Lincoln was constantly criticized, but he hardly ever responded to it. Once one of his advisors told him of a criticism and said, "Mr. Lincoln, what are you going to do?"

He said, "I'm going to live in such a way as to prove that the accusation is a lie."

That takes a big person. It takes patience. It takes confidence that, in the end, the truth will win out. But be confident; the truth comes to the surface in time, and it buries criticism and it demolishes strongholds.

Keep Your Eye on the Goal

If a fight breaks out in the middle of a basketball game, a good coach instructs his players not to get involved in the fight. The player may protest that his manhood is at stake, but the coach says, "Our goal is to win the game, not to give bloody noses. If you get involved in a fight and get thrown out of the game and then we are beaten, they get the last laugh. Remember, your objective is to win the game."

When people are critical of you, you're tempted to get involved in a skirmish because your self-esteem is involved. Remember your ultimate objective. It may mean swallowing your pride. It may mean putting up with some minor irritations. Just keep your eye on the goal. Paul says our goal is "building you up rather than pulling you down" (2 Corinthians 10:8). If you respond to criticism, you've got to tear the critic down. But if your goal is to build up other people (even the critics), then don't respond.

Abraham Lincoln appointed Edwin Stanton as his Secretary of War. Stanton had been one of Lincoln's most severe critics in the entire country. He once even called Lincoln a buffoon.

Lincoln's advisors were incredulous at the appointment. They protested and reminded the President of Stanton's remarks. But Lincoln ignored both Stanton's criticism and his advisors' protests. He kept his eye on the goal, which was to win the war and to build people up, not to pull them down. After President Lincoln was assassinated, it was Edwin Stanton who said, "There lies one of the greatest leaders of men this country has ever seen."

Paul says our goal is to please God, not men. "We do not dare to classify or compare ourselves with some who commend themselves. When they measure themselves by themselves and compare themselves with themselves, they are not wise" (2 Corinthians 10:12). If your goal is to please people, then you're always going to be vulnerable to criticism, and you're going to fall victim to one of two traps.

One trap is that of commending yourself. You begin to brag on yourself to impress people. You always get into trouble when you brag on yourself.

Two ducks and a frog lived in the same pond, and they became good friends. When the pond started to dry up, the ducks got ready to fly to another pond, but the frog was doomed.

The frog got a great idea. He said, "You two ducks hold on to the ends of this twig and I'll clasp on in the middle with my powerful jaws, and you can just fly me out of here to another pond."

They grabbed hold of the twig in their bills, and the frog grabbed hold of the middle with his jaws. They took off and it worked great. What a sight it was!

A farmer below looked up and said, "What a terrific idea! I wonder whose idea that was."

The frog said, "It was mi-i-i-i-i-ine!"

If you're out to please and impress people, if you're going to boast on yourself and commend yourself, you will fall. Self-praise invariably leads to deep trouble.

The second trap that Paul warned against is that of comparing ourselves with others. He said those people who "measure themselves by themselves and compare themselves with themselves . . . are not wise" (2 Corinthians 10:12).

The owner of a factory set his watch every day by the clock in the jewelry store window. One day he listened to the radio and realized his watch was ten minutes slow. He stopped to tell the jeweler that the clock in the window was off, and the jeweler said, "Oh, it can't be. I set it every day by the noon whistle at your factory."

When a person measures himself by himself, he's not wise. The standards start slipping and eroding away. That's exactly what's happening in our culture. If your goal is to please people, then you're going to have to compromise your principles, and you can never please them completely because their standards are changing. You're constantly vulnerable to their criticism. But if your goal is to please the Lord, then human criticism isn't so devastating. If somebody criticizes you, listen to it and evaluate it. But if you're doing God's will, just go on. It's not people you're trying to impress. It's the Lord Jesus Christ's opinion that really matters.

Paul concluded by saying, "It is not the one who commends himself who is approved, but the one whom the Lord commends" (2 Corinthians 10:18). Keep your eye on the goal. The goal is to hear the Lord say, "Well done, good and faithful servant."

The perfect example of how to handle criticism is, of course, Jesus Christ. At His lowest moment, as He was dying on the cross, His critics came out of the woodwork. "You who are going to destroy the temple and build it in three days, save yourself! Come down from the cross, if you are the Son of God!' . . . 'He saved others,' they said, 'but he can't save himself!'" (Matthew 27:40, 42).

Jesus had all the power of the universe at His fingertips. He could have called ten thousand angels in a minute, but He was gentle. He responded to the critics by saying, "Father, forgive them, for they do not know what they are doing" (Luke 23:34). Three days later, the truth emerged victorious. Jesus came out of the tomb. He burst Satan's stronghold of sin and death, and the truth lives on. May we proclaim it!

Beware of
False Prophets

2 Corinthians 11:1-15

P.T. Barnum said, "There's a sucker born every minute." History verifies that it is pretty easy to fool the public.

In 1983, publishers throughout the world began intense bidding for reprint rights to a sensational journalistic discovery, *The Secret Diaries of Adolf Hitler*. The temporary hero of that literary coup was Gerd Heidman, a reporter for a German magazine. Exactly where he had obtained the diaries, whose existence had not been suspected up to that point, seemed less important than their apparent authenticity. Experts pronounced the handwriting identical to Hitler's signature on a number of documents. The paper on which the diaries were written showed the typical discoloration from aging. The bidding soared beyond the three-million-dollar mark, when suddenly the diaries were exposed as a carefully orchestrated scam by a well-known European forger named Konrad Kujau. He had not only forged the diaries, but also the documents that established their authenticity. The papers had simply been touched up with tea to make them look older. Not surprisingly, it was later discovered that the inspections supposed to determine their authenticity had been superficial at best. It's almost as if nobody wanted to find out the truth.

According to an article in *U.S. Air* magazine, the history of hoaxes demonstrates that people are vulnerable in two areas — gullibility and greed. The excitement and the sheer potential of something like Hitler's secret diaries are intriguing. People simply want to believe, so they toss normal caution and research to the wind.

There have been incredible hoaxes in history. In 1835, Robert Locke reported in the New York *Sun* that a seven-ton telescope had discovered life on the moon. The telescope, he said, was so powerful that he saw buffalo-like creatures and winged monkeys. The circulation of the paper skyrocketed nearly ten times as they presented this evidence in series form. Women in New England began a fund to send missionaries to the moon. But it was all a hoax.

Old biology books talked about the Piltdown Man, discovered in 1911. A skull appeared to be part ape and part human, and was acclaimed to be the missing link in the chain of evolution. Nearly fifty years later, further investigation disclosed that the upper part of the skull was actually a medieval human, and the jaw bone was a twentieth-century orangutan whose teeth had been filed down to resemble that of an ape. The archaeologist and the evolutionist had egg on their faces.

Howard Hughes' supposed autobiography a few years back was written by Clifford Irving. *Time* magazine and *Life* magazine were drawn into that hoax.

In 1980, Rosie Ruiz jumped into the Boston Marathon a mile or two from the end and claimed to have won the race.

A sign in a window of a New York City store read, "Don't be fooled by imitators who claim to be going out of business. We've been going out of business longer than anyone on this block!"

There have been scores of incredible hoaxes. People fall victim every day. But the most dangerous ongoing scam in history is the perpetrating of a counterfeit gospel. In 2 Corinthians 11, Paul dealt with the danger of being duped by false prophets. Satan, the adversary of God, has sought to pull people into believing a false Christianity. While some of the hoaxes I've mentioned are almost harmless, this one has devastating consequences because eternal life is at stake.

Revelation tells us that, in the end, the false prophet will be thrown into Hell. As Paul said, "Their end will be what their actions deserve" (2 Corinthians 11:15). It's important that we be able to discern the true gospel from the spurious.

Be Jealous for the Truth

"I am jealous for you with a godly jealousy. I promised you to one husband, to Christ, so that I might present you as a pure virgin to him" (2 Corinthians 11:2). We normally think of jealousy as a negative emotion. When jealousy is a resentment of another's success, that's poisonous. But there is also a healthy jealousy. There is a proper desire for loyalty on the part of people we love.

A preacher came home from a religious convention to discover that his wife was ground down with jealousy. He couldn't figure out why until she showed him the telegram that he had sent from the other city. The telegram read: "Having a good time. Stop. Wish you were her. Stop."

A wife who suspects that her husband is flirting with another woman has a right to be jealous. She doesn't love him if she isn't. God says, "You shall not make for yourself an idol. . . . You shall not bow down to them or worship them; for I, the Lord your God, am a jealous God" (Exodus 20:4, 5). God will not tolerate any rivals. He wants exclusive loyalty from us.

Paul told the Corinthians he was their spiritual father. They of the church were the bride of Christ, and he promised them to one husband, Jesus. He had the responsibility to make sure that they were pure. He was jealous that they were true to Christ and did not allow the enemy to defile them.

When we're dealing with important issues, we want people to be jealous for the truth. When we fly on a plane, we want the pilot to be jealous for the truth. When we're operated on, we want the surgeon to be careful about the truth, not casual about it. When we build a house, we want the contractor to follow the blueprints jealously.

When things are important to you, you're jealous for the truth. But the Corinthians did not have that jealousy. Paul said, "If someone comes to you and preaches a Jesus other than the Jesus we preached, . . . you put up with it easily enough" (2 Corinthians 11:4). Christianity deals with eternal life. That's the single most important issue in the world. Paul urged his readers to be jealous for the truth of Christ. False teachers become careless with the truth.

Who do you think are the most dangerous false teachers in America today? Would you say the teachers of the Moonies or the Jehovah's Witnesses? Or maybe you'd say the health-and-wealth media preachers. How about the leaders of the New Age movement? I think the most dangerous false prophets in America are television producers of TV comedies and dramas that subtly come across with their universalistic philosophy that everybody is going to be saved or their humanistic ideas that there is no right and wrong. Every day they preach their liberal gospel to millions, and people just casually soak it up.

The *American Family Association Journal* recently reproduced the dialogue from the television program, "Highway to Heaven," in which Michael Landon plays Jonathan, an angel on earth doing good deeds. Here's an excerpt of the dialogue between Jonathan and his friend, Mark. Look how casually the truth is twisted into error.

"I tell you, Jonathan, I don't know what's happening to religion in this country," Mark says. "We've got one guy saying if you don't send me money by a certain time, God's going to take me, and we've got another guy who hired this high-priced attorney to try to get his ministry back after they caught him fooling around. I bet you the Boss is fed up with it."

"Ah, power changes people, Mark. Religion and politics, they're great places to gain that power."

"Well, it wouldn't change me."

"I wouldn't be so sure about it."

"Come on, Jonathan, you know me better than that. If I had the power I'd get people to do the right thing."

"Do what's right according to whom?" Jonathan says.

"Well, according to what I know to be right," Mark says.

"Yes," says Jonathan, "but who are you to tell people what's good or bad, right or wrong. What makes one person so right, you know what I mean?"

"Yeah, I guess I do," Mark says. "Ministers going around saying, 'Believe as I believe or you won't go to Heaven.' Like all those other religions that have been around for thousands of years, they don't count. You know, I saw this guy on TV running up and down waving his Bible and calling other people's religions garbage."

Jonathan responded, "Yeah, it's a little tough to have love and peace in the world when you tell people, 'Believe as I believe, or it's the end of your immortal soul.'"

That's being casual with the truth! He's saying there is no absolute standard of right and wrong. That message is subtly impacting the minds of millions of people in America.

Listen to what the Bible says. Jesus Christ said, "I am the way and the truth and the life. No one comes to the Father except through me" (John 14:6). No one else died for you. No one else rose from the dead. No one comes to the Father except through Jesus. If that sounds exclusive to you, realize you're listening to Jesus Christ. There is no television producer who has died for your sin and rose from the grave.

Or listen to what Peter said. "Salvation is found in no one else, for there is no other name under heaven given to men by which we must be saved" (Acts 4:12). The early Christians did not die because they believed in Jesus. The Romans did not imprison, crucify, and execute Christians because they believed in Jesus. The Romans believed in many gods. They had many religions. What would one more matter? The early Christians were martyred because they believed in Jesus *only*. They would not acknowledge that

Caesar was god. They would not acknowledge that the other gods were just as good as the one true and living God. They kept insisting that there was no way to be saved other than through Jesus Christ. "There is no other name under heaven given to men by which we must be saved" (Acts 4:12). For that, they died.

We, too, must be jealous for the truth.

Be Alert to Satan's Schemes

"I am afraid that just as Eve was deceived by the serpent's cunning, your minds may somehow be led astray from your sincere and pure devotion to Christ" (2 Corinthians 11:3). Satan took three steps in changing Eve's mind and deceiving her. The first step was to question God's Word. He came to her in the garden and said, "Did God really say, 'You must not eat from any tree in the garden?" (Genesis 3:1). He always begins with the mind; he questions the logic of God's Word.

The second step was to deny God's Word. Eve said, "We may eat fruit from the trees in the garden, but God did say, 'You must not eat fruit from the tree that is in the middle of the garden, and you must not touch it, or you will die.'"

"You will not surely die," the serpent said to the woman (Genesis 3:2-4).

The third step was to reverse God's Word. He said, "God knows that when you eat of it your eyes will be opened, and you will be like God, knowing good and evil" (Genesis 3:5).

He questioned God's Word, he denied God's Word, and then he ended up saying just the opposite of what God's Word said. Eve yielded and she died.

That's not just an antiquated story. The very same thing is happening all the time today. Satan doesn't have to change his tactics because they work so well. "Has God said it's wrong to get drunk? Really? It's not wrong. Everybody does it; it's fun to get high.

"Has God said you ought to spank your children when they disobey? That doesn't make sense. That's not true. Children ought to be allowed to do as they please. After all, they have rights. Just the opposite is true. People who spank their children are cruel."

"Has God said the husband is to be the leader in a marriage? Come on, that's not true. Just the opposite is true. Assert yourself and you'll be fulfilled; you've got rights."

"Has God said greed is evil? That's not true. Greed is good. Success is good."

"Woe to those who call evil good and good evil, who put darkness for light and light for darkness, who put bitter for sweet and sweet for bitter" (Isaiah 5:20). The leaders of a major denomination in America have apparently concluded that there is no such thing as sexual sin. They published a one-hundred-ten-page report called *Sexuality, A Divine Gift,* and sent it to their churches in all parts of the country. The report charges that the church's historic moral teaching that sex belongs in marriage is riddled by conflict and confusion.

The report absolutely reverses the truth of Scripture.

> Traditional theological systems are so often couched in terms of sinfulness and morality that we need a new more sacramental focus on God's loving gifts rather than dwelling on human failings. When sexual intimacy is recognized as a Christian sacrament, our bodies become the means by which God teaches us what it means to give ourselves without holding back, to love another person with generosity and enthusiasm. The attempt to use guilt to control sexual behavior should be seen as not only futile, but also as a denial of the goodness of God's gift.

Included in the package with the report are some pornographic pictures depicting homosexual relationships.

To their credit, many local congregations within the denomination are outraged by the report. It's the reverse of God's Word. "Has God said that sex belongs in marriage? That's not true. When you're totally uninhibited with any kind of relationship, you're really fulfilled."

Be alert to Satan's strategy of false teaching. He questions the logic of God's Word, he denies its validity, and then he asserts that just the opposite is true. He substitutes his lie for God's truth. Paul warns that the end for those who follow Satan's lies instead of the truth will be just what their actions deserve.

Be Discerning About Your Leaders

This section of Scripture gives five contrasts between Paul and the false prophets. It provides five ways you can discern a true prophet from a false prophet.

First, the true prophet preaches a familiar gospel, but the false prophet introduces a new one. Paul warned against a teacher who "comes to you and preaches a Jesus other than the Jesus we preached" (2 Corinthians 11:4). We sing that song, "Tell me the old, old story of Jesus and His love."

The old gospel doesn't change. God created man, man sinned and fell from God, God sent Jesus to die on the cross, and then He raised Him from the dead. "Whoever believes and is baptized will be saved" (Mark 16:16). The true preacher relies on the power of that gospel. It may not be the most revolutionary, it may not elicit intellectual raves, but it is the power of God unto salvation. The false prophet is always trying to introduce a new Jesus. Beware of the false prophet who claims a book other than the Bible. One of the characteristics of the cults is that they always have another book that they claim to be just as inspired as Scripture. Beware of the false prophet who claims a personal revelation from God. When you hear somebody say, "God spoke to me," or, "God told me to tell you this," let that be a red flag. God can do anything He chooses to do. But if you are so gullible that you immediately accept as the Word of God anything that someone claims is a divine revelation on a personal basis, you are vulnerable to all kinds of deceptions.

Let the Scripture be your square for truth. Beware of the prophet who receives an understanding of Scripture that is radically different from the orthodox position of 2,000 years. When somebody says, "I've found out a new truth about this Scripture that has never been seen before," that's sometimes pretty egotistical. We need to be growing and learning, but if an idea disagrees with what Bible-believing Christians have said for 2,000 years, beware. "See that what you have heard from the beginning remains in you. If it does, you also will remain in the Son and in the Father. And this is what he promised us—even eternal life" (1 John 2:24, 25).

Second, the true prophet relies on substance; the false prophet relies on charisma. "I may not be a trained speaker, but I do have knowledge" (2 Corinthians 11:6). A true prophet has content; a false prophet has primarily good oratory, pleasing appearance, and a dynamic personality.

Our age is vulnerable to charisma. We like to see people on the tube who come across with personality and projection. One feature said people who listened on the radio to the Nixon-Kennedy debate in 1960 were convinced that Nixon had won, but those who watched it on TV thought Kennedy had won because Kennedy came across with so much more charisma and personality on television. Ever since that time, we've been careful to package our politicians according to charisma and style. Abraham Lincoln would probably never get elected today because he was awkward and wasn't an eloquent speaker.

We Christians need to think more deeply when we evaluate leaders. Evaluate people by substance, not by style. When you are finished listening, ask yourself, "What did the speaker say?" not just, "Did he say it well?" Ask yourself, "What was the substance?" not just, "Was it funny?" Does it have meaning?

"Do not consider his appearance or his height. . . . The Lord does not look at the things man looks at. Man looks at the outward appearance, but the Lord looks at the heart" (1 Samuel 16:7). We need to begin to see people from God's perspective—not, "Is she attractive?" and, "Does he have a dynamic personality?" but, "Do they speak the truth?" "Do they have something of substance?" "Are they people of character?"

Third, the true prophet has a servant's heart; the false prophet has a greedy heart. "Was it a sin for me to lower myself in order to elevate you by preaching the gospel of God to you free of charge?" (2 Corinthians 11:7). When Paul came to Corinth to start this new church, he didn't exploit people by taking up an offering to meet his own personal expenses. He worked with his hands as a tentmaker. He did receive missionary funds from Macedonia, and he said, "I robbed other churches by receiving support from them so as to serve you" (2 Corinthians 11:8). Nobody could say that Paul was taking advantage of them. He wasn't ripping them off.

Don't be gullible. Don't give because of an emotional appeal or a good speech. Don't allow yourself to be exploited. The true prophet has a servant's heart; the false prophet uses any gimmick he can to take advantage. When you give, give sacrificially; but give to that which is true. "When I was with you and needed something, I was not a burden to anyone, for the brothers who came from Macedonia supplied what I needed. I have kept myself from being a burden to you in any way, and will continue to do so" (2 Corinthians 11:9).

My wife's father has a hobby of woodworking. Almost every summer my wife will get out a woodworking magazine and go through it, and then she'll visit her father and say, "Daddy, you see this little knickknack here? Isn't it nice?" At Christmastime, she gets a present; he's made it for her! She opens it up and says, "Oh, Daddy, this is wonderful—how did you know?"

I know Christian leaders who exploit their congregations that way. It's not just the media preachers. I know of preachers who drop subtle hints. "Boy, I sure would like a trip to the Holy Land." "Sure could use a new piano." "We've been having it really tough in our home lately." And then the raise comes or the surprise trip to the Holy Land; "Well, how did you know? That's so wonderful; how did you ever suspect?"

Paul said he kept himself from being a burden *in any way*. He did not exploit people, he said. A true prophet has a servant's heart, not a greedy heart.

Fourth, a true prophet exalts Christ; a false prophet promotes himself. Paul asked them to put up with his foolishness because he was going to have to defend himself. He felt uncomfortable doing that. Paul was humble, and it seemed out of character to have to boast about himself. He said, "As surely as the truth of Christ is in me, nobody . . . will stop this boasting of mine" (2 Corinthians 11:10). He did what was unpleasant because he would do whatever it took to exalt Christ.

False prophets love to promote themselves. It comes naturally. Beware of the person who always has his or her name in lights. Be careful when one person has his name on the Bible college, on the literature, and on the media ministry. Be wary when you hear someone say, "I've written this book and the deepest truths are in this book—it will change your life. You must buy this." True leaders should be able to say with John the Baptist, "He must increase, but I must decrease."

Fifth, a true leader is transparent; the false leader masquerades. "For such men are false apostles, deceitful workmen, masquerading as apostles of Christ. And no wonder, for Satan himself masquerades as an angel of light" (2 Corinthians 11:13, 14). The true leader doesn't have to wear a mask. There's a genuine humanness and spirituality that's apparent. False teachers have to have an air of mystery about them. Beware of those who appear super pious. Beware of those who never admit their weaknesses. Beware of those who cover up their past.

A Boston preacher saw a group of boys around a stray dog, and he asked them what they were doing. "We're seeing who can tell the biggest lie," they said. "The one who tells the biggest lie gets the dog."

"Why, boys!" the shocked minister said. "When I was your age, I never even thought of telling a lie!"

"I guess the preacher gets the dog," said the crestfallen boys.

You never see a counterfeit nine-dollar bill because there's not a real one. Satan is an imitator. He is going to do his best to get as close to the authentic as he possibly can. His servants masquerade as angels of righteousness: they quote Scripture, they talk of morality. We have to be discerning. Examine their doctrine—is it consistent with Scripture? Evaluate their life-style—is it godly and humble or immoral and extravagant? Ask the tough questions. "Test the spirits to see whether they are from God" (1 John 4:1).

I'm told the Federal agents who detect counterfeit bills don't study the counterfeits—they spend most of their time studying the real currency. They become so familiar with it that the spurious is immediately discerned. We can't spend all our time studying all the cults, but we can be jealous for the truth. We can be so aware of Satan's schemes that, when the false prophets come on the scene, we can tell the difference.

U.S.A. Today reported that the treasury department has introduced a new one-hundred-dollar bill that cannot be duplicated. It has a "security thread," a tiny polyester strip that is only visible when the bill is held up to the light. The light must shine *through* the bill, not *on* it, for the thread to be seen, and this makes it difficult to copy.

Jesus said, "I am the light of the world" (John 8:12). When Jesus is allowed to shine in all His splendor and glory, He exposes the counterfeits of this world.

The best way to expose false teachers is to exalt Christ. "For there is no other name under heaven given to men by which we must be saved."

Credentials of a Committed Christian

2 Corinthians 11:16-33

A YOUNG CHRISTIAN enlisted in the Army just after graduation from high school. His friends from church were concerned about his faithfulness to the Lord amidst all the military pressures. When the young soldier came home on leave from boot camp, his friends asked about his testimony. "Did the other guys ridicule you for being a Christian?" they asked.

"Oh, no! There was never a problem," was his disappointing answer. "I guess they never knew that I was a Christian."

Do the people you associate with in the world mark you as a follower of Jesus Christ? It's easy in this era of casual Christianity to blend in with the crowd. It's easy just to be a nominal believer; there's never any rejection, never any ridicule. But Jesus made it clear that a committed Christian should be easily distinguished in the world. He said, "You are the light of the world. A city on a hill cannot be hidden. . . . Let your light shine before men, that they may see your good deeds and praise your Father in heaven" (Matthew 5:14, 16). Some obvious characteristics should identify us as followers of Jesus Christ.

The apostle Paul was not one to brag, but he was at times forced to produce his credentials as a Christian leader. In Corinth, his credibility had been undermined by false teachers who claimed to be superior to him. They ridiculed Paul as unqualified to lead. The false teachers had even led some of the Corinthians away from the true gospel. In this letter, then, Paul attempted to reestablish his credibility.

He felt uncomfortable talking about himself this way. It did not sound like the Lord; it sounded like boasting. But he reluctantly did so—not to

187

exalt himself, but to save the weak Corinthian believers from being led into false teaching. Proverbs 26:5 may have been on his mind: "Answer a fool according to his folly, or he will be wise in his own eyes." Sometimes you have to debate on a shallow level because that's where people are. That's the reason Paul said, "Let no one take me for a fool. But if you do, then receive me just as you would a fool, so that I may do a little boasting" (2 Corinthians 11:16). Paul had to debate with these false teachers on their own level.

This passage presents four credentials of a committed Christian. It's a good one for examining the depth of our commitment. If you are a young Christian, then these are the goals to which you should aspire. If you've been a believer for a long time, here is the proof of your faith. If you've decided in your heart that you don't want to be a casual Christian, that if you're going to do this thing you're going to do it right, then I hope that this look at Paul's credentials will motivate you to a deeper level of service.

Integrity in Relationships with People

Paul began with documentation of how the false teachers were being dishonest with the Corinthians. "You even put up with anyone who enslaves you or exploits you or takes advantage of you or pushes himself forward or slaps you in the face" (2 Corinthians 11:20). "They enslave you," he said. They take you captive with their false doctrine. The false teachers were teaching these Christians that they had to go back to the Old Testament rules of not eating certain meats and observing feasts and Sabbath regulations. They were leading them back into the bondage of the Old Testament law.

Shallow people are inclined to follow somebody who is dogmatic. They're vulnerable to being enslaved by rules. That is the reason cults are so powerful. They take advantage of people's ignorance and insecurities, and they enslave them. The Corinthians were being enslaved by the "Judaizer" cult, and Paul was disturbed that they could not see what was happening to them. They were being exploited. They were being led into bondage.

Some people are vulnerable to being exploited by the greedy motives of their leaders. In 1982, a television preacher told his audience that God had given him a vision that he was going to usher in the second coming of Jesus Christ. "Please send $25.00 to this cause — VISA and MasterCard accepted," he said. Thousands of people responded.

Jesus said, "Watch out for the teachers of the law. . . . They devour widows' houses and for a show make lengthy prayers. Such men will be punished most severely" (Mark 12:38, 40). There are still religious leaders who take advantage of widows and others who are lonely and vulnerable. Because it is profitable, they lead astray and exploit people.

Paul said, "They take advantage of you." The word here pictures a fish being caught on a hook. They bait the hook and it looks appealing. They promise prosperity and family unity and freedom, but they are just being opportunistic. They want to hook you and destroy you. Isn't it unbelievable that people will give hundreds of dollars to an astrologer to predict the future and dictate their choices of behavior? Paul said, "They are taking advantage of you."

"They push themselves forward," he said. They're not interested in you; they just want to promote their own egos. They long to see their names in lights.

"They slap you in the face." Many teachers in the first century would hit their students to show their own superiority and to keep the students under subjection. The false teachers in the church were publicly embarrassing some of the Christians by hitting them or insulting them. Not much of that kind of abuse goes on today, but still some Christians are absolutely intimidated by their leaders.

A group in Louisville not long ago took the Bible teaching about the "pastor-shepherd" to such an extreme that members of this group would not do anything until they got permission from their shepherd. They wouldn't move, change jobs, or even paint their homes without getting their decision approved by the shepherd. One of the pastors led a group of five or six families to leave Louisville altogether and move to a new location. Slowly, some of them began to break away, but they trembled at the idea of going contrary to what their shepherd had to say. People are still gullible and vulnerable to false teachers.

One of Paul's credentials as an apostle was that he had not manipulated his followers. He sarcastically exclaimed, "To my shame I admit that we were too weak for that!" (2 Corinthians 11:21). They may have thought his gentleness was weakness, but that wasn't true. He was honest with them. He did not try to exploit them or take advantage of them.

One of the most salient credentials of a Christian is integrity, an integrity that should be obvious to the world. We're living in a time when everybody is concerned about moral breakdown. We see the loss of values in the military, in government, in athletics, and even in the church. The motto seems to be, "Do unto others before they do it to you." People think you've got to lie and cheat and steal or you're not going to get ahead in this world.

Wayne Smith told about a man who was applying for special insurance, and the insurance agent asked him, "How old is your mother?"

He said, "She's dead."

"How old was she when she died?"

"She was forty-one."

"What did she die of?"

"Tuberculosis."

"How old is your father?"

"He's dead."

"How old was he when he died?"

"Forty-three."

"What did he die of?"

"Heart attack."

The agent tore up the form and said, "You're a terrible risk! There's no way you can get this special insurance; your heredity is not good."

So the man went to another agent, and the agent asked the same questions: "How old is your father?"

"He's dead."

"How old was he when he died?"

"Ninety-four."

"What did he die of?"

"He fell off a horse, playing polo."

The agent said, "How old is your mother?"

"She's dead."

"How old was she when she died?"

"Ninety-one."

"What did she die of?"

"Childbirth."

We have the idea that we have to twist the truth to get ahead in our world; that's the way people operate. There's not much integrity anymore. But the Christian is to be a person of contrast. We're to be a counter-culture. We're to be people of integrity. "Therefore each of you must put off falsehood and speak truthfully to his neighbor" (Ephesians 4:25). The best definition of integrity I've ever heard is simply, "Doing what you say you're going to do."

Jesus said, "Let your 'Yes' be 'Yes,' and your 'No,' 'No'" (Matthew 5:37). That means if you vow that you will be faithful to your mate until death do you part, you do what you say; be faithful. If you sign a contract that you are going to pay a designated amount on the fifteenth of the month for a particular item, then pay your bill on time. Christians ought to have the best credit rating in town! If you take a job and agree to be at work every morning at eight o'clock, then be there on time every day and do a full day's work. If you say you'll be responsible for a certain task in the church or in the community, then do it without having to be prodded or complimented. That's integrity; it's doing what you say you'll do.

Jesus warned that, if we couldn't be faithful in the little things, He could not entrust us with major responsibility. (See Matthew 25:14-30.) We can't allow principles of ethical conduct to erode in the television programs we watch, the expense account we turn in for reimbursement, or even the parking spaces we choose.

We are sometimes tempted to think that, since we have been Christians for a long time, or since we hold positions of leadership, we're exempt from some of the basics. We seem to believe we have "diplomatic immunity" and can ignore certain rules that we consider to be insignificant. But we're not the exception to the rules; we're the example. That means we pay even closer attention to detail and adhere even more closely to the basic principles of morality — even when no one sees or when most people would excuse us.

One Sunday after church, I took my wife and my teenage son out to eat. My wife and I got the salad bar with our meals, but my son did not. As I sat down to eat, he reached over and took one of my two strawberries and ate it. I tried to explain calmly that it was not very thoughtful for him to eat my strawberry. He said, "Dad, just go back and get another one." So I tried to explain why it was unethical for someone who had not paid for the salad bar to get something from the salad bar — even if it's just one strawberry. Have you ever tried to explain to a teenager why one strawberry is a big deal?

Now you may be thinking, "Come on, that's petty." I don't think so. I think that's integrity. Jesus said, "You have been faithful with a few things; I will put you in charge of many things" (Matthew 25:21).

Now, I am not suggesting that we become legalistic or so fastidious that we take the joy out of life. But we must give attention to the details of integrity and morality. It's in the erosion little things that life caves in. And it's the shoring up of the little things that keeps us strong.

One of our sectretaries has a plaque on her desk. It reads, "Great occasions for serving God come seldom. Little ones surround us daily." Paul said, "Whatever you do, whether in word or deed, do it all in the name of the Lord Jesus Christ" (Colossians 3:17). That's integrity.

Tell the truth. Follow the rules—even in little things. That's one of the characteristics of a mature Christian.

Painful Sacrifices

The false teachers had evidently claimed to be superior to Paul in status. So Paul asked, "Are they Hebrews? So am I. Are they Israelites? So am I. Are they Abraham's descendants? So am I" (2 Corinthians 11:22). "If you're comparing pure Jewish blood, I can stand up to any man," Paul said.

Perhaps they boasted they were native Palestinians. But Paul could trace his Hebrew heritage, too. "Circumcised on the eighth day, of the people of Israel, of the tribe of Benjamin, a Hebrew of Hebrews" (Philippians 3:5). He had been "brought up" in Jerusalem, where he studied under Gamaliel, one of the most outstanding Jewish leaders of the day (Acts 22:3), and was "advancing in Judaism beyond many Jews of my own age" (Galatians 1:14). The Jewish teachers who opposed Paul had nothing on him when it came to ancestry.

But when it came to really proving his credentials as a servant of Christ, Paul didn't talk about status, he talked about scars. He listed all the sacrifices he'd made for Christ. "I have worked much harder," he said. Hard work is one of the credentials of the committed Christian servant. I've "been in prison more frequently." Paul wasn't in prison because he had broken the law; he was in prison because he had preached the gospel. I've "been flogged more severely. . . . Five times I received from the Jews the forty lashes minus one. Three times I was beaten with rods" (2 Corinthians 11:23-25).

The Jewish law said no man could be hit more than forty times because that was life-threatening. If a flogger hit a man more than forty times, he himself was to be flogged. So when a person was flogged, the one with the whip would count out loud and stop at thirty-nine—just in case he miscounted. Paul had suffered that flogging of the Jews five times. If someone wanted to know Paul's credentials as a leader, he could have taken off his shirt and bared his back, displaying the scars where he had been lacerated because he had dared to preach Christ.

Three times Paul had been shipwrecked. "I spent a night and a day in the open sea," he said (2 Corinthians 11:25). Imagine spending twenty-four hours clutching onto some log or plank of a ship, bobbing up and down in the sea, having lost all your belongings, wondering whether you were going to live or die! Paul had to wonder at times, if he was doing God's will, why didn't God protect him better?

> I have been constantly on the move. I have been in danger from rivers, in danger from bandits, in danger from my own countrymen, in danger from Gentiles; in danger in the city, in danger in the country, in danger at sea; and in danger from false brothers. I have labored and toiled and have often gone without sleep; I have known hunger and thirst and have often gone without food; I have been cold and naked (2 Corinthians 11:26, 27).

Look at the phrase, "I have been constantly on the move." When I first started in the ministry, I thought I would like to be a traveling evangelist and go to different churches a week or two at a time and preach and then move on. In my first year, I preached a two-week revival meeting at a church in Appalachia. The host preacher thought it would be a good idea for me to get acquainted with people by staying in a different home every night, so I had to live out of a suitcase.

I would eat three meals at three different homes every day. I stayed at homes where I slept on the couch and had no privacy. I stayed in homes that didn't even have inside plumbing. One night before I went to bed, I told my host that I needed to use the rest room. The guy grabbed a flashlight, went out on the back porch, and shined the flashlight down the path. He waited on the porch while I kept walking and walking. Finally he called, "Any place out there will be okay!"

About that time I decided I didn't want to be a traveling evangelist. I took a church in Louisville and I've stayed for more than twenty-five years. I'm soft!

Paul said, "I've been constantly on the move." He was not on the move like a modern evangelist, traveling from one friendly city to another. Paul was under constant threat. Robert Hughes says, "These were not simple misfortunes of someone who took a series of vacations. They were the sufferings accrued as an ambassador of the Lord."

One of the credentials of a committed Christian should be sacrifice. There ought to be some scars. Paul's experience is foreign to us. We're not accustomed to making very much of a sacrifice; we have everything so easy today.

I found the income tax forms made public by one of the presidential candidates in the 1988 election very interesting. They showed that the candidate had made over $200,000 in the previous year and had given a little bit more than $2,000 to charitable institutions—less than one percent of his income. Considering he was a preacher, that's not much of a sacrifice, is it? We can't find too much fault with him, however, because most of us aren't accustomed to making sacrifices. When somebody suggests sacrifice, we protest vigorously. But when people really believe in something, they're willing to suffer for it.

Our newspaper carried this one-sentence filler recently. It was entitled "No Sacrifice Was Too Great":

> *Richmond, Virginia* – Thomas Nelson, signer of the Declaration of Independence, ordered the state militia to bombard his own house because it was believed to be the headquarters of Lord Cornwallis, a British general.

During the Revolutionary War, a patriot ordered his own house destroyed—at a time when there was no insurance. He did that to advance the revolutionary cause. Today, we live in a free country because people sacrificed their lives, their fortunes, and their sacred honor.

There are still a few people who are willing to make a significant sacrifice for Christ. I know of a Christian opera singer who backed out of a musical he had always wanted to participate in because the dance in it was too lewd. I know of another Christian, a former professional football player, who turned down a lucrative contract with a beer company because he didn't want to entice people to drink. I know of a Christian who resigned his job with no alternative available because, he said, "I just cannot participate in the under-the-table deals that are necessary to succeed in this field."

Years ago, when our church had a special offering, we had an auction. People were asked to sacrifice goods they had in their homes that were of value. One man drove up to the auction site on a beautiful motorcycle. He got off the motorcycle, put the helmet on it, and walked away. A reporter called him to ask why he had donated his motorcycle.

He said, "That's the most precious non-essential item I have in my possession. We were asked to make a sacrifice, and I'd never done that before. I just wanted to demonstrate that Christ and the church meant more to me than anything."

Maybe you aren't called upon to sacrifice anything material. Maybe you're not called upon to be beaten for your faith, because you live in a free country. But even in the little things, if we are going to be toughened up as genuine believers of Christ, there need to be some scars.

Maybe our sacrifices will be reflected on our calendars. If you have a scheduled church activity and there's an important basketball game, go to the church activity. For us sports fans, that's a supreme sacrifice! If you're in a choir and they decide they're going to practice a half hour longer, go ahead and make the sacrifice of your time without squealing as if you've been nailed to a cross. If you have an opportunity to witness to friends or family members and they object, go ahead and give your testimony even if they ridicule you. If the church needs housing for somebody, open up your home even if it means hours of cleaning or inconvenience in getting up earlier. If you have the capability of teaching children, quit being satisfied with sitting comfortably in the pew and give up the time to study and teach. When the church has a special offering, sacrifice something, even though you may never have done it before. There ought to be some scars in your pocketbook, too.

People say, "If I sacrifice, my life will be miserable." No. Sacrifice for Christ leads to a life of joy, fulfillment, and fellowship. Jesus said, "Whoever wants to save his life will lose it, but whoever loses his life for me and for the gospel will save it" (Mark 8:35).

That's what He did for us. He said, "The Son of Man came to seek and to save what was lost" (Luke 19:10). Then He did what He said He was going to do—He went to the cross and sacrificed His all for us. He asks that we follow His example. That is what proves we are genuine believers in Christ.

Concern for the Church

Paul wrote, "Besides everything else, I face daily the pressure of my concern for all the churches" (2 Corinthians 11:28).

I love being a preacher. Almost everything I do I enjoy. But I have to admit, this ministry has pressure. Our congregation has needed some large offerings to buy property or eliminate indebtedness. We don't want to pressure people. We don't want to turn people off or alienate visitors by constantly talking about money. Financial stress is frequently a cause for pressure on a ministry, just as it is on marriages. But, to be honest with you, money is not a great pressure of mine.

The greatest pressure I experience is people. When Christian people fail, when they fall short, I feel responsible. I think, "Maybe if we'd just got them plugged into a small group, or maybe if I had taught them better, they wouldn't have done that." When marriages fall apart, I lie awake at night wondering why. Should we have done better in premarital counseling? Should I preach more on the family? Was there something more we could have done?

Paul felt awesome pressure in his ministry because he was responsible not for just one church but for the many he had established. Many of those churches faced overt persecution and problems unlike any we have today.

He wrote to the church of Corinth earlier, "I appeal to you, brothers . . . that all of you agree with one another so that there may be no divisions among you" (1 Corinthians 1:10). He wrote to the church of Galatia, "I am astonished that you are so quickly deserting the one who called you by the grace of Christ and are turning to a different gospel" (Galatians 1:6). He pleaded with two women in the church of Philippi to agree with each other in the Lord and to stop their bickering (Philippians 4:2). He wrote to the church of Colosse, "I want you to know how much I am struggling for you" (Colossians 2:1). He wrote to the church at Thessalonica, "When I could stand it no longer, I sent to find out about your faith. I was afraid that in some way the tempter might have tempted you and our efforts might have been useless" (1 Thessalonians 3:5).

Paul loved the people in those churches. He agonized over their faithfulness. That's why he said to the Corinthians, "Who is weak, and I do not feel weak? Who is led into sin, and I do not inwardly burn?" (2 Corinthians 11:29). As we mature in Christ, we ought to have a deepening love for the church.

I know some Christians who ridicule the church. They've rejected the church. They think that's a mark of sophistication. People carried placards that read, "Jesus, Yes; The Church, No," at a Christian conference a while back. Now, the church certainly has faults that need to be improved, but a mature believer loves the church unashamedly, in spite of its imperfections.

Paul Harvey talks about marital love in three stages. First there is romance. The couple is infatuated with each other and wants to be together twenty-four hours a day. Love is blind at first, but then infatuation gives way to the second stage, which is tolerance. We find out that our partner has faults; we get on each other's nerves, and we just put up with each other. Then comes the third stage, mature love, in which we love each other in spite of our imperfections. We've gone through deepening experiences together.

The same kind of transition in love can be seen in children growing up. A little boy idolizes his dad—there's almost a romantic love—his dad's a hero. Then he gets to be a teenager, and his dad is ignorant. The teen sees all the mistakes his father makes; he can't stand his dad; he thinks about leaving home. Then, in his twenties, he begins to develop a new appreciation for Dad. Even though he isn't perfect, he really is special.

I see Christians going through those transitions in their attitude toward the church. When they first come to the church, they love it blindly. "Oh! This is the most marvelous place there ever was!" When they've been in church for a while, the infatuation wears off and they begin to see that the leaders have feet of clay and not everything meets their needs. They become critical and flirt with the idea of leaving.

One of the credentials of a mature, committed Christian is an unapologetic love for the church. "Sure, the people are imperfect," he realizes, "but so am I. They're doing better and they're seeking to grow. They're saved by Christ, and so am I."

Jesus said, "All men will know that you are my disciples, if you love one another" (John 13:35). Let me suggest five practical ways we can express our love for the church.

First, *attend the services regularly.* "Let us not give up meeting together" (Hebrews 10:25). One new couple at our church had gone down to their cabin at Rough River Lake (a campground some ninety miles from Louisville) every summer weekend for years. They still go, but now they get up at four o'clock every Sunday morning and leave early so they can come to church. If you love the church, you want to be there.

Second, *minister to hurting people sympathetically.* "Who is weak, and I do not feel weak?" Paul said (2 Corinthians 11:29). A few years ago, twenty-seven people were killed in a bus accident near Carrollton, Kentucky. The church they came from was not far from the church where I preach. Our hearts ached for the families of those people. We hurt for that church. Somebody said, "Compassion is *your* pain in *my* heart." Paul wrote elsewhere, "If one part suffers, every part suffers with it" (1 Corinthians 12:26).

Third, we can *esteem the church leaders highly.* "We ask you, brothers, to respect those who work hard among you, who are over you in the Lord and who admonish you. Hold them in the highest regard in love because of their work" (1 Thessalonians 5:12, 13). If you love the church, you love the leaders. If you're always second-guessing the leaders, if you imply they've got some kind of hidden agenda and that you could do a lot better, you don't really love the church. Respect those who are your leaders.

Fourth, *live up to its principles consistently.* If you love the church, you ought to abhor the idea of embarrassing it. Your constant prayer ought to be, "Lord, don't let me bring disgrace on the church. Don't let me give the enemies of God an occasion to blaspheme."

Fifth, if you love the church, *speak positively about it.* I know Christians who criticize the church almost all the time. They go home every Sunday and complain about the style of music, or the length of the sermon, or their boring Sunday-school class, or the crowded parking lot. They think it's a mark of maturity to see the faults and complain.

The church is the bride of Christ. If you love Christ, you're reluctant to criticize His bride. Have you ever been to a wedding where you knew and loved the groom, but you didn't know the bride? You didn't criticize the bride; you looked for something positive to say about her. In a situation like that, you don't say, "I thought your bride was a little overweight—I was surprised." You don't say, "Your bride lacks poise; her hand really trembled when she lit the candle," or, "Your bride has a nasal twang in her voice, and when she gave the vows it was abrasive." If you do that, you may get punched in the nose—and you will certainly lose a friend! You want to love the bride and find something positive to say about her, like, "Your bride is lovely; I hope you two will be very happy together."

The church is the bride of Christ. If you love the groom (Jesus), you will look for positive things to say about the bride (the church).

> Husbands, love your wives, just as Christ loved the church and gave himself up for her to make her holy, cleansing her by the washing with water through the word, and to present her to himself as a radiant church, without stain or wrinkle or any other blemish, but holy and blameless (Ephesians 5:25).

Christ, the groom, loves the bride, the church, so much that His love is blind. He's covered over our sins; He sees us as perfect. If we love the Lord, we're going to love His bride.

An unusual thing happened to Bill Geiger, the preacher at my parents' church in Pennsylvania. He picked up the telephone to make a call and he couldn't get a dial tone, but he could hear people talking in a normal conversation in their home. As he listened, he recognized the people as two members of his church, JoAnn and Chuck Peterman, having a conversation at the table.

When Bill told his wife about it, she said, "I called JoAnn an hour ago and evidently when I hung up, the line didn't break. You've got a direct line, a bug, into their home."

"I knew I wasn't supposed to, but I listened," Bill said. "They were talking about the church. And they were talking about me. I really listened carefully, and fortunately, everything they said was good."

I was in the church when Bill used that story as a sermon illustration, but at first he didn't tell the congregation who it was he heard on the other end. He said, "I picked up the phone and I heard two church members on the other end talking about the church, and they were talking about me." A hush came over that congregation like you wouldn't believe! Then he said, "It was Chuck and JoAnn Peterman, and they were talking positively," and the whole congregation breathed a sigh of relief!

If your minister bugged your home and taped your conversation about the church, would your speech give evidence of your love for the bride of Christ, or would it reveal ridicule and betrayal? If somehow a stranger were listening to the conversation around your dining room table, would it be obvious to him that you were a Christian? "All men will know that you are my disciples" Jesus said, "if you love one another" (John 13:35).

Humility in Service

Paul says, "If I must boast, I will boast of the things that show my weakness" (2 Corinthians 11:30). Sometimes a person's weakness becomes his greatest asset. A fellow walked into the First Christian Church and said, "Look, I'm not a beggar, but I'm without a job and I need money. I'm willing to work." So they put him to work mowing the grass, and they gave him other tasks to do. For three days, he worked hard at all kinds of jobs. They were so impressed that they said, "Look, we'll hire you as a janitor. Just fill out these employment papers."

He said, "I can't read or write."

"Well, if you can't read or write, I guess we can't hire you as a janitor," they said. They gave him a check for his services.

The man was tenacious. He took the money, and he bought some fruit and set up a fruit stand alongside the road. With his profit he bought more fruit, and pretty soon he had a very profitable fruit stand. In fact, over a period of several years, he made more than a million dollars.

One day, he took the money in cash down to the local bank and said, "I want to set up a savings account."

"Wonderful!" they said. "Just fill out these forms."

He said, "I can't read or write."

"You can't read or write?" the banker said. "Do you know where you'd be today if you were literate?"

"Yes," he said, "I'd be the janitor at the First Christian Church!"

Sometimes our weaknesses can be our greatest assets. Some of the people God uses the most effectively are weak, unimpressive people. Look back at the Old Testament prophets. Some of those men were farmers, sheep herders, and fig pickers. But still God used them. The twelve disciples in the New Testament were not impressive men. They were accused of being unlearned, ignorant Galileans by the sophisticates of their day, but still God used them. The reason God used them, and the reason He uses us in our weakness, is to demonstrate that the power comes from God, not from us.

But Paul was different. Paul wasn't a weakling in the eyes of the world. He was quite impressive. He had all the right credentials. He was a Hebrew, a Pharisee, a Roman citizen, the son of wealthy parents, educated in the school of Gamaliel, a rising star in the political sphere. Paul was arrogant, too proud at first to submit to Christ. So he became an intimidator, a persecutor of Christians, breathing out threats and slaughter against the church in Jerusalem. And when he ran out of Christians there to persecute, he headed for Damascus to arrest and imprison the Christians there.

Before God could use Paul, He had to point out Paul's weakness. He had to humble him.

God never saves a strutter, He saves the childlike. God never uses a superstar; He uses servants. Paul thought of himself as a superstar. God needed Paul, so He began a series of events to break him down and help him understand how weak he really was. As he rode toward Damascus, a bright light struck him and knocked him to the ground.

Few experiences are more humbling than to fall down in front of people. Once, at the end of the first of three Sunday-morning worship services, I introduced a video we were going to see. As the lights were turned off, I started down the steps, but I missed the last step, stumbled, and fell flat on my face right at the feet of our music minister.

I bounced back up. It was dark, so I hoped that nobody had seen. But people had seen. Several asked me if I would do it in all three services, they thought it was so entertaining. It's embarrassing and humiliating to fall down in front of the people you're trying to lead.

So there was Paul (actually *Saul* at that time), with the authority of the high priest, proudly leading a group of soldiers into Damascus—and boom! A bright light struck him to the ground, and he heard a voice asking, "Saul, Saul, why do you persecute me?"

He called out, "Who are you, Lord?"

A voice said, "I am Jesus, whom you are persecuting. Now get up and go into the city, and you will be told what you must do."

Saul got up and realized he was blind. This man who was going to ride arrogantly into Damascus now had to be led there by the hand. For three days he could not see. A disciple named Ananias came to him, healed his blindness, and taught him about Jesus. Then Saul got up and was baptized. Educated, arrogant, sophisticated Paul had to get into the water and be immersed as a sign of submission to Jesus. (See Acts 9:1-19.)

I suspect Paul had to struggle with ego at first in his Christian life. When he started giving testimony in Damascus, it appears that he was too forceful and proud, and he infuriated the Jews instead of winning them. They plotted to kill him, and they guarded the city gate. In order for Paul to escape, his friends crunched him into a shipping basket and lowered him over the wall. "In Damascus the governor . . . had the city of the Damascenes guarded in order to arrest me. But I was lowered in a basket from a window in the wall and slipped through his hands" (2 Corinthians 11:32, 33).

Robert Hughes wrote, "A man who had once been in the highest circle of his nation had become a lonely figure, bobbing up and down in a make-shift elevator, scraping against the city wall, and then fleeing into the night." That's the way Paul began his ministry. God had humbled him. Later he said, "If I must boast, I will boast of the things that show my weakness." He wrote to the Philippians, "Whatever was to my profit I now consider loss for the sake of Christ" (Philippians 3:7).

One of the most evident traits of a committed Christian should be humility. Humility is not insecurity and it is not cowardice. Humility simply means there's a constant awareness of the need for God in your life. Humility means that we say, "Regardless of my title, I am still a sinner, and only Christ can forgive me. I may look good on the outside, but I am mortal. Only Christ can help me live forever." Humility means you're willing to take a back seat in order to advance the cause of Christ. It means that you aren't easily offended if you are not in the limelight, if you're not asked to sing the solo, give the keynote speech, or be the chairman. Humility means, if you succeed and all the charts on your business are going upward, you don't become proud and boastful. You just thank God that He's gifted you and give Him thanks. It means that, if you are failing, if your life or your family is falling apart, you don't quit, wallow in self-pity, or blame other people. You just say, "God, by Your strength, I'm going to hold on." It means that, when you are criticized, you don't lose control or retaliate. It means that, if you're in charge, you lead as a servant.

Some members of our church went to a conference in Chicago. We all stayed at the same hotel. One of our men went to the desk clerk and said, "Would you please give me change for a dollar?"

The man said, "I'll give you change, but don't say 'please.'"

"Why?"

"You Christians have been so nice to us this week," he said. "We have the regular people coming in next week, and you're spoiling us, so don't say 'please.'"

The world is not into humility. The world is into pride. The expression of the Marlboro Man or the liberated woman is haughty—the curled lip, the defiant sneer, the cynical expression, and the condescending spirit are common. A humble spirit, to the world, is a sign of weakness. "There are three things you never do," said the ad. The last one was, "Never let 'em see you sweat." Don't let people know you've got weaknesses.

But the Lord tells us to take off the mask, be real, admit our weaknesses. The Bible says, "God opposes the proud but gives grace to the humble" (James 4:6; cf. Proverbs 3:34). If you are arrogant, God will find a way to humble you.

One way He does that is through your family. Your family members know the real you. If you try to appear more than you are, they will humble you. When I come home at the end of the day, my boys don't welcome me by saying, "Oh, Dad, you have such wonderful insight into the Scriptures! Welcome home." They say, "Dad, you're a half hour late! You were supposed to be here so I could use the car. Where have you been?" My wife doesn't say, "Oh, welcome home, great purveyor of truth. Come on in." She says, "You're tracking grass into the house; take your shoes off." I think God gave us families to keep us humble—and the family will do it, too!

A second force that God uses to humble us is failure. The Bible says, "So, if you think you are standing firm, be careful that you don't fall!" (1 Corinthians 10:12). When we get too proud, God will let us fall. Years ago, Charlie Shedd, a great Christian author and speaker, developed a speech he called, "How to Raise Your Children." It was a great sermon, he said. He was in great demand and was paid tremendous fees, going every-where with his speech, "How to Raise Your Children." But then one day he had a humbling experience. Charlie and Martha Shedd had their first child. It wasn't long, they said, until that tremendous speech was a total wreck; it didn't make much sense when they were up with a crying baby at 2:00 A.M. Charlie edited the speech and gave it a new title: "Some Suggestions to Parents." He said he wasn't in much demand, and the fees weren't as high, but he kept on. Then they had their second and third chil-dren, and later the children became teenagers. He altered his text and the title one more time, and it came out, "Feeble Hints for Fellow Strugglers." It doesn't sound nearly as impressive, but I suspect Charlie Shedd's last ef-fort was more realistic and more used of God.

The family and experiences of failure should humble us. The more ma-ture we become in Christ, the more there ought to be evidence of a ser-vant's heart.

Paul had that all through life. Paul, the one we think was the great Christian, referred to himself as "the chief of sinners." He said, "I'm a servant; I'm a slave of Christ." Listen to the word of Jesus:

> You know that the rulers of the Gentiles lord it over them, and their high officials exercise authority over them. Not so with you. Instead, whoever wants to become great among you must be your servant, and whoever wants to be first must be your slave—just as the Son of Man did not come to be served, but to serve, and to give his life as a ransom for many (Matthew 20:25-28).

Ruth Harms Calken, in her poem "I Wonder," points out that the great proof of humility is willingness to remain anonymous in service.

> You know Lord how I serve You with greater emotional fervor in the limelight.
> You know how eagerly I speak for You at women's clubs.
> You know how I effervesce when I promote a fellowship group.
> You know my genuine enthusiasm in a Bible study.
> But how would I react, I wonder, if You pointed to a basin of water and asked me to wash the calloused feet of a bent and wrinkled woman day after day, month after month, in a room where nobody saw and nobody knew.

The humble person is willing to serve without recognition.

Is it obvious that you're a Christian? Are you genuinely humble in your service for the Lord? Is your concern for the church apparent? Are you self-sacrificing with the things that God has entrusted to you? Are you honest in your relationships with people?

Lt. John Blanchard was a young soldier stationed at an Army base in Florida during the first part of World War II. One day, he was reading through a book he had borrowed from the base library. He was impressed with some of the notes written in the margin. They were written in feminine handwriting, and they were so tender and so thought-provoking that he looked back at the flyleaf to see who had been the previous owner of the book. He found it was a woman named Hollis Maynell.

Blanchard did some research and found her address in New York. He wrote her a letter telling her how much he appreciated her insights in the book. The next day he was shipped overseas, but for the next thirteen months, John Blanchard and Hollis Maynell corresponded back and forth. They developed a tremendous relationship through their correspondence, and found that they had much in common and they thought very much alike. They began to realize they were falling in love with each other, though they had never met. Blanchard asked Hollis Maynell if she would send a picture, but she refused. She wrote, "If you really care about me, it wouldn't matter what I look like, because it's character and what's inside that really counts."

After thirteen months, the day finally came when he was to meet her. They made arrangements to meet at Grand Central Station in New York City at 7:00 P.M. on a particular night. She said, "You'll be able to identify me by the red rose I'll be wearing in my lapel."

Lt. Blanchard waited with anticipation. Finally, a group of people got off a train and were coming toward him. Out in front was a slender blonde woman with great poise and beauty. She came in a pale green dress that looked like the freshness of spring, and his heart leaped out of his chest as he started toward her.

Then he saw that she did not have a red rose in her lapel, even though she was looking directly at him. As she went by, with a provocative smile she said, "Going my way, soldier?"

Suddenly, he felt a strong desire to follow her, but then, right behind her, he saw Hollis Maynell. She was over forty years of age, had graying hair, and was vastly overweight, but she was wearing a rose in a lapel of her wrinkled coat. She had gray eyes and a kindly expression, but he was so disappointed.

Everything within him wanted to chase after the beautiful blonde, who was now disappearing. But then he remembered the relationship he had developed through those letters, and even though this probably wouldn't develop into marriage, he realized maybe it would develop into something very meaningful—a friendship, a companionship he had not known before.

So, without hesitation, he handed her the book, which identified him to her, and reached for her bag and said, "Are you ready to go to dinner?"

"Young man, I don't know what this is all about," she said, "but that blonde woman begged me to put on this red rose, and she said that if you asked me out to eat with you, I should tell you were supposed to meet her in the restaurant across the street. She said it was some kind of a test."

Lt. John Blanchard passed the test. Would you? He passed the test of being a person of integrity, of doing what he said he would do, and of possessing a willingness to make a sacrifice of that which seemed immediately pleasurable.

Would you?

The Lord promises that, when you do, you'll receive a reward. "Whoever wants to save his life will lose it," He warns, "but whoever loses his life for me and for the gospel will save it" (Mark 8:35).

Paul believed the Lord's promises. His faith was obvious to everyone. First, he was a man of integrity. He did what he said he would do. Second, he was willing to make sacrifices for Christ. "If you want to know whether I'm a legitimate leader," he said, "look at my scars." Third, he was concerned for the church, concerned enough to put his life on the line for the good of the church. And finally, through it all, he maintained a genuine humility in his service.

God never saves a strutter. He never uses a superstar. He saves those who are humble. He uses servants.

Great Expectations

2 Corinthians 12:1-10

Has this ever happened to you? A friend says, "You just have to see this movie—it's the greatest movie I've ever seen. I laughed until my sides split. You've just got to see it." So you go to that movie, and your level of anticipation is so high that the film just doesn't quite measure up. Later, you realize the movie was good, but your friend's buildup made your expectations unrealistic.

Sports fans also suffer from unrealistic expectations. The UCLA basketball teams won a series of national championships under coach John Wooden. When Wooden retired, he was succeeded by an excellent coach, Gene Bartow. Bartow had a terrific record at UCLA, but he didn't win a national championship. In two years, he was forced out. That program has never fully recovered because nobody can fulfill the unrealistic expectations of the fans and the alumni.

Unrealistic expectations can be devastating to a marriage. I really get concerned when I counsel with starry-eyed young people about to get married. They expect so much—they are bound to be disappointed.

"It's going to be so wonderful," she says. "He's everything I've ever dreamed of."

"And she's everything I've ever wanted!" he says. "I can't wait for the wedding."

About six months later, I notice they're really struggling. She's discovered that he's self-centered, and he's discovered that she expects to be the center of attention all the time.

Someone told me that, when the wedding march begins, the bride sees three things—the aisle, the altar, and him, and from that time on her motto

is, "I'll alter him." And when it doesn't work that way, there is disillusionment and difficulty.

Unrealistic expectations are dangerous to the Christian, too. Some
people anticipate that, when they give their lives to Christ, all of their
problems will be eliminated. They begin the Christian life with such unrealistic hopes that they are quickly disappointed. A preacher friend told me
that several days after he'd baptized a brother and sister, ages ten and
eleven, their mother called the church office. "Preacher, it isn't working,"
she said. "They still fight sometimes." I wonder if we in church don't inad-
vertently promote that idea on occasion. Our sermons and our testimonies
leave the impression that once a person gives his life to Christ, he'll find
instant and permanent peace, and if one has trouble in his home, it will
immediately be eliminated.

We sing choruses like, "I've found happiness all the time, wonderful
peace of mind, when I found the Lord." Really? Happiness *all* the time?
Christ does bring peace, joy, harmony, and happiness, but if we aren't realistic about the time that it takes and the struggles that are involved,
people could be disillusioned.

When God converted Saul of Tarsus, He said, "This man is my chosen
instrument to carry my name before the Gentiles. . . . I will show him how
much he must suffer for my name" (Acts 9:15, 16). God didn't begin Paul's
Christian life by promising peace, but suffering; not ease, but service. We
would do well to present the Christian life realistically so that people can
understand what is expected.

In 2 Corinthians 12:1-10, Paul spoke both of his glory and of his pain.

An Occasional Mountaintop Experience

Paul talked about the "spiritual highs" that had been his. He said he
had "visions and revelations from the Lord" (2 Corinthians 12:1). In order
to establish his credentials, Paul reflected on the mountaintop experiences
he'd had in the past fourteen years. He'd had a number of visions. First,
Jesus had appeared to him on the road to Damascus. Later, a man from
Macedonia appeared to him in a vision saying, "Come over . . . and help
us" (Acts 16:9). In Corinth, Jesus spoke to him in a vision and encouraged
him to continue his ministry there (Acts 18:9-11). And on his way to Rome,
when it was obvious the ship he was on was in danger of being shipwrecked, an angel appeared to him to comfort him (Acts 27:23).

But the greatest revelation he had came when he was caught up into
Heaven. "I know a man in Christ"—Paul is relating his own experience,

but his distaste for boasting caused him to speak in the third person—"who fourteen years ago was caught up to the third heaven" (2 Corinthians 12:2). This had happened fourteen years earlier, and this was Paul's first mention of it. If this had happened to me, I'd be in the pulpit the next morning talking about it, but Paul was humble.

The first heaven is the atmosphere, where the birds fly, which we can see. The second heaven is the universe, where the stars and the planets are found. This, too, we can observe and explore (i.e., with telescopes, satellites, and rockets). The third heaven, however, is another dimension that we cannot see or explore—and that we cannot spoil. It is the dwelling place of God. It's where Jesus went when He said, "I go to prepare a place for you." Paul says he was "caught up to the third heaven," and there he heard "inexpressible things, things that man is not permitted to tell" (2 Corinthians 12:4).

What a contrast this experience was with the one when Paul was let down in a basket over the Damascus wall to escape. Here he's caught up to the third heaven where he could meet the Lord. It was such a mystical experience that he did not know whether he was still in his body or out of his body.

We've heard a great deal about out-of-the-body experiences. Dr. Elizabeth Kubler-Ross and Dr. Raymond Moody, two psychiatrists, did a study in which they interviewed 500 people who were declared clinically dead and then were brought back to life.[19] The people described encounters they had. They were attracted to a being of light or they saw something terrifying. One man who was blind told that out of his body he could see, and he described what the operating room looked like and who came in and out of the room. When he was resuscitated, he couldn't see. Raymond Moody told of a woman who suffered respiratory arrest. She said she looked down, saying, "Leave me alone," as she watched the doctors pounding on her body. She encountered such peace that she did not want to return. One doctor told about a man who was pronounced clinically dead but was then resuscitated. The man sued the doctor for bringing him back to his miserable existence.

I'm not sure how to interpret those out-of-the-body experiences. Some suggest that Satan is masquerading as an angel of light (cf. 2 Corinthians 11:14), using people's hallucinations to transmit false messages about salvation. Others suggest that God is giving us additional evidence in these

[19]*Life After Life: The Investigation of a Phenomenon, Survival of Bodily Deaths* (St. Simons Island, GA:Mockingbird, 1975, 1981.)

skeptical times to counter the most unbelieving. But one thing is sure, these accounts verify that there is a spirit world beyond the physical senses. There is life outside the body.

Paul had some kind of a mystical experience—in the body or out of the body, he didn't know—but he was caught up into Heaven. It may have occurred when he was near death, and it may have been just a revelation from God, but whatever the experience, it was an uplifting one that he remembered forever.

There will be a few occasions in your Christian life when you will be on the mountaintop spiritually. I can remember how clean and close to God I felt when I was baptized as a young boy. I can also remember times at the end of a week at Christian service camp, after we had been apart from the world and had studied the Word of God all week long, when I felt extremely close to the Lord. I can remember as if it were yesterday the time, in my senior year in high school, when I decided to go to Bible college to study for the ministry. What a sense of peace I had about that decision. I knew that I was doing God's will, and I remember thinking I would live the rest of my life above the temptations that would come to others. I was dead wrong, of course, but I felt on top of the world then. Sometimes I feel on the mountaintop after a church service.

But maybe for you it was when your child was born, or when, after a long siege of prayer, you learned a critically ill family member was going to recover, or when you got a job you had been praying about for a long time.

The Southland Church in Lexington had the Cathedrals Quartet in for a concert some time back. The next week, the church printed a letter one man had written about the experience. He said,

> I've been to a Super Bowl, a Peach Bowl, three Kentucky Derbies, two Final Fours (including Kentucky vs. Duke in '78), seventeen boys' state tournaments, Kentucky political rallies, a World Series, a Billy Graham Crusade, the Hawaiian Islands twice, and Tater Day in Benton, Kentucky, but I've never enjoyed myself or been as blessed as I was during both performances of the Cathedrals Quartet yesterday. The atmosphere in God's presence was tremendous.

I love quartet music, but I don't know that I'd go that far—better than the Hawaiian Islands? Still, that man was on a spiritual high!

It is important that you understand that mountaintop experiences are occasional. If you expect the Christian life to be one continuous high, you're going to be disillusioned—they are rare. Paul said this had happened to him fourteen years before, and it apparently had never happened again. Emotional and spiritual highs are to be remembered, but they are not to be reproduced. They are to be savored, but they are not the standard by which you measure the level of your spirituality.

Back in 1986, the Louisville Cardinals beat Duke for the national collegiate basketball championship. That night, after eleven o'clock, I went out in the streets and yelled with my neighbors. My sons got streamers and signs and put them on the car and drove around the neighborhood beeping the horn. The next morning, I drove to the church in that car and people saw the streamers and beeped and waved. It was great.

But what would people think of me if I went out in the street tonight at 11:30 and started leading Cardinal cheers at the top of my voice? Even my neighbors who were U of L fans would say, "I wonder what he's been drinking in the Communion juice." Or if I put red streamers on my car, and when people asked, "What's that for?" I'd say, "U of L beat Duke!" Even if they were Louisville fans, they'd think that was a little strange—that was years ago!. Some people in my congregation would start looking for another church.

Emotional highs are a rare experience. It's not normal to expect them all the time. That's true for spiritual highs, too—they are rare. People who go around every day shouting, "Praise the Lord! Hallelujah!" all the time are a little strange to me. Christianity has some mountaintop experiences, but they are rare. Savor them, rejoice in them, but don't expect to experience them all the time.

When Jesus was transfigured, He stood in dazzling white with Moses and Elijah beside Him. Peter said, "Lord, it is good for us to be here. If you wish, I will put up three shelters—one for you, one for Moses and one for Elijah" (Matthew 17:4). Instead, Jesus led them down to the bottom of the mountain, where there was a demon-possessed boy who needed healing.

Peter wanted to build a memorial so they could hold on to their spiritual high. Jesus reminded them there was work to be done in the valley.

If you expect the Christian life to be one continuous high, you're vulnerable in two areas. First, you're vulnerable to depression. When you come down from a great emotional experience, you begin to ask, "What's wrong with me? Why isn't my walk with God as close as it was when I was in camp? Doesn't He love me any more? Have I strayed?"

Second, you're vulnerable to manipulation. If you evaluate your walk with God by your emotional high, there's a constant temptation to try to reproduce that high artificially. A television program, *Promise to Heal*, told the true story of a couple who got involved in a faith-healing movement. Their son had diabetes. In a frenzied service, the preacher convinced them that their son had been healed and that they should claim healing. They did. They threw away the boy's insulin. When he got weaker and weaker, the father's faith began to waver, and he started looking for the insulin, but then they got hyped up again and were convinced that all they had to do was pray and claim healing. But the boy died. Instead of accepting it, they were led in another frenzied worship service. This time, the preacher said God was going to do a greater miracle—He was going to raise him from the dead. In one of the most pitiful scenes of the program, the father realized that he had been duped. He'd been manipulated into a spiritual high that was artificial. The parents were put on trial for murder, but the judge said, "It's the minister who should be on trial here."

I know Christians who spend a great deal of time and money attending one concert after another, or one seminar after another, trying to reproduce a spiritual high they experienced at an earlier one. The desire for a spiritual high can become almost like an addiction.

Mountaintop experiences are wonderful if they are authentic, but understand that they are rare. Don't try to reproduce them artificially. Be satisfied with the ordinary, too. Continue to trust God in the valley as well as praise Him on the mountaintop.

Normal Human Difficulties

"To keep me from becoming conceited because of these surpassing great revelations, there was given me a thorn in my flesh, a messenger of Satan, to torment me" (2 Corinthians 12:7). Every time I read that I wonder what Paul's thorn in the flesh was. Some people speculate that it was epileptic seizures, a speech impediment, fleshly temptations, an estranged wife, hateful persecutors, constant earache, or grotesque physical appearance.

I think his thorn in the flesh was one of two things. It could have been frequent migraine headaches that were the aftermath of malaria. Paul had traveled in the eastern Mediterranean where malaria was a dreaded disease. After his first missionary journey, he had a doctor, Luke, as a constant companion. The word for thorn actually means "stake." Paul suggested he had a sharp stake twisting in his body. One man who had suffered from malaria once described the headache that accompanies it as being like a red hot bar thrust through the forehead. That describes a thorn in the flesh. If Paul suffered recurring migraine headaches that just almost reduced him to putty—that would be a humbling experience.

The second possibility, and I think this is the more likely, is that Paul's thorn in the flesh was poor eyesight. When God struck him down on the Damascus road, he was left blinded for three days. When Ananias healed him, maybe it was a partial healing. Perhaps God allowed him to be left with poor eyesight as a constant reminder of that experience. Paul said the Galatians would have plucked out their eyes and given their eyes to him if they could have (Galatians 4:15). He ended his letter to the Galatians by saying, "See what large letters I use as I write to you with my own hand!" (Galatians 6:11).

When you become a Christian, you're going to experience the normal difficulties of life. Some would suggest that, if you are a believer, you should never be sick, you should always be healthy and wealthy. A sick Christian, they say, is a disgrace to God. But the Bible makes it clear that God does not exempt His people from pain. If He did, people would follow Him strictly for selfish purposes. Jesus said, "He causes his sun to rise on the evil and the good, and sends rain on the righteous and the unrighteous" (Matthew 5:45). Jesus said, "In this world you are going to have trouble." Paul said, "There was given me a thorn in my flesh."

"There are two kinds of coaches in the NFL," said Bum Phillips just after he was released by the Houston Oilers. "Them that's been fired and them that's going to be." There are two kinds of Christians, too: those who hurt and those who are going to. Just because you take your children to Sunday school doesn't mean they will never use drugs. Just because you are a Christian doesn't mean you'll never get cancer. Just because you tithe does not mean you will never feel the tension of financial strain. Just because you marry a Christian doesn't mean you're going to live happily ever after. Just because you're driving to church doesn't mean you won't ever have an accident.

Warren Wiersbe says there are three main reasons Christians suffer. First, we suffer simply because we're human. We live in a fallen world. Our bodies age just like everybody else's. The world is full of sin and we live in its fallout. If another man gets drunk and gets confused and drives his truck the wrong way on the interstate, he may hit a bus full of Christian young people. They are not exempt. It's not because God is a tyrant causing grief, it's because we live in a fallen world of sin and we have to experience the results of it.

Second, we suffer because we ourselves are disobedient and foolish. I watched a man writhe in pain from lung cancer. He had smoked three packs a day from the time he was thirteen years old. His daughter was distraught at her dad's suffering and said, "Why is God doing this to him?"

I didn't say it, but I thought: "God's not doing that to him. He's afflicted himself by foolish behavior earlier in life." Sometimes our pain is a direct result of our own rebellion against God. We bring it on ourselves as surely as a little child who touches a hot stove, in violation of his parents' warnings, brings pain on himself.

Third, suffering is a tool God uses to build godly character. Sometimes suffering is not a punishment, but a training ground. Parents sometimes allow their children to go through hurt to build their character. They bring their little one to church and leave him in the nursery or preschool department. The child doesn't want to stay there—he cries, he wants to be with his parents because it's more secure. But if children were never put through any kind of hurting experience, they would grow up to be maladjusted and insecure people, so parents let them hurt.

> Our fathers disciplined us for a little while as they thought best; but God disciplines us for our good, that we may share in his holiness. No discipline seems pleasant at the time, but painful. Later on, however, it produces a harvest of righteousness and peace for those who have been trained by it (Hebrews 12:10, 11).

Paul said, "To keep me from being conceited . . . there was given me a thorn in my flesh" (2 Corinthians 12:7). God knew how to counterbalance Paul's blessing with a burden, so he wouldn't be an egomaniac. God was developing in Paul a right balance.

Roy Lauren has said there is no such thing as painless power. Power is always the result of pressure, fire, constriction, or tribulation. Water power is the result of a massive building up of water that is then forced under great pressure through turbines to generate electricity. Steam power is the result of fire that heats the water until it expands and pressures a cylinder to turn. Gasoline power is the explosion of volatile gasoline in a chamber, which forces the piston to turn the crankshaft and creates motion.

The same principle applies in the Christian life. Physical suffering and mental anguish create pressure that produces spiritual power, and there can be no spiritual power without pressure. God told Paul, "My power is made perfect in weakness" (2 Corinthians 12:9). If all of life went smoothly, we would have no spiritual power. A. W. Tozer said, "It's doubtful that God uses anyone greatly until He has hurt him significantly."

The Sufficiency of God's Grace

"Three times I pleaded with the Lord to take it away from me" (2 Corinthians 12:8). Paul thought, "I don't need this affliction. It makes no good sense that I should have to suffer like this. I'll have no ego problem if God takes it away. I'll be grateful." So on three separate occasions Paul pleaded, "Heal me, Lord," but his request was not granted.

One of the things you can expect in the Christian life is a "no" answer to prayer. Some people give the impression that, if you really have faith and you pray, then what you want is automatically going to happen. There is tremendous benefit to prayer, but it's not an immediate guarantee of everything you desire. There are times when God answers our prayer with "No. It's going to be better if you don't have this." That's not the way we want it, but that's the way it happens.

An airplane pilot announced over the intercom, "We have lost one of our four engines. But don't worry; we'll be able to make it to our destination with three engines, and you will be reassured to know there are four pastors on board."

One passenger leaned over to the stewardess and said, "I'd rather have four engines and three pastors, wouldn't you?"

Most of the time we'd like life to go smoothly and not to have to pray or rely on God. That's the very reason He lets us hurt—so that we'll rely on Him, and pray, and that His power will be made perfect in our weakness.

Did you ever wonder how long you should pray for something if it is not answered affirmatively? Luke 11 says keep on asking, keep on seeking, keep on knocking, and you'll find. In George Mueller's prayer journal was the name of one man for whom Mueller had prayed every day for nearly forty-three years, and finally the man became a Christian. When do you conclude that God is saying, "No—it's time to quit praying about that and go on"?

My advice is just to keep on praying until it's obvious that God says no. Our church prayed for over a year that our old building would be sold. Eventually, there were no more potential buyers, and we began to observe that the day care and kindergarten programs meeting in that building would be more effective if they remained in that facility. So we concluded the Lord was saying, "Quit praying and start fund raising."

Paul prayed intently for relief for three different periods, and each time there was no relief. Then God answered Paul, "My grace is sufficient for you."

Wiersbe says, "God didn't give any explanation, He just gave a promise. 'My grace is sufficient.' God often meets our needs not by eliminating the problem but by transforming the person. We pray for exemption from pain, and God gives us more power to endure. We prefer it the other way, but His grace is sufficient."

"God is faithful," Paul assures us. "He will not let you be tempted beyond what you can bear. But when you are tempted, he will also provide a way out so that you can stand up under it" (1 Corinthians 10:13).

I've been with people through the death of loved ones, desertion by their mates, financial collapse, and other troubles. I've seen every time, in the life of the believers, a level of strength that was not their own.

I'll never forget—though it happened more than a decade ago—the time I drove to a local hospital to meet one of our couples who had just learned that their little six-year-old boy had leukemia. As I drove, I thought, "Lord, there is no way any parent can cope with this. They've got to be so angry at You they'll just collapse. They won't be able to hold up. They're going to expect me to have some answers, Lord, and I don't know what to tell them."

I met them in a little counseling room and discovered they both were calm. They smiled and said, "Thank you for coming." The mother said, "Before you say anything, Bob, we want to say something to you. We're doing OK. God's helping us out. You're probably worried about what to say. You don't have to say anything; we just thank you for coming."

Where did they get that strength? Not on their own! The Lord gives us grace sufficient for any problem that we endure. He says, "My power is made perfect in weakness."

That's the reason the Bible says, "Don't worry." Jesus said, "Do not worry about tomorrow, for tomorrow will worry about itself. Each day has enough trouble of its own" (Matthew 6:34). He doesn't say, "Don't worry about tomorrow because there won't be any problems." He says, "Don't worry about tomorrow because, if you get some big problems, I'll see that you have big grace. I'll supply your every need. You just trust in Me and, whatever the problem is, I'll see that you have the strength to endure."

Nancy Speigelberg wrote this prayer: "Lord, I crawled across the barrenness to You with my empty cup of uncertainty, asking any small drop of refreshment. If only I had known You better, I would have come running to You with a bucket."

> He giveth more grace when the burdens grow greater;
>   He sendeth more strength when the labors increase.
> To added affliction he adds his mercy;
>   To multiplied trials, his multiplied peace.

When we have exhausted our store of endurance,
  When our strength has failed 'ere the day is half done,
When we reach the end of our hoarded resources,
  Our Father's full giving is only begun.

His love has no limit; His grace has no measure;
  His pow'r has no boundary known unto men.
For out of his infinite riches in Jesus,
  He giveth, and giveth, and giveth again![20]

You can expect some mountaintop experiences. You can expect some hurt, too. But you can expect whatever the hurt, His grace is sufficient.

---

[20]Annie Johnson Fint, "He Giveth More Grace." Copyright © 1941, renewed 1969 by Lillenas Publishing Company. Used by permission.

Telltale Signs of a Carnal Christian

2 Corinthians 12:11-21

A LOCAL SPORTSCASTER SAID that, for him, the start of the Indianapolis 500 was the most spectacular event in sports. To see thirty-three low-slung, sleek, turbocharged automobiles roaring around Turn 4 and zooming across the starting line at 200 miles per hour to start the world's most famous race is an incredible event. But of the thirty-three cars that started a recent race, only eleven actually finished. Over half the cars got knocked out of the race by either a wreck or some kind of mechanical difficulties. In some instances, something as minor as the failure of a ten-dollar bolt could force a car out of the race.

As impressive as the start is, the important part of the race is finishing. The financial rewards and honors do not go to those who start well, but to those who finish well. So the driver and the pit crew are constantly watching gauges and evaluating the performance of the car so they can prevent a breakdown and make necessary adjustments along the way.

Many people who start in the Christian life don't finish. One of the saddest characters in the Bible is Solomon. He began his life with noble motives, but he wrecked along the way in indulgence and compromise. In the New Testament, Paul spoke of a former co-worker by the name of Demas, who dropped out of the race: "Demas, because he loved this world, has deserted me" (2 Timothy 4:10). Jesus said, "No one who puts his hand to the plow and looks back is fit for service in the kingdom of God" (Luke 9:62).

It is not enough to start the Christian life well. We need to plan to finish well. The reward is not given at the beginning, but in the end. Revelation 2:10 says, "Be faithful, even to the point of death, and I will give you the crown of life."

219

A Christian may drop out of the race dramatically because there is a wreck in his life along the way. Another just kind of coasts to the sideline because little things have gone wrong and he fizzles out. But whatever the cause, we all need to be alert to the telltale signs that trouble is brewing in our lives, and we need to make the adjustments that are necessary.

In 1 Corinthians 3:3, Paul addressed the Corinthians as "worldly" Christians. The word translated *worldly* really means "fleshly." It's the word the King James translators rendered *carnal*. These carnal Christians were selfish; they wanted blessing without sacrifice; they wanted power without restraint. They were more concerned about the things of the world than they were the things of the Spirit, the temporal more than the eternal, the physical more than the spiritual.

So Paul warned them about regressing in the Christian life. In 2 Corinthians 12, he had to warn them again. This time, he mentioned four telltale signs of a carnal Christian. When you see these characteristics developing in your own life, beware! If you don't make adjustments, it could be just a matter of time before you're sitting on the sidelines watching others, and wondering what in the world happened to your marriage, your family, or your spiritual life.

Lack of Appreciation for Spiritual Leaders

Paul said, "I have made a fool of myself." He was talking about having to go back and list his credentials. Don't you feel a little foolish when you make out a resumé or you have to brag on yourself? If you don't, you should. Paul said, "I have made a fool of myself, but you drove me to it. I ought to have been commended by you, for I am not in the least inferior to the 'super-apostles,' even though I am nothing" (2 Corinthians 12:11).

They should have commended Paul. He was a humble man. All the time he had labored among them, he had never bragged about himself or thrown his weight around. He was humble, and they took him for granted. He was really a powerful man. "The things that mark an apostle — signs, wonders and miracles — were done among you with great perseverance" (2 Corinthians 12:12). One of the signs of being an apostle was the ability to perform miracles, to heal people, raise the dead, speak in languages that the speaker had never studied, and foretell the future. Paul had done all those signs among them, and he had done them consistently.

He was generous. He had served the Corinthian church without demanding a salary. "I was never a burden to you," he said (2 Corinthians 12:13). Other churches that Paul had started supported him financially, but he labored in Corinth without taking up any love offerings because he didn't want to be a burden, and he didn't want anyone in that totally pagan culture to think that he was in it for the money.

He was loving. "Now I am ready to visit you for the third time, and I will not be a burden to you, because what I want is not your possessions but you" (2 Corinthians 12:14). They could not accuse Paul of exploiting them. He loved them and he treated them with integrity. He said the reason he didn't take up an offering was that he felt like their spiritual parent. "Children should not have to save up for their parents, but parents for their children" (2 Corinthians 12:14).

I have a son who is in ministry and another who is in college. They both have incomes, but, when we go out to eat, they never reach for their wallets. When we go out to play golf, they just stand around and wait for me to pay. That's the nature of things; I expect to pay. I don't want them to pay, but I do want them to be grateful.

Paul said, "I will very gladly spend for you everything I have and expend myself as well. If I love you more, will you love me less?" (2 Corinthians 12:15). Instead of appreciating Paul, the Corinthians had taken him for granted. They suggested he wasn't really good enough to be paid. They were giving all kinds of compliments to the false apostles and were taking Paul for granted. That's one of the signs of carnality.

When I was in high school, I took my father for granted. He was a wonderful, gentle, humble person who treated me well. But during my sophomore year in high school, I became enthralled with a carnal man who took me hunting. I was impressed with his athletic ability and with his sense of humor. I would brag about him all the time—I just idolized him. Finally, my sister took me aside and said, "Bob, you need to quit talking about this new friend all the time; you're hurting Dad." Looking back, I realize how that was so, and I realize my father was such a better person. He loved his family and was faithful to us, and he loved the Lord. But because he was humble, I took him for granted.

I see that same characteristic in spiritual babies and retarded Christians. They take humble Sunday-school teachers, elders, church staff, spiritual parents, musicians, and accompanists for granted. At the same time, they're swept off their feet by superficial, charismatic leaders who are self-promoting and exploitive. It's hard to understand.

One of the characteristics of spiritual maturity is appreciation for the people who have contributed to your life. Christian leaders should not be idolized, but they ought to be regarded with a sense of gratitude. There ought to be evidence of reciprocal love.

The Messengers Quartet at the Southland Church in Lexington has sung almost every Sunday morning for twenty-eight years. For twenty-eight years they have practiced every week and presented a quartet number during the offering. One of their members recently got cancer, and the congregation wanted to show their appreciation. They gave him and his wife a free cruise to the Caribbean. But when the time for the cruise came, he was too sick to go. They asked him what they could give him instead, and he said, "I would like the number-one gospel quartet in America to come and sing at Southland." That was the Cathedrals Quartet. It cost the church people $4,000, but they brought the Cathedrals in and had a wonderful concert. It was their means of expressing their love to a man who had contributed to their spiritual life for so many years.

The Bible says we are to give honor to whom honor is due. (See Romans 13:7.) One of the signs of a carnal attitude is a lack of appreciation for the humble spiritual people who labor among you.

Immediate Suspicion of Other People's Motives

The Corinthians had not only taken Paul for granted, they were impugning his motives. They were accusing Paul of being deceptively humble. They suggested that he had refused support from them because, in the end, he was going to take up an offering for the poor in Jerusalem and he would probably pocket a great deal of that money. Paul was annoyed with them for such infantile pettiness. He responded sarcastically, "Crafty fellow that I am, I caught you by trickery!" It was ludicrous. "Did I exploit you through any of the men I sent you? I urged Titus to go to you and I sent our brother with him. Titus did not exploit you, did he? Did we not act in the same spirit and follow the same course?" (2 Corinthians 12:16-18). Yet there were still shallow people who suspected the worst from Paul.

There are carnal Christians today who are immediately suspicious of everybody. "Well, that singing group came in, but they really milked us. They're just in it for the money."

"That missionary is a con man. I bet he's over there taking a vacation."

"Yeah, that guy stopped by and said he needed money for something to eat. I'll bet he's out drinking it up right now."

"Well, he's going to church and he got baptized, but I bet he's just going there so he can make more sales in insurance."

"Yeah, the preacher's on an ego trip; you can tell it by his expression."

"She's singing because she loves to strut up front."

Let's admit there are con artists in the church; there are people on ego trips; there are people who exploit for money or take advantage. We need to be alert and aware, and we shouldn't be naïve. But if our first reaction to people is always suspicion, if we're skeptical of everyone, if we're cynical about everything that goes on, that's a sign of carnality. "Love always . . . trusts" (1 Corinthians 13:7). Look for the best in people first.

Not only is it a sign of carnality to see the worst, but sometimes it's a sign of stupidity. A tough-minded manager walked through his shipping department and saw a young man lounging on a shipping crate, almost asleep. He said, "Young man, what do you make a week?"

"I make $150 a week."

The manager took $150 out of his wallet and gave it to the boy. "Now get out of here and don't come back," he said. Then he went directly to the head of the department and demanded, "Who hired that young man?"

"Nobody," the supervisor said. "He's just a delivery boy waiting for a package."

If you're skeptical of everybody, you may think that shows your sophistication, but it could be a sign of carnality and stupidity. Our attitude as Christians should be that people are innocent until proven guilty. I'll trust that you are for real until you prove otherwise. "To the pure, all things are pure, but to those who are corrupted and do not believe, nothing is pure. In fact, both their minds and consciences are corrupted," Paul said (Titus 1:15). If you always suspect the worst in people, it may be that your own heart and mind are corrupted. We say, "It takes one to know one."

William Barclay repeats a story from H. L. Gee "of a tramp who came begging to a good woman's door."

> She went to get something to give him and found that she had no change at all in the house. She went to him and told him, "I have not a penny of small change. I need a loaf of bread. Here is a pound note. Go and buy the loaf and bring me back the change and I will give you something." The man executed the commission and returned and she gave him a small coin. He took it with tears in his eyes. "It's not the money," he said, "it's the way you trusted me. No one ever trusted me like that before, and I can't thank you enough."[21]

Barclay says, "It is easy to say that woman took a risk that only a soft-hearted fool would take, but she had given that man more than money; she had given him something of herself by giving her trust."

[21]William Barclay, *The Letters to the Corinthians* (Philadelphia: Westminster, 1954), p. 292.

Do you trust people? You're going to be taken on occasion, but I'd rather be taken once in a while than to go through life cynical, suspicious, and guarded. To the pure, all things are pure. To the carnal, all motives are questionable.

A Sour Disposition That Divides the Church

When you become a Christian, it's supposed to make you sweeter in spirit. I wish more Christians understood that. "I am afraid that when I come I may not find you as I want you to be," Paul wrote, "and you may not find me as you want me to be. I fear that there may be quarreling, jealousy, outbursts of anger, factions, slander, gossip, arrogance and disorder" (2 Corinthians 12:20). These eight unholy attitudes are signs of carnality in the life of a church or an individual. Left unchecked, they are devastating to the harmony of the church.

The first is *quarreling*. One commentator translates it, "There may be 'fussing.'" There are people who are always fussing about little things. It's too cold in the sanctuary; no towels in the bathroom; the lights are too dim; the song was too long—just fussing and quarreling all the time.

As a result, there's *jealousy*. Jealousy is the spirit that begrudges another person the possession of anything that is denied to oneself. Envy is the characteristic of the mean and little mind. The Bible says, "Rejoice with those who rejoice; mourn with those who mourn" (Romans 12:15). If you're a jealous person, you're always pouting because you find somebody who has more, and you don't want anybody to have more than you.

There are *outbursts of anger*. The Bible says the fruit of the Spirit is self-control. A sign of carnality is a lack of control. A carnal person can be sweet and nice when everything's going his way, but when he gets a bad call in a ball game, when somebody cheats him out of money, when somebody criticizes his children, or any time the pressure's on, there's a personality transformation and he goes to pieces. He gets red in the face and screams and says things that are out of line and writes nasty letters. After it's all over and he has ventilated, he feels bad and apologizes. He wishes that the event had never happened.

One guy said, "I lose my temper on occasion, but it's all over in a minute." So's a tornado! But somebody still has to clean up afterward. "Better . . . a man who controls his temper than one who takes a city" (Proverbs 16:32).

Then there are *factions*. There are all kinds of factions in the world. You're either in the labor camp or in the management camp; you're either liberal or conservative, Republican or Democrat. People bring that same spirit into the church. They're always asking, "Are you premillennial? Are you inerrantist? Are you Calvinistic? Are you baptismal regenerationist? Are you for the preacher or for the deacons? Are you for gospel music or contemporary? Are you for clapping or saying 'Amen'?" Some people love to stir up division. That's a sour disposition. That's a sign of carnality.

Then there's *slander* and *gossip*. Slander is easier to cope with than gossip, because slander is in the open while gossip is in secret. Gossip sabotages the other person. J. Vernon McGee said, "You can get people to believe anything if you just whisper."

There's also *arrogance*. Conceit is admirable in today's world. People boast about themselves, athletes brag on themselves, politicians promote themselves, businessmen put out glowing resumés about themselves. The world is concerned about titles and status. But the Christian is not supposed to be arrogant, but humble and gentle in spirit.

Jesus told the people not to act like the Pharisees and teachers of the law, for they loved the honors of this world, to be treated with respect and be called "Rabbi." He said, "The greatest among you will be your servant. For whoever exalts himself will be humbled, and whoever humbles himself will be exalted" (Matthew 23:11, 12). The world has an arrogant spirit; the Christian ought to have a gentle, humble spirit.

One other indication of a carnal disposition is what Paul calls *disorder*. That's the word for anarchy or tumult. This word speaks of everybody doing his own thing, nobody respecting the leader enough to follow. Carnal Christians are quick to disregard the instructions of leaders. "Hey, nobody's going to tell me where to sit." "Nobody tells me what I'm supposed to sing." "Nobody tells me where to park."

It's a matter of pride. The church and the Christian home ought to be places of cooperation with leaders in a spirit of peace and tranquility. But carnal Christians have a sour, mean disposition. And they never grow out of that. They never make the connection between being born into the family of God and being changed in attitude.

"The fruit of the Spirit is love, joy, peace, patience, kindness, goodness, faithfulness, gentleness and self-control" (Galatians 5:22). The carnal Christian never catches on.

Continued Participation in the Sins of the Flesh

Paul said, "I am afraid that when I come again . . . I will be grieved over many who have sinned earlier and have not repented of the impurity, sexual sin and debauchery in which they have indulged" (2 Corinthians 12:21). The Corinthian church was made up of people from the most corrupt background imaginable. The city of Corinth was a seaport town in ancient Greece—the link between two major commercial and military sea routes. Corinth was like San Francisco, Atlantic City, and Las Vegas all rolled into one. The sailors loved the port at Corinth because it was where the action was. To "live like a Corinthian" in the first century was synonymous with hedonism.

The word *debauchery* means a rebellious spirit that has lost all sense of shame. Debauchery means to disobey without a twinge of conscience. William Barclay says the Corinthians lived in a society that did not regard even adultery as sin. It was just natural and expected that a man would take his pleasures where he could. In the middle of this cesspool, Paul started a church. It was rather like a flower growing out of a dung heap. People were converted to Christ in Corinth out of this disgusting background. Earlier Paul had said,

> Neither the sexually immoral nor idolaters nor adulterers nor male prostitutes nor homosexual offenders nor thieves nor the greedy nor drunkards nor slanderers nor swindlers will inherit the kingdom of God. And that is what some of you were. But you were washed, you were sanctified, you were justified in the name of the Lord Jesus Christ and by the Spirit of our God (1 Corinthians 6:9-11).

"That is what some of you were!" Some of the Corinthians had been homosexuals, some had been drunkards, some had been swindlers, some had been adulterers. They came from horrible backgrounds. It was wonderful the way Christ had changed them. But some of them were apparently regressing back to their old ways of the flesh. Paul was concerned that they hadn't really repented of those things—they hadn't really changed the direction of their lives. Paul understood their background. He was sympathetic, but since they had come to Christ, he had taught them a better way to live. They were not to get sucked back into their former life-style.

Our society is becoming more and more like Corinth. I think thirty years ago America was predominantly a Christian culture. Today it is a predominantly pagan culture. In a crowded hospital waiting room, a young man came in with a girl and introduced her to a woman seated opposite me.

"This is my new fiancé," he said loudly, with no sense of shame. "We're going to get married in a couple of weeks. We've been living together a couple of years and we think it's time to get married."

A woman who was apparently a relative said, "Well, I understand. You don't want to rush into anything. Just be sure."

He said, "Well, I talked to my Mom about it and she said the same thing, but she said maybe it's time now."

Twenty-five years ago, some people were living together, but they were a little embarrassed about it. You didn't hear it boasted about. Now it's commonplace, and if you hold to traditional, Biblical values, you're in the minority in this country. Ours has become a pagan culture—but we are winning people to Christ out of that background.

The church is winning people to Christ out of the background of drug abuse, immorality, violence, and dysfunctional families. Some of the people in the church of whom I'm the proudest are people who came from the worst backgrounds. They know that Christ has changed them, and they know that they are welcome in the church. But I worry about them, too. It is so easy, since they're familiar with that life-style, for them to regress.

The adversary is relentless. He knows when you're down, he knows your points of weakness, and he knows where you're vulnerable. Peter said, "Be self-controlled and alert. Your enemy the devil prowls around like a roaring lion looking for someone to devour" (1 Peter 5:8).

We don't expect people to be on a par with the apostle Paul in the first year, or to be completely mature in three or four years, but you are to repent. You are to turn from that old life-style. I know that it still appeals. I know that the world looks temporarily exciting out there, but remember what it does to you.

J. Wallace Hamilton asked the question, "If you get where you are going, where are you going to be?" What direction are you going? That's the question. If you're regressing into those old sinful ways, if you're taking two steps forward and three steps back, I urge you to repent.

A little lamb and his mother passed the pig pen every day on their way to the pasture. The lamb looked longingly at the pigs wallowing in the mire, and he asked his mother if he could go and play in the mud.

She'd say, "No, sheep don't wallow."

But he would look over at those pigs in that mud. It looked like so much fun; on hot days, the mud looked cool.

One day, when he was older, he let his mother go on a little bit ahead of him. He jumped over the fence and started playing in the mud. The cool mud on that hot day felt so good around his ankles, so he went in a little deeper. It got up to his belly and he was cooling off. But wool and mud don't mix well, and it began to cake on his wool until he realized he was stuck; he couldn't get out. His pleasure had become his prison.

He began to cry for help, and finally the farmer came and took him back out to pasture.

His mother said, "Sheep don't wallow."

Christians aren't to wallow in the mire of sin, either. It may look appealing, but remember where it leads. It traps, it addicts, it enslaves, it destroys. It may be temporarily pleasurable, but it is eternally damning. Don't get caught back in that old life-style.

A newspaper clipping gave the obituary of a pornographic film star several years ago.

> Pornographic film star, John Holmes, who boasted thousands of sexual conquests on and off the screen, died Saturday night at the VA Medical Center, a business associate said. He was 43. Adult producer William Anderson said the cause of death was not immediately known. Holmes was variously reported to have had colon cancer, to have been gravely ill with AIDS, and to have been a drug addict. According to a fellow actor, he was also heavily involved with alcohol. He had spent a considerable amount of time in jail as a result of his 1982 arrest in the unsolved murders of four people. "Those factors would open up anyone to any disease," said Bill Margold, who appeared in films with him. Margold, who also directed some of Holmes's films, called him the pioneer in X-rated films. "Without the king, I don't think X-rated films would have the popularity they have today."

Let me ask you something—how would you like to be John Holmes today? Ask him in Hell: "Was the pleasure worth it, was the money worth it, was the notoriety worth it?" If you get where you're going, where are you going to be?

God wants us to repent and to leave that old life behind. Not because He's a tyrant trying to prevent us from having fun, but because He wants us to have the very best life possible on earth. He wants us to live forever with Him in Heaven. So it's not enough to start well; we have to work at finishing well.

Maybe the Christian life, the straight life, appears boring to the unbeliever, but in reality it's exciting. There's a constant presence and blessing of God. It's certainly the wisest life. It leads to eternal reward.

Are there any danger signs emerging that would threaten to prevent you from finishing the race? Make the correction so that you can finish well and say one day with the apostle Paul, "I have fought the good fight, I have finished the race, I have kept the faith. Now there is in store for me the crown of righteousness, which the Lord, the righteous Judge, will award to me on that day—and not only to me, but also to all who have longed for his appearing" (2 Timothy 4:7, 8).

I went to visit my Aunt Isabel in Melbourne, Florida, recently. I hadn't seen her for over a decade. She is 93 and lives in a nursing home. I was pleased that she was alert and in fairly good health. She had been a good Christian. We talked and reminisced for twenty minutes, and then I said, "Izzy, I'd like to have prayer with you."

After we had prayer together, I said, "Well, I've got to go. I'll see you later."

She patted me on the arm and said, "I probably won't see you again down here, but I'll see you one day up there."

I think she is finishing well. I want to, too. I want to hear one day, "Well done, good and faithful servant! You have been faithful with a few things; I will put you in charge of many things. Come and share your master's happiness!" (Matthew 25:21).

I want to finish the race!

Standing for the Truth

2 Corinthians 13:1-14

> Pilate . . . summoned Jesus and asked him, "Are you the king of the Jews?"
> . . . Jesus said, "My kingdom is not of this world. If it were, my servants would fight to prevent my arrest by the Jews. But now my kingdom is from another place."
> "You are a king, then!" said Pilate.
> Jesus answered, ". . . For this reason I was born, and for this I came into the world, to testify to the truth. Everyone on the side of truth listens to me."
> "What is truth?" Pilate asked (John 18:33-38).

THAT DIALOGUE BETWEEN JESUS AND PILATE was a foretaste of the debate that has continued down through the centuries. The Christian insists that there is an absolute truth. The Christian believes that God created the world, man sinned and alienated himself from God, but Jesus Christ came to earth as God's truth. He died for our sins and arose from the grave. The Bible contains God's accurate record of Jesus Christ and His instructions on how we are supposed to live.

The unbeliever, on the other hand, insists that there is no absolute truth. Truth has to be left up to the individual. It's all relative, the unbeliever says. Who are we to say whether we are created or whether we evolved? Who are Christians to try to impose their religious beliefs on other people? Everybody ought to be free to believe what he wants to believe and to do what he wants to do.

The history of mankind is a tug-of-war between these two divergent philosophies. One is humanism; the other is Christianity. One says, "I will live according to the way I feel." The other says, "I will live according to what God's Word says." The conflict between those two philosophies is intensifying in our day.

Dr. James Dobson and Gary Bauer have written a pertinent book that demonstrates how vital it is, for the sake of our children, that we take this confrontation seriously. The book is *Children at Risk*, and in it the authors point out that there is a "civil war" being fought in America today over values, and to the winning side will go the next generation of children.

It is not just a matter of individual religious beliefs that we're talking about here. It's a matter of what is true and what is false. It's a matter of what is healthy and what is disease ridden. It's a matter of life and death. It's a matter of Heaven and Hell. For the sake of our children and for the sake of the future of this world, which is in danger of collapsing, we'd better stand up for what is right. If the trumpet gives an uncertain sound, the Bible says, who will prepare for battle?

Paul was a man who did his best to stand up for what was right regardless of the circumstances. In the final chapter of 2 Corinthians, he summarized his letter and encouraged his readers to stand firm in the truth. Five principles from this passage will help us as we stand for truth in the midst of a pagan world.

Truth Requires Confirmation

"Every matter must be established by the testimony of two or three witnesses" (2 Corinthians 13:1). Paul was coming to them for a third time, and he was going to deal with the improprieties in their church. But he assured them that his judgment would not be superficial. He wouldn't rely on rumors. He would examine the facts and rely on a series of witnesses to confirm the truth.

In following this procedure, Paul was following Old Testament instruction. For example, the Bible says, "One witness is not enough to convict a man accused of any crime or offense he may have committed. A matter must be established by the testimony of two or three witnesses" (Deuteronomy 19:15). In the New Testament, it says, "Do not entertain an accusation against an elder unless it is brought by two or three witnesses" (1 Timothy 5:19).

I think that is the reason we have four witnesses to Jesus Christ in the New Testament—Matthew, Mark, Luke, and John. All four give testimony, like four people in a courtroom giving witness, about Jesus Christ: that He died for our sins and that they saw Him alive after He had died. We have good evidence for believing that Jesus is the truth.

We're to confirm the truth by reliable witness. We're not to accept hearsay; we're not to believe every rumor that circulates; we're not even to entertain an accusation if it's not confirmed. Either prove the rumor with undeniable testimony or reject it. That simple principle will save you and the church a lot of hurt.

There will always be rumors circulating—the preacher's new house has a bowling alley in the basement and his wife is moonlighting at the race track to pay for it—or something. All kinds of rumors circulate about what's going on in the church, but don't believe rumors. Confirm them or else reject them. Have reliable testimony from two or three witnesses.

One area in which Christians really need to practice confirmation of the truth is in discerning the news. We can be so gullible in reading the newspaper or watching a reporter on television that we get sucked into anti-Christian opinions just because of the reporters' bias. The news can be distorted by emphasis or innuendo.

Marvin Olasky is a Christian and a journalism professor at the University of Texas. He is the author of the book, *The Prodigal Press*. He wrote, in an article in *Moody Monthly*,

> We Christians need to know how secular journalists perceive their work and be able to point to examples how some are covering up and manipulating the news. Many journalists see themselves as altruists doling out positive publicity to those causes they think are worthy.

As an example, Olasky cited Karen DeYoung, foreign editor of the *Washington Post*, explaining her positive coverage of the Sandinistas when they seized power.

> Most journalists are eager now to seek out guerrilla groups, leftist groups, because they assume such groups must be the good guys. . . .
>
> In the 1970's Geraldo Rivera reported for ABC in Panama. He said that, when a violent incident threatened Senate ratification of a treaty relinquishing U.S. control of the Panama Canal, "We downplayed the whole incident. That was the day I decided that I had to be very careful about what was said because I could defeat the very thing, the passage of the treaty, that I wanted to achieve."
>
> According to ABC executive producer Abe Weston, network abortion stories in the early 70's followed a formula. First, dramatic photos of bruised, unwanted babies, or shots of a silhouetted woman telling how she nearly died after an illegal abortion. Then, when the case for legalized abortion was

powerfully presented, an opponent of abortion would be given a chance to make the pro-life side of the case, usually without dramatic pictures, inserted merely as a talking head. Equal time, yes, but not equal impression.[22]

Olasky said these problems in American journalism are not present because of some conspiracy, but as the result of a materialist world-view hostile to Christianity. Most journalists see leftist guerrillas, homosexual parades, and anti-Christian textbooks as the good news of our era. They do not want to stand in the way of liberation. Until that world-view changes, there will be few improvements in news coverage. We need to become much more discerning and zealous for the truth in listening to and reading the news.

Is John F. Kennedy really the modern folk hero that he's made out to be in the press some three decades after his assassination? Is the problem really a defective bus, or is it the drunk driver? Does a fifty-person gay rights march merit front-page coverage when six thousand in worship are not even mentioned?

Olasky says it takes time to be a smart consumer of the news. We do not glorify God by being sheep walking peacefully toward the wolves, even if the shepherd says the journey is for our own good. Make sure you confirm the truth. Don't be sucked in by rumor or innuendo.

Truth Necessitates Confrontation

"On my return I will not spare those who sinned earlier" (2 Corinthians 13:2). Paul was going to confront the rebellious Corinthians face to face. He had done everything he could to avoid that confrontation. He had sent them an earlier letter, he had sent Titus as an ambassador to straighten things out, and now he was sending this letter in hopes that they would repent. But, as a last resort, he said he would not spare those who had sinned — and that word *spare* means to spare in battle. In short, Paul was declaring war on those who opposed the authority of God's Word.

Truth sometimes requires confrontation with those who oppose it, and that's not easy. If you've ever had to confront somebody who was in the wrong, you know you don't sleep the night before; your palms get sweaty; your voice quivers. It takes tremendous courage. It's the easiest thing in the world just to let it slide and say, "I'm probably blowing this out of proportion. It will get better in time." But if we are really concerned for

[22]Marvin Olasky, "Views of the News," *Moody Monthly* (June, 1988), p. 12.

people and we're concerned about the truth, sometimes we must face the issue head on.

David Augsburger wrote a book called *Caring Enough to Confront*. You don't have to read it to discern its basic premise: if you care, you confront. Maybe you suspect your teenage son or daughter is toying with drugs or has an alcohol problem. You've put off confronting because you don't want to alienate them, but maybe it's time you sat down on the edge of his or her bed and had a serious talk. Maybe you've got a friend that you suspect is cheating on his wife. You see some things going on that you know just aren't right. You don't want to lose a friend, but maybe it's time, for the sake of that family, that you talked it over. Maybe you hear about some things being taught in the local school that violate Christian values and need to be confronted. It's hard to walk into the principal's office or to stand up and speak at a PTA meeting, but maybe you're the one person who can prevent disaster before it's too late.

Confrontation with the truth is much better than gossip about suppositions. "If your brother sins against you, go and show him his fault, just between the two of you. If he listens to you, you have won your brother over" (Matthew 18:15). It's risky—if he doesn't listen, you may lose a friend. But more important is your stand for truth.

Truth is Based on Christ's Resurrection

The Corinthians were apparently sneering, "Who is Paul to tell us how to live? Paul is weak. He's unimpressive. He's not nearly as powerful as some of our other teachers." Paul said they were "demanding proof that Christ is speaking through me" (2 Corinthians 13:3).

Paul responded that he came representing Jesus Christ, whose Word is true regardless of what they thought of him. "He is not weak in dealing with you, but is powerful among you. For to be sure, he was crucified in weakness, yet he lives by God's power." That truth stands regardless of rank, status, or public opinion. "We are weak in him, yet by God's power we will live with him to serve you" (2 Corinthians 13:3, 4).

If you ever stand up for the truth, people are going to say to you, "Who are you to tell other people how to live?" "Who is Bob Russell to tell people how they ought to behave?" Good question—I'm not the most intelligent or educated person. I'm not the most influential. I don't have a lot of titles, and I don't have all of my life together. My family still struggles with problems, and I don't overcome every temptation that comes my way. Maybe I'd be better off if I just kept my opinions to myself.

But wait a minute! There was a unique event in history that makes all the difference in the world. Jesus Christ conquered the grave. When He came out of the tomb He said, "All authority in heaven and on earth has been given to me. Therefore go and make disciples of all nations" (Matthew 28:18, 19). So I don't really represent myself or my own opinions. I represent Jesus Christ. He said, "Heaven and earth will pass away, but my words will never pass away" (Matthew 24:35). He said, "You will know the truth, and the truth will set you free" (John 8:32).

Some friends were on the expressway when they saw a man drive down the ramp the wrong way and come on the interstate in the wrong lane. Memories of the school bus accident in nearby Carrollton, Kentucky, in which a driver going the wrong way on the interstate struck a church bus and killed twenty-seven people, were still fresh in their minds, and their hearts leapt into their throats. They immediately pulled off the expressway and called the police and tried to stop him.

Now, you could protest, "Who were they to try to impose their driving standards on other people? After all, they're not perfect drivers, either." No—you would say, "If they really care and want to prevent disaster, they'd better stand up for what's right."

So it is with our knowledge of the truth in Jesus Christ. When men and women go the wrong way, they're heading toward disaster for themselves and for others. In the words of Peter and John, who were told not to speak about Jesus anymore, "We cannot help speaking about what we have seen and heard" (Acts 4:20).

In his first letter to them, Paul told the Corinthians,

> The message of the cross is foolishness to those who are perishing, but to us who are being saved it is the power of God. For it is written:
>
> 'I will destroy the wisdom of the wise;
> the intelligence of the intelligent I will frustrate.'
>
> Where is the wise man? Where is the scholar? Where is the philosopher of this age? Has not God made foolish the wisdom of the world? For since in the wisdom of God the world through its wisdom did not know him, God was pleased through the foolishness of what was preached to save those who believe (1 Corinthians 1:18-21).

Truth is not based on our intellect or on our power, but on the death, burial, and resurrection of Jesus Christ. And that doesn't change!

A ship's captain was awakened in the middle of the night and informed that the lights of an approaching vessel were dead ahead and threatening to ram the ship. The captain came on deck, looked at the oncoming lights, and ordered this message sent on the radio: "We are a U.S. warship. Alter your course ten degrees."

But immediately the radio message came back: "Alter your course ten degrees."

The captain became angry. He picked up the radio microphone and barked, "I am Captain MacGregor of the United States Navy. I command you to alter your course ten degrees."

But back came the reply, "I am Seaman Fourth Class Richards of the United States Coast Guard. Alter your course ten degrees."

The lights came dangerously close. The captain was enraged. He radioed back, "I am a battleship! Alter your course ten degrees!"

Back came the reply, "I am a lighthouse! Alter your course ten degrees."

Paul said we can't do anything to oppose the truth. It's absolute. So, rather than oppose it, we need to spread it. Jesus said, "You are the salt of the earth. . . . You are the light of the world" (Matthew 5:13, 14). We're supposed to make a difference.

Maybe we don't have the greatest education, and maybe we aren't the most articulate spokesmen, but we do stand solidly on the truth of Jesus Christ, and that does not change. There comes a time when every person, regardless of influence, status, or rank, is going to have to bow before Him. The Bible says there's going to come a day when every knee shall bow, and every tongue will confess that He is Lord (cf. Philippians 2:10, 11). Failure to acknowledge truth can result in disaster. We don't apologize for the truth, because it's based on the resurrection of Jesus Christ from the grave.

Truth Demands Self-Examination

"Examine yourselves to see whether you are in the faith; test yourselves" (2 Corinthians 13:5). Over and over in Scripture we are urged—before we ever confront anybody else, before we ever condemn anybody else—to examine our own hearts. Jesus said,

> How can you say to your brother, "Let me take the speck out of your eye," when all the time there is a plank in your own eye? You hypocrite, first take the plank out of your own eye, and then you will see clearly to remove the speck from your brother's eye (Matthew 7:4, 5).

That's probably the thing that has disappointed us the most about the televangelist scandals of the past few years. We have wondered how in the world certain media preachers could have been so critical of others when the same type of sin they condemned was flagrant in their own lives.

Paul urged the Corinthians to examine themselves. They had been focusing on Paul when they should have been evaluating themselves. The quest for truth always begins with oneself, not other people. The Bible says, when you come to worship and to come around the Lord's Table, "a man ought to examine himself" (1 Corinthians 11:28). Don't examine other people. Don't evaluate the performance. Examine yourself.

Some people want to come in to church and nudge somebody and say, "How did you like the special music? How did you like it when the screen came down this morning? Preacher keep your attention? Did you like that chorus?" It's as if we're evaluating a performance. But our attitude when we come to worship should be, "Oh, Lord, search my heart. I fall so far short. Teach me. Let there be something from this service that causes me to be more deeply committed to the truth." If that's your spirit, if you're examining yourself, then you're open to being taught and molded by God.

I heard of a man who said he'd been attending church for fifty years and had never heard a sermon from which he couldn't gain something. He said, "I'll have to admit, I've had some close calls on occasion!"

If you're really examining yourself, you're going to receive something, and you're going to be deepened in the truth.

Truth Must Be Balanced With Compassion

We sometimes think of the apostle Paul as hard-nosed, but the last few verses show how he oozed with compassion. "We are glad whenever we are weak but you are strong; and our prayer is for your perfection" (2 Corinthians 13:9). He was more concerned about others than for himself. "I write these things when I am absent, that when I come I may not have to be harsh in my use of authority—the authority the Lord gave me for building you up, not for tearing you down. . . . Aim for perfection, listen to my appeal, be of one mind, live in peace" (2 Corinthians 13:10, 11).

The letter ends with a famous benediction that includes all three persons of the trinity: "May the grace of the Lord Jesus Christ, and the love of God, and the fellowship of the Holy Spirit be with you all" (2 Corinthians 13:14). It is so important that our love for the truth be balanced with a love for people. Once, when Jesus was rejected by the Samaritans, James and John said, "Lord, do you want us to call fire down from heaven to destroy them?" (Luke 9:54). Some people are so zealous for the truth that they appear to be angry all the time. They hate people. They get red in the face and they shout and call their opponents names. We'll never successfully communicate the gospel of Christ by the use of ugly moods and bad temper. You never proclaim the love of God with a clenched fist.

But some people go to the opposite extreme. They get so caught up in loving people, they compromise the truth. A young man asked a girl to marry him. She said, "I'm not going to marry you until you've got $10,000. We're not going to start off on a shoestring."

Five years later they both were still single. "Are you ready to marry me now?" he said.

"How much money have you got?"

"Twenty-five dollars."

She said, "That's close enough!"

It's so easy for time and weariness to erode away principle. Some people get so passive that they don't want to believe anything or stand for anything. Churches are caving in because there is so much permissiveness in our world. William Banowsky said, "It is not unusual to meet people who think that not to believe in any truth is a primary condition required of democratic citizens in order to be tolerant of one another." There's a vast difference between being tolerant and being permissive.

John Stott said, "Love without truth is sentimentality. Truth without love is fanaticism. Love balanced with truth is Christianity." Our zeal for truth should always be communicated in love. Jesus prayed that His followers would be sanctified in the truth and that they would be united in love (John 17:17, 21). Paul urged the Ephesians to be "speaking the truth in love" (Ephesians 4:15). That's our goal as Christians: to have strong convictions and not to waver where the Bible speaks, but also to have a spirit of love and compassion for people. In fact, there's a slogan that says, "In matters of faith, unity; in matters of opinion, liberty; in all things, love."

John Gough told of being in a church service one day and hearing a hoarse discordant voice behind him singing, "Just As I Am." He cringed, he said, because this man was the worst singer he had ever heard. There was no melody and no tune. After three stanzas, the organist mercifully played an interlude. As it was being played, Gough says he felt a hand on his shoulder. The man with the terrible voice asked him, "Could you tell me the first phrase of the next stanza? I think I could get it if I just had the first few words." John Gough said he looked around into the face of the terrible singer, and he saw that the man was blind. He passed onto him the next stanza of "Just As I Am:"

Just as I am, poor, wretched, blind;
Sight, riches, healing of the mind,
Yea all I need, in thee to find,
O Lamb of God, I come! I come![23]

John Gough said when that next stanza began, he didn't hear the discordant notes any more. That blind man was singing, "Just as I am, poor, wretched, blind, I come."

We need to stand for truth, because if the trumpet gives an uncertain sound, who is going to prepare for battle? But we need to understand that people are imperfect. They're poor, they're blind, they're wretched, and they need healing. If we can combine truth with tolerance, we'll represent well the Christ who came not to call the righteous, but sinners to repentance. "If you hold to my teaching, you are really my disciples. Then you will know the truth, and the truth will set you free" (John 8:31, 32).

[23]Charlotte Elliott, "Just As I Am," 1834.